COMBAT CORPSMAN

COMBAT CORPSMAN

Greg McPartlin

BERKLEY CALIBER BOOKS, NEW YORK

THE BERKLEY PUBLISHING GROUP
Published by the Penguin Group
Penguin Group (USA) Inc.
375 Hudson Street, New York, New York 10014, USA
Penguin Group (Canada), 90 Eglinton Avenue East, Suite 700, Toronto, Ontario M4P 2Y3, Canada (division of Pearson Penguin Canada Inc.)
Penguin Books Ltd., 80 Strand, London WC2R 0RL, England
Penguin Group Ireland, 25 St. Stephen's Green, Dublin 2, Ireland (a division of Penguin Books Ltd.)
Penguin Group (Australia), 250 Camberwell Road, Camberwell, Victoria 3124, Australia (a division of Pearson Australia Group Pty. Ltd.)
Penguin Books India Pvt. Ltd., 11 Community Centre, Panchsheel Park, New Delhi—110 017, India
Penguin Group (NZ), Cnr. Airborne and Rosedale Roads, Albany, Auckland 1310, New Zealand (a division of Pearson New Zealand Ltd.)
Penguin Books (South Africa) (Pty.) Ltd., 24 Sturdee Avenue, Rosebank, Johannesburg 2196, South Africa

Penguin Books Ltd., Registered Offices: 80 Strand, London WC2R 0RL, England

This book is an original publication of The Berkley Publishing Group.

Cover design by Steven Ferlauto
Photo Credit: Bettmann/Corbis

PRINTING HISTORY
Berkley trade paperback edition/November 2005

Library of Congress Cataloging-in-Publication Data

McPartlin, Greg.
Combat corpsman / Greg McPartlin—Berkley trade pbk. ed.
p. cm.
"A Berkley Caliber book."
ISBN 0-425-20582-7 (pbk.)
1. McPartlin, Greg. 2. Vietnamese Conflict, 1961–1975—Personal narratives, American. 3. Vietnamese Conflict, 1961–1975—Medical care—United States. 4. United States. Navy. SEALs—History. I. Title.

DS559.5.M435 2005
959.704'37—dc22
[B]

2005052511

PRINTED IN THE UNITED STATES OF AMERICA

10 9 8 7 6 5 4 3 2 1

With many thanks to Faye Walters, who turned my scratches on paper into neatly typed stories, and to Teresa Patterson, without her this world would not have been written.

—Greg McPartlin

Contents

COMBAT CORPSMAN

1

Pay No Attention to the Man Behind the Curtain

IT had been a rough day at the office. Dirt, sweat, and blood covered me from head to toe. I was tired, and the wound in my shoulder felt as if it went all the way to the bone. My prisoner was in worse shape, having taken several rounds in his gut. All I wanted was to get back to our base at SEAFLOAT and tend to my wounded prisoner. Technically successful, the operation had netted a high-level Viet Cong chief without losing any of our own. The degree of success, however, depended on whether the prisoner survived. I managed to stabilize him during the helicopter flight back. After we set down, I climbed wearily from the chopper onto the deck of our massive floating base, only to find myself face-to-face with the business end of a 16mm Arriflex. A quick look around confirmed my worst fears. Despite being anchored in the middle of a two-mile-wide river, we had been invaded. But not by the Viet Cong—a TV news crew lay in ambush. Of the two, newsmen were worse. At least I was allowed to shoot VC.

Against my better judgment, I left my Stoner machine gun in its place across my back, gritted my teeth, and pushed past the Arriflex camera to escort my prisoner to sick bay. My first priority was to make certain this particular VC chief would live long enough to talk. I must have looked even worse than I felt, because the newsman quickly retreated.

When I returned from sick bay some time later, feeling a little groggy and light-headed from blood loss, I was again assaulted by the camera's fisheye stare as the lens was shoved into my face. A microphone held by a freshly shaved man with TV good looks blocked my escape route. He must have come straight from an air-conditioned suite in Saigon because he was just beginning to sweat. I shifted my weapon slightly to relieve the stress on my injured shoulder, and wondered if this man realized he stood between me and a long, cool, shower.

"So what's your name, soldier?"

"McPartlin. What's yours?"

"Morley Safer." He nodded toward sick bay. "How's your prisoner?" He must have seen the hesitation on my face. "It's okay. We're here with Admiral Zumwalt. His aide said we could look around here at SEAFLOAT."

"Uh huh." I tried to sound noncommital. I heard that Admiral Zumwalt had planned a visit to see his son Elmo, a Swift Boat commander with our base, but I didn't realize he was bringing a herd of newsies with him.

"Your prisoner . . . ?"

"He'll live." I turned to walk away, hoping he would get the message, but he became as tenacious as delta river mud, sticking right to me.

"So what's your first name, McPartlin?"

"Greg."

"And what's your rate?"

"I'm a Navy SEAL." That was at least something I was proud to share, and something he probably already knew.

"Do you have a rate?"

"E-5"

"That's your rank. What's your rate?"

This guy definitely did not get the message.

"HM2, Corpsman," I snapped and kept walking. He continued to follow close behind me.

"So what's that on your back?" He gestured toward my Stoner.

I stopped and turned to face Mr. Safer, releasing my weapon with my good arm while wishing I could show it to him up close and personal.

"This," I said, "is my Stoner 5.56mm belt-fed, gas-operated machine gun. It has a rate of fire of around one thousand rounds a minute." I did my best to sound like my instructor back at Coronado.

He appeared to admire the weapon for a moment, then fixed his intense newshound gaze on me. "So what is a medic doing with a machine gun? That isn't standard corpsman equipment."

I just looked at him, unable to believe he would ask a question like that in the middle of a war. Especially *this* war. "Well then, think of it as a surgical instrument capable of making up to a thousand incisions per minute."

Rather proud of my impromptu response, I couldn't hide my grin as I resumed walking to our living area, or "hooch," as it was called in the native dialect.

"Hey," he called after me, "don't you know it's against the Geneva Convention for a corpsman to carry anything more than a sidearm?"

I stopped, turned and looked him in the eye. The smile drained from my face to be replaced by a sneer of disgust. I stepped toward this sack of shit in his starched clean cammies and leaned in until my face was only inches from his, silently reminding myself that throttling reporters went against more than the Geneva Convention. As I glared at him, the sweat started to bead up on his forehead. I could smell his Aqua Velva aftershave and I wanted to be certain he could smell the stench of sweat, shit, and dried blood that permeated my clothes and body. I wanted this pretty boy, who probably never slept outside of a nice hotel, to get a good whiff of life in the bush. During the mission, I had given CPR to the wounded prisoner, who had regurgitated in my mouth, so I knew my breath was far from minty fresh.

"And I suppose you think I should wear a big red X on my helmet as well? Who the *fuck* has heard of the Geneva Convention out here? Certainly not Charlie!"

Before the startled Mr. Safer could reply, Admiral Zumwalt, who must have seen the newsman accost me, stepped in and saved him. While still maintaining the guise of the generous host, he smoothly confiscated the film from the protesting Mr. Safer and passed it to his aide.

"Gentlemen," he announced, making certain he had the attention of the entire news crew. "These men," he gestured to include me as well as the members of my platoon who had started to gather in the area, "are Navy SEALs. They and this area of SEAFLOAT are off limits to you or any other members of the press. They do not exist. You never saw them. And, to quote a cliché, if you ask them anything else, they'll have to kill you." He smiled as he said it—possibly to underline the humor of his words—but the smile was predatory. Mr. Safer glanced over at me. I grinned dangerously, letting him know that I would be only too glad to carry out that threat, cliché or not.

I watched for a moment as the cowed newsmen left the area, then resumed my march to our hooch. My buddy and tentmate Wayne Bohannan stopped me long enough to take charge of my Stoner so I could shower and get my wound attended. Just outside the showers, the admiral's aide caught up with me.

"Doc, the admiral would like you to know that we all agree with what you said to the reporter. It's how we all feel. But," his eyes twinkled, "he also says you are definitely not going to get that appointment as the public affairs officer."

I laughed and gave him a thumbs-up, then turned and climbed into the shower, web gear and all.

Under the cool spray, I began peeling off the last thirty-six hours along with my cammies and gear, watching as the water turned dark from dirt and blood. I thought about what the reporter had said. I understood his point, but I sure as hell didn't agree with him. The Geneva Convention was useless in a war where the enemy considered any means justifiable in the pursuit of their goal. To someone who used children to deliver bombs, a red cross was a nice clear target, and a wounded soldier simply provided a lure to force another target into range. In Vietnam, anyone who did not go into the bush prepared to fight became a liability for his entire unit. This proved especially true within a SEAL unit. I understood that. But I also realized that someone who had never been in battle would have a hard time understanding why a medic needed to be able and willing to kill. Fact remained, I had been trained to kill as efficiently and effectively as to heal. Both skills usually ended up saving lives, and I had few regrets. But I hadn't started out to be a killer. I had started out as a healer.

2

Just Another Wasted Youth

I had always planned to be a doctor. Medicine ran in the family. My grandfather, who died before my birth, became the first white doctor in the Dakotas and helped found the Mayo Clinic. My grandmother worked as a nurse. So, it seemed natural to me to follow their path. My dad, on the other hand, wanted me to follow in his footsteps and become an advertising executive. As much as I admired his talent for coming up with catchy slogans, I had absolutely no interest in becoming a glorified salesman. Advertising had no life-and-death struggle. But the thought of battling death the ways doctors did fascinated me.

I was very young when I first came into contact with death. Unlike many other children, illness and death held no horror for me. As a third grader, I helped my grandmother with her medications. When the other kids were hanging out at the playground, it was not unusual to find me at my favorite haunt, the funeral home.

I discovered the Wenban Funeral Home almost by accident. The winters in Lake Forest, Illinois, were fiercely cold. Only thirty miles north of Chicago on Lake Michigan, we always caught the full force of the same bitter winter winds that made Chicago famous as "the windy city." But even as a youngster, I refused to blithely accept extreme discomfort. I saw no reason to suffer if there was an alternative. This particular fall afternoon was blustery and biting cold. In an effort to escape the wind, I decided to cut through the showroom of the Wenban Buick dealership, which lay along the route to my home. I ducked into the showroom to find that it was not only warmer, but full of new Buicks. I wound a slow admiring path through the shiny new cars then stepped out the rear door and back into the teeth of the wind. Behind Wenban Buick, on a side street, I spotted the Wenban Funeral Home, and the promise of additional warmth. I knew George Wenban owned both establishments because my father had created their most memorable advertising campaign. He had made the Wenbans famous with the slogan "Buy a Buick or Drop Dead."

The funeral home's garage was open, so I scurried through the doorway to find a treasure trove parked inside. The new Buicks in the dealership had been interesting, but they were nothing compared to the fleet parked in the garage. There was a hearse, a limo, and even a flower van. I walked slowly around each one, examining every detail.

Then I saw it—the ambulance—complete with a shiny paint job and a huge rack of lights on top. I stopped in my tracks and stared.

In a town as small as Lake Forest at that time, it was normal for the funeral home to have an ambulance, but I had never seen one up close before. Every detail of its design fascinated me.

The mortician, Sonny Wenban, found me there, mesmerized by the car. Fortunately, he understood, and instead of calling my parents, he let me sit in the front seat. I thought it was a perfect fit. I couldn't wait for the time I would be old enough to drive one. Sonny assured me that I would be a good ambulance driver. I was determined to prove him right. Despite the difference in our ages, we developed a friendship based on our mutual appreciation of fine cars.

From the garage, it was only a short walk through the funeral parlor itself. It did not bother me that someone lay on display in the parlor. I did stop briefly to pay my respects—though it was mostly to see who was being mourned—then made my way out the front door. The detour proved to be not only warmer, but also a block shorter than my regular route home. Not to mention the fact that it had much greater scenic value.

As a result of this discovery, an almost daily visit to the Wenban Funeral Home became part of my regular routine during the school year. As an Irish Catholic kid, I viewed death and the wakes that inevitably followed as just another excuse for grown-ups to drink and party. I saw dead bodies every day. Ambulance runs were much more interesting. If the ambulance passed nearby on a run, lights flashing and siren wailing, I always tried to follow it on my bike to get a look at the victim and watch the medics work.

Grandmother, who lived with us at the time, knew my heart. She was old, diabetic, and crippled but her mind remained as sharp as a tack. She used to quiz me on medical terms to expand my vocabulary. Her nursing background made her a wonderful teacher. By the time I was nine, she even let me give her the insulin shots myself. I felt like a real doctor.

My mother was not quite so understanding. She believed children should be protected from the harsh realities of life. As the youngest of three boys, I was the one for whom she felt most protective. She had no interest in the medical profession, and was definitely not a fan of what she referred to as my "ghoulish" behavior. Of course, I did little to help myself in her eyes.

One day I got into trouble with the nuns at school. Not unusual by itself, but this time it was particularly bad. They called Mother. I knew I would need to do something nice for Mom to help redeem myself. After giving the dilemma some heavy thought, I realized that Dad always brought flowers home when he was in hot water, and it seemed to work. I knew Mom liked flowers, so I decided that flowers would be a proper apology for me, too. And I knew just where to get them.

It didn't take me long to find the perfect bouquet, full of most of her favorite varieties. I took them home and handed them to her while making the proper noises of apology. Inside, I congratulated myself on my bright idea.

But instead of accepting my apology and forgiving me, her stern expression turned slowly darker as she examined the flowers, until her face was thunderous with fury. I couldn't understand what was wrong. I knew I had chosen flowers she liked. Then I realized the problem. I had forgotten to remove the sympathy card.

Even on later occasions when I carefully selected what I was certain were normal type flowers and made certain to remove any incriminating cards, somehow Mother always knew I had "borrowed" them from the funeral home. She made it very clear that she did not approve of children—especially *her* children—hanging around the funeral home like "ghouls." Since neither of my brothers were involved, that could only mean me. For the most part, I ignored her comments and simply tried not to draw her attention to my activities. What she didn't know couldn't hurt.

But I forgot my plan one night at dinner, in my eagerness to join in the otherwise adult conversation. Mom always loved to hear any news about anyone she knew, but when the talk turned to such gossip, I usually felt left out, since I never willingly chose to spend time with most of Mother's friends. That particular evening I grew tired of being ignored. Everyone else droned on at great lengths about people and places of no interest to me. Even my brothers, Fred and Jeff, seemed to have something witty to say. Finally, I had had enough.

"Hey Mom," I interrupted, "I saw your friend, Mrs. Miller, today."

"Oh really? How did she look?" Mom was always concerned with appearances. In this case, it was easy to tell the truth.

"Real good. She looked real good."

"Did she have anything to say?"

"Not to me," I answered around a mouthful of mashed potatoes. "They were just wheeling her into the viewing room."

After that, Mom started picking me up after school, on her way to the A & P. It marked the end of my daily visits to the Wenban's Funeral Home, but not the end of my love affair with medicine.

Fortunately for me, my older brother Fred shared some of my interests. By the time I was in eighth grade, Fred started spending his breaks from college working as a volunteer fireman and an ambulance driver. It didn't take long for me to convince him to let me go along. At first, I just observed, but by the time I turned fourteen and started high school, I had received my Red Cross Advanced First Aid Certificate and began working as a full-scale ambulance attendant on weekends.

By the time I was sixteen, I was considered one of the more experienced ambulance drivers on the North Shore. I worked for Village Ambulance Service. It was the perfect job—every teenage boy's dream—I had a legal right to drive fast and feel good about it. I was definitely the only kid in town with his own ambulance parked in the high school lot. Better yet, the emergencies didn't stop just because I was in school. Many times I was beeped to go on a call in the middle of class. Of course I had to rush to the rescue while leaving my poor classmates behind. It worked so well that I occasionally arranged to have the Highland Park answering service beep me even when no emergency actually existed.

This was particularly effective in the middle of exams, especially the ones for which I had neglected to prepare.

Beep! Beep!

"Excuse me, Mrs. Jameson, I have to go."

"Mr. McPartlin, it's the middle of the test! You can't just leave!"

"Sorry, ma'am. I am sure the victim would be willing to wait to be rescued until I finish your test."

"Very well, Mr. McPartlin. You may go. But I expect you to be available for a makeup exam tomorrow!"'

Somehow I usually found a way around the makeup exam as well. Not so good for my grades, but great for my ego and peace of mind.

The owner of Village Ambulance Service was notoriously cheap. Rather than pay more medics, he cut a deal that allowed volunteer corpsmen from the Great Lakes Naval Hospital to ride along for the experience. Some of these corpsmen were being groomed for service in Vietnam. The rest would end up as bedpan washers somewhere. Their fate would depend on how they handled themselves in emergency situations. The Navy needed these corpsmen tested and evaluated by a professional and I, a seventeen-year-old high school kid, was the professional doing the evaluations. Fortunately, I looked older than my years.

If looks were not enough, I had an ace in my pocket, literally. My oldest brother Jeff, four years my senior, had managed to "lose" his driver's license—and on his twenty-first birthday, of all things. I never told him I had found it. So, if anyone decided to check, I needed only open my wallet to show proof that I was twenty-one.

By the mid-sixties, Fred had graduated from college and become a Marine Corps aviator. He was my hero—tough, smart, and a Marine pilot. Fred trained all over the country in preparation for deployment to Vietnam. He was an A-4 pilot, the best of the best. I was very proud of him. Whenever he came home, he would give me his old Marine Corps T-shirts. I wore them everywhere, wanting everyone to know that my brother was a Marine. Even better if they thought they were mine.

For myself, I hadn't given the military or Vietnam much thought. My GPA in school was certainly not going to get me a Rhodes scholarship. Athletic scholarships were out of the question as well. Notre Dame thought the Irish jigs from the South Side were more desperate to play football than those of us from the North Shore Ivy Leagues. My family didn't have the money to send me outright, so for me, college was pretty much out of the picture. The fact that the only other choice was the draft did not occur to me.

It didn't help that my attitude toward authority was anything but commendable. I couldn't take the teachers seriously when they seemed so far away from the real life I experienced as an ambulance driver. What did calculus or grammar have to do with life and death? Such knowledge did not keep my customers alive. Most of my teachers knew I used my job to avoid class, but there was little they could do about it. By the time graduation rolled around, I had had enough of school and school had had enough of me.

Dean O'Dair, who was probably as glad to see me go as I was to leave, wrote a touching note in my Lake Forest High School yearbook: "Good luck, you'll need it. You'll probably be the first in your class killed in Vietnam."

I mustered an absolutely serious expression and thanked him for a very touching send off. Later that night, I backed over his mailbox.

3

Driving 'em Wild

OKAY, I had graduated. Now what?

I decided to turn to something I knew well—fast cars.

The summer of 1966 found me spending most of my time at Waukegan Speedway, driving stock cars and working for Village Ambulance Service. Our company had the ambulance contract for the speedway. Every weekend I worked in the infield as part of the safety crew. I felt at home there. I knew all the owners and drivers from working the same contract the year before. They were all "good ol' boys" hailing from places like Waukegan, Kenosha, Grayslake, Libertyville, and other Westside villages. Not at all like the snobs from home in Lake Forest.

Don't get me wrong, Lake Forest is a beautiful, very affluent village. Its palatial estates are home to many notables with seats on the Board of Trade. Names like Schweppes, Armour, Swift, and Marshall Field adorned the ornate mailboxes that lined the better streets of Lake Forest. Since I did not aspire to attend Brown, Yale, Columbia, or Harvard, I really wasn't made to feel comfortable in their presence. So I took my fun—and their daughters—to Waukegan Speedway on the weekends.

At the speedway, many of the drivers let me do hot laps with their cars. But it wasn't the same as having one of my own. I honed my skills on their cars and saved up my pennies until I had enough to buy a car. I bought a beat-up '55 Ford wreck for $75 at a police auction. The old Ford was barely worthy of being called a car, must less a race contender. Determined to make it race-worthy, I spent everything I had on it. I installed a roll bar, put in a safety harness, knocked out all the glass, and installed a steel mesh windshield. Two hundred dollars and a lot of sweat later, it still looked like a junker, but I saw only my own beautiful race car. I was ready to set the track on fire.

Three weeks later, well into the racing season, the Ford was a wreck in fact as well as name, and I hadn't won a penny. Desperate to regain my losses, I decided to enter it in the $250 winner-take-all, figure-eight demolition derby. Now, demolition derbies are not as much about racing as they are about smashing things—both cars and the people who drive them. I had always known I was a little off, but once the word got out that I had entered the derby, most of my friends insisted that I was certifiably crazy.

The day of the race I joined the other drivers in the pit area. As I scanned the other drivers, I realized that my friends may have been right. These nuts I was preparing to drive against all looked like the extras out of *Deliverance*. Most of them had more tattoos than teeth. All of them were liberally covered with scars—no doubt received both on and off the track—which they bore proudly. I had no wish to look like them. As I readied my car I began to question my own sanity.

Fortunately, they all knew me, and must have guessed that I was in over my head. Each one stopped by to promise that they would not hurt my pretty young face. I noticed that they made no such promises about my car.

I was prepared for a serious, hard-fought battle of steel against steel. When the signal came, I drove into the race with all the bravado youth could supply, determined to stay for the long haul. About thirty seconds later, an old Packard, backing up at about thirty-five miles per hour, hit me head-on. With a shriek of rending metal, the whole front of my car collapsed under the impact of the Packard's reinforced back bumper. My car was totaled. My short racing career was over.

The following week, lacking a race car, I returned to my post in the speedway infield. It was just me and a new young corpsman, a serious young man only two days out of training. We sat in the ambulance while the race went on around us. It was his first day of ambulance work, and he was enjoying the view our VIP infield seats provided.

About 9:00 PM, the track announcer broke into the race: "Will the medical team please report to the grandstand. Ambulance to the grandstand." I did not hide my surprise. Usually, our emergencies were all on the track. Clueless, I drove the ambulance off the infield, across the track, and behind the grandstand. A crowd of people had gathered in a cluster around someone on the ground.

As I collected my gear, someone shouted, "Some lady is having a baby!"

No problem, I thought, *I've seen this one done before. I can do it.* I ran over to check her out. She was a young blond woman, probably mid-twenties, with four youngsters still in tow. She remained very calm, despite her obvious pain, determinedly chewing her gum while holding on to the oldest child's hand.

"Everything's going to be fine, ma'am," I reassured her as I took her vital signs.

"I thought I could hold off until the end of the race. My husband's driving. Car 53." She flashed a proud smile before the next contraction wiped it from her face. Then she bit down hard on her wad of gum, chewing fiercely until the contraction passed. "Johnny would have taken me to the hospital after the race. I really thought I could hold, but this baby's comin'. I can't hold him back. This baby ain't going to wait for Daddy."

"No sweat," I reassured her as we loaded her into the ambulance, "we will take you now, and your husband can follow us with the kids."

The corpsman got into the back with the woman and I backed the ambulance up and headed out of the track with sirens blaring and tires screeching. St. Theresa's Hospital was only a mile away. I knew we could make it easily before the baby came.

As I was exiting the highway to St. Theresa's, the woman, instead of being relieved, became distressed. "Not here," she yelled, "I'm military, we have to go to Great Lakes!"

Great Lakes Military Hospital was another fifteen miles away. I didn't think she would make it that far.

"Okay, you're the boss! But it is going to take another fifteen to twenty minutes even under lights and sirens."

"I can make it!" This gum-chewing, trailer-park momma was tough.

I floored the gas pedal, determined to do my part to get her there on time. About five minutes out, I yelled back to the corpsman, "Has her water broken?"

"I'll check." The serious young man turned to our patient. "Are you thirsty, ma'am? Would you like a glass of water?"

I had forgotten that this kid was just out of Corps school, where they taught battle dressings, not babies. I turned off the siren, pulled the ambulance over onto the shoulder of the road, and jumped in back while throwing the corpsman out.

"You! Drive. I'll handle the patient."

He looked bewildered, but relieved. As he pulled back onto the road I turned my attention to our young momma. Oh, her water had broken, all right!

"I'm sorry." She started apologizing as I placed sterile sheets under her midsection. "I just couldn't hold out no more."

As I put on my gloves, the baby was crowning. By the time we reached the gate, I was holding a crying baby girl in my arms. As the corpsman pulled the ambulance into emergency, I had the umbilical cord clamped, the nose and mouth cleared, and the baby was breathing just fine. The Great Lakes duty nurses, doctors, and corpsmen all ran out to the ambulance and took over. As I handed the baby to one of them, I felt almost like a proud papa myself.

The father met me as I returned from cleaning up in the head. He was a bear of a man still wearing dust and grease stains from the track. He grabbed me in a big hug while mumbling his appreciation in incoherent sobs like a child.

"Thanks," I said, pulling away, "but I still have to charge you an additional $25 for the extra mileage."

This doctor stuff isn't too hard, I thought, driving back to the track. I have a talent for it. Maybe I should get my act together and get in school.

Unfortunately, it was too late. The choice to attend school or not was no longer mine to make.

4

"Be All You Can Be" Didn't Sit Well With Me

THE war in Vietnam continued to heat up. More and more American boys received their draft notices every day. I was 1-A, prime cannon fodder, and the draft was breathing down my neck. Fred was already flying fighter jets in 'Nam for the Marines, and I knew Uncle Sam would soon send me my own personal invitation to become a soldier. It was only a matter of time. If I waited for the draft to get me, I would have to take whatever position they decided to hand out. As one who had no desire to allow other people to control my life, I chose to enlist. If I had to go to war, I wanted to have some choice in the matter.

I decided to join Fred. He was having all kinds of adventures as a Marine A-4 pilot. I knew I could not be a pilot, but I could be a Marine. I had followed in Fred's footsteps so much of my life, it seemed only natural to follow him into the Marines as well. Feeling good about my choice, I went to the recruiter's office in Waukegan. All the military recruiters shared a bank of offices in the strip center. I chose the door with the Eagle Globe and Anchor. The motto *Semper Fi*—always faithful—was etched under it. I learned that one from Fred. I marched smartly up to the desk to greet the beefy man in an immaculate dress blue uniform, complete with the trademark blood stripe down the pants legs.

"I want to be a Marine, sir." I thought the "sir" was a nice touch.

"Excellent choice, son." He smiled and shook my hand with a firm grip. "What is it you do now?"

"I drive an ambulance."

"Well," his smile became positively gleeful. "Perfect. We always need corpsmen in the Marines."

That sounded good to me. I thought of all the corpsmen I had evaluated over the last few years. I figured I was at least as good as any of them.

"Okay, I'll be a corpsman."

"Great. Now if you will just go talk to that man over there." I looked where he indicated, and was shocked to see a tall, lanky man in the next office, wearing the unmistakable uniform of the U.S. Navy.

"But that man's a *squid*!" I protested, unable to keep the disgust out of my voice.

"That's right. He's the Navy recruiter."

"But I don't want to be a squid! I want to be a Marine!"

"Yes, I understand. But the Navy trains all of the corpsmen we use," the Marine recruiter continued, ignoring the sour look on my face. "Don't worry, son. We'll guarantee in your contract that you'll be able to go to the Marine Corps right after your training."

So that day, I reluctantly signed up with the Navy. I couldn't believe that I would have to become a squid to be a Marine. But the Navy and the Marines had been connected since the days of old when Marines first berthed on Navy sailing ships, and while they were basically separate services, they still shared certain things. Apparently, corpsmen were one of those things. I had to admit, it made more sense than having two different training programs to teach the same thing.

Boot camp proved pretty uneventful. I was still upset about having to be in the Navy, but I figured basic training was probably the same in every branch of the service. I spent those weeks being rousted up before dawn to run until breakfast, take some classes, do some more physical training (PT), go to the range, drill some more, then fall into bed to get a few hours sleep before getting up to do it all again, all while being yelled at and insulted by a drill instructor. Fortunately, I was in pretty good shape, so the physical part was not difficult. I made a few friends, but most guys kept their distance as soon as they found out I was training to be a corpsman for the Marines. Apparently, the Marines had been doing a really good job of getting their corpsmen killed or wounded in Vietnam.

Whenever discussions of eventual MOD came up, someone would always say, "Whatever you do, don't volunteer to be a corpsman. I hear their life expectancy in 'Nam is around thirty seconds or, if they're lucky, thirty feet . . . Oh, you've already volunteered? Well, can I have your girlfriend?"

Right after I completed boot camp, I went on to A-School at Great Lakes Naval Hospital. The medical instruction I received there was my favorite part of the training. I finally felt like I was doing something positive toward my chosen career. I was finally on my way to becoming a Marine corpsman. I shared my excitement with my classmates only to discover that most of them had equally strong feelings about the Marines. Almost to a man, most of them were willing to do anything to avoid Field Medical School and subsequent assignment to the Marines. It was considered the "kiss of death." It wasn't long until I began to understand why the recruiter was so glad to sign me up. I figured, what the heck, my big brother was a Marine and he wouldn't let anything happen to me. In the end, there were only four of us from my Corps class who actually volunteered at our enlistment to go with the Marines—Tom, Ed, Corry, and me.

At field medical, as we learned battle dressing and triage, I discovered I was usually way ahead of my classmates. I often silently thanked my ambulance-driving days and all those budding corpsmen for giving me a head start. I tried not to think of the doom-and-gloom predictions of my classmates.

Once I had completed my training and became a qualified corpsman, I was finally sent to the Marine Corps and assigned to the Third Marine Force Reconnaissance Battalion. I soon discovered that Third Recon was definitely not your mama's regular Marine Unit. Third Force

Recon was one of the elite special-forces units—the "eyes and ears" of the Corps. The job of Force Reconnaissance companies was to conduct preassault and postassault reconnaissance in support of the combat force. In Vietnam, they had to get into the thick of things deep in the bush and bring back intelligence concerning enemy concentrations or troop movement that made the difference for the main units of grunts to follow. Reconners were often dropped in small groups into the heart of hostile territory to count enemy activity, or to call in target coordinates for the bombers or heavy artillery. The problem with collecting this type of recon in a thick jungle-covered country was that they had to get almost nose-to-nose with the enemy to count them.

As a field corpsman, I was expected to go into the bush with my fellows in Force Recon, so, along with the rest of my unit, I participated in a very rugged training regimen designed to prepare us for whatever the Viet Cong might dish out. We thought we were ready for anything. We were wrong.

My platoon was deployed to Vietnam in early 1968, just in time for the bloody TET Offensive. TET was the Vietnamese New Year, held in late January, and had always been deemed a time of cease-fire and celebration—at least until I got there. That year, the Communists decided the holiday was a perfect time to stage an all-out offensive against urban centers throughout South Vietnam. The offensive was all the more unexpected because of a buildup of forces that led the American leadership and General Westmoreland to believe that any real assault would be aimed at Khe Sanh, near the demilitarized zone, or DMZ. Most Marine battalions and a large deployment of support forces were being relocated to the north to hold Khe Sanh. Everyone else was preparing to enjoy the holiday truce. The result was that the North Vietnamese and the Viet Cong caught the American and South Vietnamese forces with their pants down.

The North Vietnamese and Viet Cong forces were driven back with extremely heavy losses, but allied forces also suffered losses, especially those out front, like 3rd Force Recon. Ironically, I learned later that several Marine Recon patrols had noticed and reported the buildup in advance of the offensive. But for some reason, the experts behind the lines completely disregarded their information. Marine Reconners were constantly plagued by desk-bound bureaucrats who often refused to believe the intel reconners spent their blood to gather.

At the time, I only knew that we arrived expecting a lull because of the impending holiday, and found ourselves embroiled in a months-long firefight as our area of operation was inundated with enemy contact. The battalion suffered its heaviest losses of the entire war that month. During the thirty-one days of January 1968, at least thirty-four Reconners died and seventy-two lay wounded. The Marines, including the Reconners, bore the brunt of the brutal fighting in Hue and Khe Sanh.

I saw very little frontline action. I was too busy getting lots of on-the-job training as the dead and wounded poured in. Unfortunately, most of my training consisted of learning how to put guys in body bags. Sometimes the casualties came in as unrecognizable pieces. The stench of death became the only smell in my life. My medical training seemed all but useless. It got to the point that I felt I was more of a "corpseman" than a corpsman.

One unusually bad day, I noticed something familiar about the body I was tagging and bagging. On closer inspection I realized it was Ed. Only a few days later, Tom bought it, and I had to process him as well. Out of the four of us from my class, at least two were already down. I never heard from or saw Corry again, so for all I know I was the only survivor among us.

After only three months "in country," my recon platoon was called back to the States. We had lost too many men to remain active as a functioning unit. Most of my friends were dead or injured. My adventures in Vietnam had taken the gloss off my image of the Marine Corps. Somehow, *Semper Fi* no longer seemed like a romantic motto. I didn't want to be faithful anymore. It wasn't that I didn't want to serve my country. I just wanted to get away from the Marines.

Once back at Camp LeJeune, I approached the chief corpsman. He was an imposing older man who gave the impression of being Corps to the bone. But he was the only one who could help me.

"Chief, do you think there might be some other position available for me?"

He studied me closely for a moment. "You mean something outside of the Marines?"

"Yes sir." I waited, half expecting him to berate me for daring to want a different assignment rather than sticking it out for the glory of the Corps. He made a show of looking at my records, then fixed me with a penetrating stare.

"Have you ever head of the Navy SEALs?"

I quickly dredged my memory for anything I had heard about the group. Remembering information about squids had not been high on my priority list once I had completed corpsman training, but a little bit of Navy had rubbed off on me.

"Yeah, they're some kind of UDT unit. Don't they specialize in underwater demolitions or something?"

The chief's gaze intensified.

"Can you swim?"

"Chief." I looked him right in the eyes. "To get away from the Marines? I can walk on water."

5

A New Deal as a SEAL

AS it turned out, I was only partially right about the SEALs. They were much more than the Underwater Demolition Teams (UDTs) that spawned them. The original UDTs, created during World War II, were used to help clear and prepare the beaches for the D-Day invasion. Their primary focus was on underwater mapping and explosives. The SEALs, on the other hand, were designed to be a special-forces covert unit that could function not only in the sea, but from the air, and on the land as well. The name comes from an anagram for Sea, Air, And Land.

I didn't know it when I volunteered, but the SEALs were considered the most ruthless and efficient of all the American Special Forces. Officially commissioned in 1962 by President Kennedy, SEAL Teams began as a detachment that could infiltrate enemy territory in small groups. While the Teams, as they were often called, were primarily designed to specialize in maritime and riverine environments, they were actually expected to be able to function in any environment, and to be used to conduct clandestine and counterguerrilla operations wherever and whenever such operations were needed.

I also didn't realize that the physical requirements for the SEALs were considered the toughest in the U.S. military. Even though I had already passed the Marine elite forces training program, and proven my abilities during three months in 'Nam, I was still put through a grueling series of tests, both mental and physical. Fortunately, my training with Third Force Recon had toughened me even more than growing up in the Chicago area. I qualified without too much difficulty.

If I had not been a corpsman, I would have been sent on to BUD/S, or Basic Underwater Demolition/SEALS, training. But in 1968, corpsmen could not receive the regular course of instruction, especially in demolitions. That policy came to haunt me later. BUD/S was the grueling, meat grinder course that separated the men who would be SEALs from everyone else. It culminated with Hell Week, five-and-a-half days of constant physical and mental punishment with an average of only twenty minutes of sleep each day. The program is designed to break those who can be broken. During the early days of the program, when someone decided that medics should not be allowed to have this training, they did not think about the facts that medics have to face the same enemy under the same conditions as the rest of the team. I knew nothing of that. I just knew that I was being sent on to a new program called Special Operations Technician in Key West, Florida, along with about seventeen other corpsmen.

I drove down from Chicago to Highway 1 and reached the Florida Keys on a hot, muggy Sunday in August. Key West is located at the farthest tip of the group of islands that make up the Keys. As the southernmost city in the United States, it is actually closer to Cuba than to the rest of the U.S. mainland. The islands of the Keys are joined together by a series of bridges and ferries and connected by Highway 1. As I drove its length, I noticed that the highway was never more than a few hundred yards away from the waters of either the Gulf of Mexico or the Atlantic Ocean. Some of the Keys were so narrow that I could see them both at the same time. A breeze blew off the waters, but the heat and humidity insured that the breeze did nothing to cool the air. Pale pink, aqua, blue, and beige buildings dotted the two-lane roadway, most of them decorated with garish signs advertising all manner of souvenirs, from shells and T-shirts to sea monsters.

I passed a multitude of bathers and boaters enjoying the water in these last days of summer. Fishermen often sat along the edge of the bridges or on boats pulled up beneath them. I remember looking at the blue-green waters and thinking how great it would be to take a cooling swim. It was the last time I would ever look forward to getting into those waters.

I found the naval base easily once I reached Key West. It was situated right off the highway along the shoreline. Like most military installations, the Key West Naval Base was filled with barren, no-nonsense, blocky buildings designed for efficiency rather than style. Unlike most bases, these buildings were all thick-walled and painted in white or pale hues. Fortunately, none of them were aqua or pink. The grounds were neatly kept with well-manicured green lawns accented by the occasional yucca plant and palm tree. A thick growth of mangrove trees formed a forest along the shallower edges of the shoreline, partially obscuring a clear view of the Gulf.

My uniform shirt stuck to my back as I unloaded my gear from the car and attempted to get my bearings. I finally located the U.S. Navy Underwater Swimmers School, marked with a small makeshift sign on a wooden post embedded in the lawn and a statue of a frogman riding a shark. Lugging my gear inside, I was grateful to find that the thick walls blunted the effect of the heat. Two formidable men in blue and gold T-shirts and khaki swim trunks, who I assumed to be instructors, stood near a table at the far end of the reception area. Some others were talking to younger men who had to be newly arrived corpsmen like me. Dick Wolfe, a big, tough red-headed corpsman I had met earlier, came in behind me and hovered at the door. Like me, Dick had served with a Marine Recon unit and survived to tell about it. We had developed a friendly but competitive relationship. Determined to be first to the plate, I stepped up to the "quarterdeck," so called because it was the main "deck" or reception area of a Navy command, and cheerfully greeted my hosts.

"Hey, guys. I'm here to check in."

The man closest to me approached with a disdainful expression on his face. I guessed him to be in his early forties from the grey that streaked his close-cropped hair, but he was powerfully built and very fit despite his age. With hands on hips he managed to tower over me even though I was probably at least as tall as he was.

"Gimme fifty!"

I just got here and they're already gouging me! I thought, as I dug around in my pockets.

"All I've got is two twenties and a ten." I pulled the money out of my pockets and handed it to him. "Here. Can I check in now?"

The room erupted with laughter as all the instructors doubled over and pointed at me. My face flushed as I suddenly realized my mistake and reached out to retrieve my money, but the instructor neatly evaded my grasp.

"Now drop and give me fifty *push-ups*," he commanded as he pocketed the money.

"That's no way to treat . . ." I started to complain.

"Pardon me!" He leaned forward so that he was yelling right in my face. "What are you trying to say? You puke! You ain't gonna last. I'll see to that. Now get down and give me fifty."

As I dropped to the deck, I wondered what I had gotten myself into. There was no doubt that my training had begun, and round one had gone to the instructor. I soon learned that the rounds *always* went to the instructors. They were on our backs and chewing our tails from the moment we arrived. Dick thanked me later for taking point so that I was the fool instead of him.

The man who so neatly humiliated me was Joe Kazmar. He became my greatest enemy over the following month. I'll always love that man. He was aided by Dick Ray, Roger Moscone, and other experienced SEAL instructors. Because of the special rule regarding corpsmen, their task was not an easy one. We couldn't attend BUD/S, but were going to be working side by side with men who had. Because a team is only as strong as its weakest member, they had to find a way to turn us into SEAL operators despite the rule. Joe and the others really had no experience in handling a rag-tag group of medics like us since we were the first group of corpsmen to go through the new program. But they were experts in preparing SEALs. Following the old adage "stick with what you know," they decided to treat us just like SEAL trainees and not worry about the fact that we were medics. To the end, they put us through every kind of hell they could imagine—and they had very active imaginations. They seemed determined to ensure that, just like at BUD/S, only the best would make it to graduation.

What followed was three weeks of the worst PT I had ever experienced. No one warned me that they were going to try to kill me *before* I went back to Vietnam. Out of the original seventeen, only five corpsmen, including Dick Wolfe and myself, lasted through the course. I wanted to walk away within the first week, but the instructors were determined to make me stick it out. I had already been to Vietnam, and had a good idea of what it took to survive there, so they were unwilling to drop me from the class. Every time I wanted to quit, they found something else for me to do.

I spent a lot of time in the water. It seemed we were always swimming, struggling to learn to handle inflatable boats in rugged surf and swift current, getting in the water, hanging in the water, or just crawling through the mud. When I wasn't getting wet, I was doing sixteen-mile runs through the deep beach sand, or straining to hold my part of a huge log high over my head for what seemed like hours. I just *knew* the instructors spent their nights dreaming up new and innovative ways to cause us pain.

One of Joe Kazmar's personal favorites among all his modes of torture was the water tread. He loved to make me swim in the cold water doing flutter kicks for hours. During these sessions, my body became one giant, frozen ache as my legs worked furiously to keep me afloat. Somehow the seaweed always tangled around my legs—like some kind of sea monster—determined to pull me under. I was equally determined to stay afloat, but this was definitely not my idea of fun. I had a suspicion that if I ever went under, no one would bother to pull me out.

During one of these torture sessions when the ocean waters were particularly cold, I finally decided enough was enough. I had nothing to prove. I had already done 'Nam and saw no reason why I should continue to allow myself to be the victim of Joe's sadistic nature.

"I quit!" I sputtered after fighting off a particularly tenacious patch of seaweed.

"Doc." Joe leaned over the gunwale of his comfortable boat, so close I could smell the coffee on his breath. "You can't quit." He yelled, "We've already gotten rid of the rumdums. We're not going to let *you* quit."

"But I said I quit!"

A slow, ferocious smile lit his face. "You can swim, or you can drown. But you can't quit."

Given those options, I decided he was right. I had to swim.

And that was how it went for weeks. By the time the first three weeks were up, the few of us who remained were getting in pretty good condition. At that time the newest class of Underwater Demolition Team Replacement (UDTR) students who had just completed their initial training at Little Creek, Virginia, joined us. At first, they looked down on us because we were not "regular" SEAL trainees. But we had been run around, worked on, and pounded into the sand so much that we soon proved we could hold our own with any of them. Together we began the underwater phase of training.

SEALs are noted for their underwater skills, but up to this point, most of our training had been focused on how to survive on the surface. The world beneath the waves is an unforgiving and alien environment. To survive there, we had to learn how to use Self-Contained Underwater Breathing Apparatus, or SCUBA gear, as well as the more stealthy—and dangerous—self-contained re-breather units. As a medic, the studies of dive physiology, and all the nasty things that can happen to a human body when something goes wrong underwater fascinated me. We spent many hours learning how to cope with all the multitude of equipment failures that can happen when you carry your life support on your back. Since most SEAL underwater operations are conducted at night or in low-light conditions, we spent many hours learning how to navigate in water so dark you couldn't see your buddy. I was usually cold and always wet, but if the seaweed monster attacked, at least I could now fight it on its own turf.

We finished scuba training in November. The UDTR students went back up to Little Creek for demolitions training—barred to corpsmen—and the four of us who had survived continued on to Lakehurst, New Jersey, for parachute training.

Jump school was something else. After all the grueling weeks in Key West, I expected more of the same. Instead, we set a new record for getting our wings. Since there were just the four of us, we received an accelerated course of instruction. The normal three-week course was shortened to three days: one day of ground school, one static line jump, and then fourteen free falls. All the jumps were done within two days. On the fourth day, we were jump qualified and were awarded the Navy gold wings to prove it. I was able to get home in time for Thanksgiving.

Despite the enforced separation from the regular SEAL trainees, our little band of medics actually managed to complete every aspect of basic SEAL training except Hell Week and demolitions, thanks to Joe and his fellow torturers. In my case, I felt I wasn't missing anything. I had done my Hell Week for three months in 'Nam. And while I hadn't learned how to make and deploy explosives, I knew how to help put the victims of those explosives back together. At the time, I thought it was a fair trade.

6

Will Jump for Beer

IMMEDIATELY after Thanksgiving, I checked into UDT 21 at Little Creek, Virginia. Several of the guys I met during dive school classes had already arrived. They were glad to see me, but my new jewelry caused quite a stir.

"Doc, where in the hell did you get the gold wings?"

"I ain't never seen wings on a medic before. Did you mug a flyboy or what?"

"Didn't have to," I retorted. "These are mine, fair and square. I'm free-fall qualified."

"No shit? We got us a jump-qualified Doc!"

Dick Wolfe checked in a few days after I did, giving UDT 21 two jumping medics, but by the time he arrived, the novelty was gone. I enjoyed being the first one in the door for once.

Being qualified allowed me to jump with the East Coast Jump Team. And I took full advantage of that fact, doing a few training jumps to learn how to handle the more sophisticated equipment used in exhibition jumps. Before I could get really proficient, however, it was time to go down to Roosey Roads in Puerto Rico for winter deployment. This was really tough duty. I had to endure the sunny weather in Puerto Rico while my family languished in the crisp Chicago winter.

We were scheduled to return to Little Creek in December. But before I could pack, our executive officer, Fred Kochey, asked me if I would consider staying on for a few months. It seemed that UDT 22, which was just beginning its deployment in Roosey Roads, was short a corpsman. Since we had two corpsmen, Dick and myself, he asked if I would consider postponing my return to fill out 22's roster. For the greater good, I agreed to make the sacrifice. So I continued basking in the sun at Roosey Roads with UDT 22 while Dick and the rest of my unit left for the frozen north.

It was almost spring when I finally got back to Little Creek. My girlfriend Vicki met me there. She and I had known each other for years, growing up in the same town. Up until then, she had been content just to be my girl, but now she wanted to be my wife. I liked that idea, so we drove to Elizabeth City, North Carolina, and got married amid April flowers.

Back in Little Creek, the situation was difficult for Vicki, because we didn't really know any couples. My idea of a night on the town was to hang out at the Jolly Roger, the Team's watering hole. Vicki, on the other hand, was not all that fond of spending her evenings with a bunch of boisterous frogmen. My marriage might have ended soon after it began if I had not run into Frank Thornton at the Jolly Roger. He was with SEAL Team Two and was already a living legend in the Teams. Frank sat holding court near the bar with a group of admirers clustered around him. He was easily recognizable because his devilishly good looks had captured the attention of every single woman in the bar—and probably some not-so-single ones as well. This in turn had assured him the attention of every man in the bar. He looked far younger than his actual years.

I made a point of going up to meet him, and we soon hit it off. He and his equally attractive wife, Lee, ended up taking Vicki and me under their wings. I not only learned a lot from Frank; I owe him and Lee for keeping my fledgling marriage from ending almost before it started. With Lee's help, Vicki met other wives in the area and we soon developed a social life outside of the Jolly Roger.

Just as I became really comfortable with the routine around Little Creek, Fred Kochey called me into his office.

"Doc, you've got to get over to the SEAL Team."

The SEAL Team Two headquarters stood only a few buildings away from the UDT billets. I expected to be assigned to the Team eventually, so this was no surprise. Besides, I had already volunteered for the *Apollo* capsule recovery team. An assignment to Team Two would still allow me to participate in that mission.

"Super. I'll get my stuff and carry it over." I turned to leave.

"Doc, I don't think you understand." Fred stopped me. "You're to report to the *West* Coast—SEAL Team One at Coronado."

"Hollywood UDT!" I was stunned. I had always assumed I would be sent to Team Two, since I was trained on the East Coast and my instructors were all from Team Two. The East Coast and West Coast SEAL Teams had maintained a constant but easygoing rivalry since the first day of their commissioning. Each of the Teams considered itself superior to the other. During my training, I had acquired the East Coasters' disdain of anything from the west.

"West Coast Pukes? No way. I want to stay here! I was supposed to be assigned to the *Apollo* splashdown crew. Uh, sir." I added the last as an afterthought. No sense pushing him too far.

"Sorry Doc. They're short a corpsman on a platoon scheduled for deployment to Vietnam, and you're it. You report to Captain Dave Schiable in Coronado by June 1st."

Vietnam. I hadn't really expected to go back there so soon. Tucked away in the comfortable environments of Puerto Rico and then Virginia, I had almost managed to forget we had a war going on.

Fred understood my reluctance to leave the East Coast Team. "It's not so bad. Your friend Dick Wolfe is already out there. Oh, by the way," he grinned, "once you're out there, you've been requested for a Temporary Assigned Duty as one of the designated corpsmen for the *Apollo 11* splashdown crew. You report to Lt. Tim Kenney at UDT 11, also based in Coronado. Your SEAL platoon doesn't deploy until October, so you've got time to go help some astronauts. I'll even authorize some basket leave so that you'll have time to get your gear out to the West Coast."

That was the assignment I really wanted. It almost made up for having to drive to Coronado. When I told Vicki about my orders, she was a little disappointed at having to leave her new friends, but understood that it was part of my being in the Navy. She helped me pack our stuff and we began the cross-country road trip to the Pacific coast.

After a very long drive, we finally arrived in San Diego. I left Vicki at our new apartment while I reported in to Team One at Coronado, a cozy little picture-perfect town located just across the bay from San Diego. I assured her we would have the weekend together, since it was Friday. There was no way they would give me an assignment over the weekend.

My certainty had not taken Chief Blackburn into account. The Chief Master at Arms of Team One, a mean-spirited corpsman who hated all other corpsmen, especially low-ranking medics like me, had other plans for me.

"Well, Doc," he sneered, "guess you're here just in time to take the weekend duty. I got a date to keep."

With whom? Attila the Hun? I sighed. *So much for a weekend with my wife.* Vicki would understand. I hoped.

The only good thing about having the duty that weekend was that I ran into Dick Wolfe.

"Man, you are the prettiest thing I've seen since I got here!" I grabbed his meaty hand and pumped it hard.

"Don't tell that to Vicki!" he laughed. "She may have second thoughts about marrying a man who thinks I look good!"

"Too late for second thoughts. Vicki is my wife now—and definitely better looking than you. But I haven't seen much of her thanks to that sorry sack of a chief."

"Gave you the duty, huh?" He gave me a sympathetic grimace. "He got me, too. He loves to jerk over young corpsmen. I understand he's not too fond of the older ones, either."

He smiled at the obscene gesture I aimed in the general direction of the chief, and then asked, "So which platoon did you get?"

"I've been assigned to Alpha."

"God, you've still got the luck!"

"What the hell are you talking about? I just got here and I'm already scheduled for Vietnam." Going back to 'Nam, especially with a SEAL platoon I hadn't even met, much less worked with, didn't exactly strike me as the best kind of luck.

"Yeah, but Alpha Platoon doesn't deploy until October. That will give you some quality time with the old lady. Might even make up for this weekend. Kilo—my platoon—is already in predeployment training at Niland. I'm shipping out before the summer's over—sometime in the next month or so. At least you've got a little time to get up to speed. I had to hit the ground running. And let me tell you, keeping up with these guys is no picnic. You think the chief is bad? As far as these SEALs in Team One are concerned, all corpsmen are just pecker-checkers. They don't believe any of us knows his way around a weapon, much less a war."

I laughed at that, Dick being one of the few corpsmen besides me who had survived a tour in 'Nam with a recon platoon. But Dick's survival record was even more impressive than mine: He had actually spent most of his tour on the front lines.

"At least I won't have to deal with Chief Blackburn much longer," he continued, slapping me hard on the back. "That pleasure will be all yours, kid!"

I hesitated to tell him that I wasn't sticking around either. Somehow I felt that telling him about my plum interim assignment to the *Apollo* splashdown crew would wreck the mood. I was scheduled to check in with Lt. Kenney on Monday. After that, Chief Blackburn would have to find someone else to pick on.

I signed in with Lt. Kenney as planned and began preparations with the splashdown crew. We were not scheduled to go out to sea until the second week in July, so I had a little free time in my schedule. I was determined to find something to keep me busy enough that Chief

Blackburn could not get at me again. Jess Tolison and the West Coast Jump Team provided the perfect solution.

Jess Tolison was a plank owner of Team Two, which meant he was one of the original members of the Team when it was first commissioned. He had spent most of his career on the East Coast and, like me, had deep feelings for the East Coast way of doing things. Jess received a transfer to the West and Team One upon accepting his commission as a warrant officer. He now headed the West Coast Jump Team.

The jump team needed one more skydiver to fill out their roster. Jess found out I was a recent East Coast transfer, and decided I might be the perfect choice for the team. He tracked me down one afternoon to find out if his suspicions were correct. Just short of medium height, Jess had a broad face and determination that reminded me of a bulldog. After swapping news about his friends back at Little Creek, he got down to business.

"So, Doc, are you free fall qualified?"

"Yeah. Why?"

He ignored the question.

"How qualified?"

"Well, I jumped with the East Coast Exhibition Jump Team." I didn't mention that I never actually got to do more than a few practice jumps with them.

"Great! That's just what I wanted to hear. We need you for the Fourth of July demonstration. We're practicing tomorrow." The next day was the 30th of June—my birthday. It sounded like a good way to make certain I was far away from the chief on that day.

"Have you got a para-commander?"

"Hell, I don't have anything." It had never occurred to me to bring a parachute with me from Little Creek, or to arrange to have one checked out, here.

"No problem. Let's go over to the loft and see if we can't fit you up."

We drove over to the parachute loft, which was not really a loft at all, but a large building where parachutes and jump gear were packed and stored. It took only a short time to find and fit the gear I needed to be able to jump with the team. Para-commanders are very specialized chutes with an elongated design that allows the jumper to control and steer the chute once it has been deployed. Regular parachutes, such as those used in most large air drops, allow for only minimal control, and are mostly victims of the wind. The much greater control allowed by a para-commander enables a skilled skydiver to land exactly on any given mark. They are designed with the altimeter and the stopwatch on the back of the reserve chute so that they can be read easily by the jumper to allow precision timing of the parachute release.

The next day, I met the rest of the team on the field as we got ready for our first practice together. It was the end of June and the jump was scheduled for July 4th. We didn't have much time.

"This is Doc Greg McPartlin." Jess thumped me on the back. "He used to perform with my old compadres on the East Coast Jump Team." I smiled and tried to look competent while struggling to remember how to rig my chute correctly

"So, Doc. You gonna show us how it's done back East?" a red-headed fellow challenged.

"Well actually, I'm still a novice, but . . ."

"I'll bet you are," a short fellow named Tom snorted. "Okay, we'll show you how we do it out here!"

I could tell they didn't believe me, not after the buildup Jess had given. As the ground receded from view below me, I thought that perhaps I might have exaggerated my experience just a bit too much. These guys all had numerous free-fall performances behind them. I only had a few days of accelerated jump school and some practice jumps with the East Coast Team. It was a little late to 'fess up now.

We exited the bird at about 10,500 feet. Cloud cover obscured the jump zone, making it difficult to get any bearings. And plummeting to earth from over ten thousand feet is a lousy time to discover that you've put the reserve chute on upside down. My stopwatch and altimeter were on the bottom of the pack, facing away from me. With the air whipping by me as I fell, I began to wonder if this birthday might be my last.

After a moment, I discovered that by stretching to look over the pack, I could still see both instruments, but they were upside down. *Good,* I thought, *No problem. I can compensate.*

We were supposed to pop our chutes at just below one thousand feet, but the obscuring cloud cover made it impossible to judge distance to the ground except by altimeter. I imagined terra firma rushing up to greet me very quickly just beyond the clouds. I strained to read the gauges, pulling my chute when I thought I had passed one thousand feet. Unfortunately, a 7 looks a lot like a 1 when it is upside down. I had misread the inverted instrument, and opened up at about six thousand feet.

Now para-commanders are easy to steer—except when you open up five thousand feet too high. There is no way to compensate for the prevailing winds at such a high altitude. Instead of proving my skills and landing right on target with everyone else, I found myself caught like a leaf in a breeze, completely helpless as I drifted all the way across San Diego Bay, surprising the longshoremen at the National Steel Boatyards. They had never seen a SEAL drop out of the sky before, especially not into the middle of their boatyard.

I gathered in my chute and waited, hoping someone would come get me. About the time I was convinced they were going to make me walk back to base, a jeep full of SEALs arrived to fetch the team's wandering parachutist.

"Uh, thanks for coming to get me."

"We don't give a rat's ass about you personally. Around here the tradition is that the last man down buys the beer. That means you, Doc. We just came to be sure we got our beer."

"I thought you knew what you were doing!" Tom bellowed as soon as I had loaded my chute into the jeep.

"Shit, that's probably the way they do it on the East Coast," Red quipped. "No wonder they sent him out here."

My face as red as Red's hair, I shot back, "Hey, I'm sorry. I never said I was an expert. I just need a little more practice."

Fortunately, they made sure I got more practice, a lifetime's worth in the four days remaining until the exhibition. But after a few more jumps I started to feel like a real part of the team. With each jump we improved dramatically, moving into and out of our formations with ease, until even Jess said we looked pretty good. The exhibition jump on the Fourth was scheduled to take place over Glorietta Bay, next to the Amphibious Base so the audience could watch from a large open area on shore. Directly across the bay lay a yacht club and a large golf course, which provided us with a clear landing zone.

The day of the demonstration, a large audience gathered all along the shoreline to watch our show. As I entered the plane, Tom poked me and said, "Looking forward to another beer on East Coast Doc, here." Everyone laughed but me.

When it came time to jump, we exited the plane in good order and quickly formed up on each other. Gathering up as we fell, we moved through the various formations almost flawlessly, ending by holding hands to create a human ten-pointed star. On the count, we broke formation and separated to pull our chutes.

I was very pleased with our performance, but Tom's comments on that first day still rankled.

I'll show these sons of bitches, I thought to myself. *I'll be the first one on the ground and make up for opening so high in practice.*

I passed 1,000 feet while my teammates deployed their chutes and disappeared from view. As I hurtled toward the ground, I thought I could hear the collective gasp of the crowd when they realized I was still falling. But I wasn't worried. I kept my eye out for the new Bay Bridge that spanned the distance from Coronado to San Diego—so new it hadn't even opened yet. At roughly 250 feet in height, I knew I would be close to my planned limit of 600 feet when I could see the bridge. Still well within safety parameters, but lower than anyone else in the team.

I'm going to be the first on the deck, I thought as I saw the bridge and released my chute. The audience got a better show than they bargained for, but I was comfortably in control of my chute when I passed the bridge. I made a clean, comfortable landing—always the most important part of any jump—and was bundling up my chute when the rest of the team touched down.

Jess released his harness and stormed over to me without stopping to bundle his chute, fury burning in his eyes. It took no time at all for him to share his thoughts, in graphic detail, on my jumping style.

"What the hell did you think you were doing?" he shouted, his square face inches from mine. "That may be the new way they do things on the East Coast, but I can guarantee you're never jumping with *my* jump team again!"

Funny thing, that style of skydiving didn't go over real well on the East Coast, either. At least I didn't have to buy the beer.

7

The Right Stuff

I didn't get much time to reflect on my Independence Day performance before I found myself again practicing to jump out of an aircraft, this time without a parachute. By mid-July, I was bobbing on the Pacific Ocean with the Apollo 11 capsule recovery team aboard the USS Hornet. We were waiting for Neil Armstrong, Edwin Aldrin, Jr., and Michael Collins to do their moon thing and come home. As the recovery divers, our job was to jump into the water once the spacecraft splashed down and secure and recover the capsule, its contents, and all its parachutes. It had become a tradition that every incoming space capsule that splashed down, since the Mercury program, was met in the water by UDT men.

Under the watchful eyes of the *Hornet*'s deck apes, we spent our days practicing the recovery maneuvers in the waters around the ship's position. The ocean temperatures were mild—and teeming with sharks. At the time, their presence didn't really bother me. During almost every dive I saw their sleek, deadly shapes either cruising nearby, or hanging in the distance, their shadowy shapes barely visible against the deep blue. The movie *Jaws* did not yet exist, so it didn't occur to me to be afraid of them. If *Jaws* had predated *Apollo 11,* it would have been a lot more difficult to get into that water. I would have been pointing out that sharks have been known to *eat* seals. But if these sharks liked seal meat, it wasn't the sort spelled with capital letters. I ignored them and stuck to my business, and they did the same.

When we weren't practicing the recovery, we joined the NASA boys on the hanger deck or up in the ward room going over the logistical details of the mission. Unlike the rest of the boat crew, who were regulation to the core, our team was very informal. We wore UDT trunks, blue and gold T-shirts, and coral booties as our everyday uniform. None of us, including Lt. Kenney, wore any rank identifying insignias. Everyone just knew us as "the Frogmen." For the most part, the crew of the *Hornet* treated us very well, but there were unfortunate exceptions.

One morning, during a combined meeting that included our team, the commanding officer of the *Hornet* and the NASA contingent, Lt. Kenney, called me over to tell me that he had a sinus problem and couldn't clear his ears. We had a practice dive scheduled for later that day, so this posed a potentially serious problem. If he could not clear his ears, he would not be able to equalize the pressure once he submerged below the surface and risked damaging or puncturing his eardrums. Fortunately, the condition could be easily remedied with a decongestant and some antihistamine. The LT asked me, as his corpsman, to get him the needed meds. Sick bay was located just behind the ward room, so I ducked out of the meeting and into sick bay.

It was about 0930, and sick call had just ended. The ship's chief corpsman, a pencil-necked geek named Jones who didn't look like he had ever seen a push-up, much less passed basic training, was just sending his last patient out the door when I arrived.

"Hey, Chief, can I get some Neosynephrine nasal spray and some Actifed tablets for my lieutenant?"

The chief puffed up as if I had just asked him for his life savings. He looked me up and down, examining my trunks and T-shirt as if I was some kind of particularly obnoxious germ he had discovered under his microscope.

"Sick call is from 0600 to 0900. Come back tomorrow."

"But he needs them now!"

"And just who the hell do you think you are? Coming into my sick bay dressed like *that* and asking for drugs? I'll decide what meds to prescribe. I repeat, sick call is over."

"Chief, I am a special operations technician with UDT-11. As such, I am fully qualified to prescribe medication." I attempted to maintain polite protocol despite the fact that this guy was getting to me.

"Oh yeah? What's *your* rank?" His dripped with condescension.

"E-5. Why?"

"Well, then, junior, if you want meds for your lieutenant, I suggest you return during sick call like everyone else. And wear a uniform!"

"Up your ass, Chief! I'll just let the boss know he will have to wait until tomorrow to come and see you in person. You're right, I'm probably just too junior to assess his illness. Funny thing, though, the government thinks I am old enough to be trusted with the astronauts!"

I was pissed, partially at myself for asking this jerk for anything. I had a whole supply of meds and equipment stowed down below in our Conex box along with all our dive gear. I was just being lazy because sick bay was so close and I didn't feel like walking that far.

I went back into the ward room, still steaming, and asked Lt. Kenney for the keys to the Conex box so I could get to my med supplies.

"I'm sorry, LT," I said in a stage whisper loud enough for anyone in the room to overhear. "I tried to get meds from sick bay, but Chief Asshole over there says if you want meds you have to come and get 'em yourself—so long as you do it during sick call, that is."

Lt. Kenney, always more of a gentleman than I, sighed in sympathy and retrieved the keys.

The CO, a no-nonsense kind of guy, must have overheard my tactfully phrased report and done some quick tail-chewing over his com, because before I could walk out of the ward room with the keys, the chief corpsman, with the ship's head doctor in tow, appeared in the doorway "to check on my Mr. Kenney." I watched the show as the doctor very solicitously examined his ears, nose, and throat. Lt. Kenney politely suffered through the exam while the much-cowed chief hovered nearby. After a few moments, the doctor made his diagnosis and ordered the chief to run back to sick bay for some Neosynephrine nasal spray and some Actifed tablets.

"Funny," I muttered so only the LT could hear, "that's exactly what I asked for earlier."

Lt. Kenney rolled his eyes at me when they weren't looking, but, with the true diplomacy of a born officer, thanked the doctor kindly for the meds and for giving his personal attention to the matter.

Despite this and other minor irritations, we were ready and eager on July 24th, when it came time for the *Apollo 11* capsule to re-enter the atmosphere after its historic journey to the Moon. According to plan, the team was split into two recovery teams in two different helicopters. On splashdown, the first unit would secure the capsule itself and see to the astronauts within. The secondary team would recover the parachutes which were expected to land some distance from the capsule. In true UDT fashion, we had all been trained to do both jobs. I was assigned to the secondary team, commanded by Lt. Kenney, with the recovery of the parachutes as our planned objective.

The winds were up that day, and I noticed the ocean swells were high as I joined the team in our helo, already wearing most of my gear and carrying my fins.

"Rough seas," Lt. Kenney warned us, signaling the pilots as he, too climbed in. I re-checked my gear as we flew approximately twelve miles downrange from the USS *Hornet,* to the spot where the NASA folks had determined that the parachutes would fall. The other helicopter remained with the *Hornet,* where the main capsule was expected to splashdown. As we hovered on station, I peered into the sky and waited, hoping to see something of the capsule before it fell out of our area.

I ended up getting a better look than expected. When the *Apollo 11* broke through the atmosphere and the chutes opened, the capsule dropped twelve miles south of the *Hornet*—approximately where NASA thought the chutes would end up and almost on top of us. As soon as the trajectory was confirmed, we became the primary capsule team, and received the green light to go in upon splashdown.

I gathered my fins, did a final check of my gear, and looked up in time to see the capsule hit the water. The pilots moved right up to the capsule's location, then dropped down as close to the water as they dared and held steady. Lt. Kenney stepped to the door and jumped in. I prepared to follow. With the waves swelling fifteen to twenty feet, I knew it was important to time our jump to land at the high point of the swell. We had practiced this maneuver, and usually only fell five or ten feet before hitting the water and popping to the surface. I watched the ocean rise up, fall away suddenly, and rise up again. I clutched my fins and jumped.

I fell the expected ten feet—and kept falling for another fifteen or twenty-five more before hitting the water. Hard. I realized that I must have missed the swell and hit a deep trough. The impact from the height plus the weight of my gear carried me deep under the waves. At that depth, instead of rising back to the surface, I just kept sinking. I knew the compression from the increasing water pressure would continue to pull me down if I didn't do something to increase my buoyancy. I pulled the emergency CO cartridge to inflate my UDT life vest and immediately popped to the surface. I could see the capsule drifting away from me, so I quickly put on my fins and swam hard to catch it. The distance refused to close. The current pulled the capsule away faster than I could swim. Determined to catch it, I put on an extra burst of speed and finally managed to grab hold of the spacecraft. I looked around and was gratified to see that the rest of the team had also reached the craft.

Only when we all reached the capsule did the true historical significance begin to sink in. *Wow, the first guys ever to set foot on the Moon are actually in that thing! And here I am, a twenty-year-old Navy frogman, and I'm part of the recovery team!* I could see by the expressions on the guys' faces that most of them were having similar thoughts.

But we had work to do. With the others, I set about securing the capsule just as we had practiced so many times. The procedure went smoothly, just as practiced with the rehearsal craft—except this capsule was not clean and shiny like the rehearsal craft. She bore blackened scars from the heat of re-entry, deep pits from space-born debris, and smelled like burned rubber.

Our first task was to secure the large orange floatation collar around the capsule. The collar kept the heavy metal capsule from sinking and also stabilized it a little bit so the astronauts would not get seasick. They had been weightless in space for a long time, and dropping into a wildly tossing ocean wouldn't do much to quiet their stomachs. We had to steady the craft quickly or it wouldn't take long for three astronauts to start hurling Tang.

Once the collar was in place, I set about my assigned task: communicating with the astronauts to ascertain if everyone was okay. I moved over to the hatch and tapped the glass porthole with my K-Bar's knife handle. Michael Collins appeared at the hatch and gave me the thumbs-up sign, then did it twice more. Three times meant all of them were okay. I relayed that fact to the hovering helicopter so that they could send the good news back to the *Hornet*. We then waited, hatch still tightly sealed, while the astronauts put on their bio-suits to protect against possible contamination from any moon germs. NASA worried a lot about moon germs, so the astronauts had to stay sealed in bio-suits until they were decontaminated. Once they were ready, they blew the explosive release bolts on the hatch and I swung open the door. A fetid stench rose from the aperture, taking me by surprise, causing me to gag. Boy, did it stink!

"Good grief! Who had the extra jalapeños?"

Michael Collins laughed and awkwardly climbed through the open hatchway. As I guided him onto a small life raft tethered to the capsule, I thought about the fact that Michael went all that way, but never did get to land on the Moon. He had to fly the orbiter while Aldrin and Armstrong rode down to the Moon's surface in the Eagle. Once on the raft, I helped him into the specially designed hoist cage and watched as he was lifted up to the helicopter above.

Next, Edwin Aldrin climbed out, to be lifted into the helo, followed by Commander Neil Armstrong. After I helped Commander Armstrong onto the hoist, I peered through the mask on his headgear and noticed that he appeared in good spirits. He looked at me and smiled.

"Welcome back safely, sir!" I yelled over the wind from the rotor wash, and snapped a crisp salute. He, in return, mouthed a thank-you and gave me a thumbs-up sign. After he was hoisted onto the helicopter, I thought, *Wow. I've just had the first conversation with the first man to walk on the Moon!*

We got the capsule back to the USS *Hornet* and secured it on board, but because we had been exposed to both the astronauts and the interior of the capsule, we were ourselves lifted aboard another helicopter and put in quarantine. The NASA doctors wanted to be certain we didn't have any of those pesky moon germs. Of course, I knew more than they did, and declared us all healthy after a couple of hours, long before the official okay.

Later, after all the congratulatory speeches were done, we watched the replay of our splashdown recovery as it had appeared on television. When it came to the part where the hatch was opened, I saw myself speaking to the astronauts.

"Hey, Doc, what's that you're saying?" Chief Jones asked.

"When?"

"Right there. As the hatch was opened."

"Uh, I'm not sure, Chief," I lied. "I think it was something like, 'We are from the government, and we are here to help you.'"

On July 29th, while the rest of the recovery team was basking in the limelight, I quietly flew off the *Hornet* to join my platoon, already in preparation for deployment to Vietnam.

8

The FNG

FROM the *Hornet*, I flew to Barbers Point, Hawaii, and from there on to North Island. The flight gave me a lot of time to think. I was finally going to meet my platoon. But I did not look forward to that meeting. I knew the men of Alpha Platoon had been in predeployment training in Niland for several weeks, and had been working together as a fighting team for more than three months. These guys would be tight as blood brothers. Unlike the Marines and most other branches of the service, SEALs always trained together and always deployed together as a platoon. It increased their effectiveness because they always knew what their teammates were thinking.

I knew from experience that newcomers to any established platoon were usually viewed as interlopers, useless deadwood, or worse. In my first tour, I often thought of any newbie that way, mostly because the new guy was usually the next man I had to put in a body bag. We called them FNGs, or, if they were straight out of training, "cherries." But this time, I was the outsider. I was about to go from being one of the lesser heroes of the *Apollo* mission to being the "Fucking New Guy."

Landing at North Island, I stopped at Coronado long enough to requisition a six-by-six truck, then began the drive to Niland. I finally arrived on July 31st. Niland was a rugged, sparse, training camp established near the Salton Sea primarily to prepare SEAL platoons for their work in Vietnam. Coronado could be warm, but the heat on the island was sweltering. As I followed the road to camp, I passed some unusual structures off to the side. It was a cluster of Vietnamese-style hooches. Apparently the camp came complete with its own mock VC village and jungle. I discovered after traveling a little farther that it also came with something much more important—a bar. I made a note to check out the latter at my earliest opportunity.

I stopped near a group of tough-looking men that had to be Alpha Platoon. My platoon. The outside temperature hovered around 114 degrees, but as I climbed out of the truck to meet them, I suddenly felt as if I had just stepped into a freezer. Twelve sets of cold eyes fastened their frigid gaze on me as if I was some kind of rancid meat.

A wiry-built man with short dark hair sat at a table shaded by a tarp, doing some paperwork. He looked to be thirty-something, with well-chiseled features, and had an air of command. I guessed he was Dick Flanagan, the officer in charge of Alpha Platoon. Despite his rank, he wore only flip-flops, a bathing suit, and a fresh white T-shirt. I immediately felt overdressed, still wearing the green fatigues and jump boots I had donned on the *Hornet.* I stepped up to the table and stood there, sweating and feeling as out of place as a whore in church. The rest of the guys lounged nearby, casually cleaning their weapons while giving me "the look." They were obviously seasoned pros—all dirty and cocky and ready for anything. I knew my ass was grass if I said the wrong thing to any of them, so I silently handed Lt. Flanagan my orders. He gave me the once-over with sharp eyes that seemed to look right through me, then took the papers I offered. I stood there while he lit up a Pall Mall and slowly opened the envelope with his K-Bar knife.

"Well, what do we have here?" he all but sneered. "A young pecker-checker right fresh from the fleet."

I gave him a puzzled glance and swore to myself I would try and grow a beard to look older. I had been told I looked more like an extra from *Leave it to Beaver* than a Navy SEAL, but that had not been a real problem before this.

"Hey, dick-smith!" a slight, blond fellow called out, using yet another derogatory term for a corpsman. "Are you here to give us our short arms inspection?"

I recognized the popular colloquial phrase for examinations for sexual diseases, but was unsure, since they certainly knew why I was there, why they were saying that to me.

"He still looks wet behind the ears," quipped a fellow sporting sunshades. "We should send this 'cherry' back to his boat until he dries off a little."

The lieutenant, ignoring the comments, began reading my orders and invited me to sit down and have a smoke. I took the chair, but declined the smoke. A few minutes later he called a powerfully built, dark-haired guy over and introduced him as Leading Petty Officer Wayne Bohannan.

"Boh," he said, "this is Doc McPartlin. They sent him out here to be our platoon corpsman."

I started to shake his hand, but he just stared into my eyes with a look of disgust, and turned away. This kind of treatment had gone way beyond the hazing I expected for being the new guy. "Hey, nice to meet you too!" I snapped.

He spun around, grabbed my hand in a bone-crushing handshake and attempted to jerk me up to his face. I immediately recognized the tactic. My brother Jeff, the toughest son of a bitch I ever knew, used to do that a lot and taught me how to defend against it. I pushed my hand as far into the handshake as I could, while squeezing his fingers and pushing down as hard as I could to try to force him down onto his knee. It was a standoff. He didn't budge, and neither did I.

Face to face, he glared into my eyes, and snarled in an unmistakable southern Florida drawl. "Just who the hell do you think you are? And what the fuck do you think you are doing here with my platoon?"

"Hey, I didn't ask for this job!" Something was definitely not right here. In my experience, corpsmen were always treated well—with good reason. We controlled the shot records, no small thing in a country as fraught with disease as Vietnam. Not to mention that when a man goes down wounded and yells for Doc, he definitely doesn't want the guy who holds his life in his hands to be his enemy.

"Mr. Flanagan." I released Bohannan's hand and turned angrily to the lieutenant, "Is there a problem here?"

"You're damn right there is!" he said, fire in his eyes as he rose from his seat to face me. "We are little more than two months away from deploying to Vietnam, and they send us the one thing we don't need—some nonqualified smart-ass fleet corpsman fresh off the boat to replace Doc Curl. Curl was bad enough, but now we're expected to risk our lives to protect your sorry ass on operations 'cause you won't know what the hell you are doing."

I met his fire with my own. "Why don't you review my service record before ripping off my head and shitting down my neck?" He glared at me, but I stood my ground, lit up a Marlboro, and watched as Lt. Flanagan slowly picked up my orders again and read my service jacket.

I knew what he would find there: Recruit Master at Arms, Great Lakes R.O.T.C.; Number two in his class, Hospital Corpsman, A-School, Great Lakes Illinois; Number one of forty-five students, Field Medical School, Camp LeJeune, North Carolina; 3rd Force Recon, Field Hospital Corpsman, Republic of Vietnam; Number two in his class, U.S. Navy Underwater Swimmer School; Special Operation Technician designated number 8492, Key West, Florida; U.S. Navy free-fall parachute school, Lakehurst, New Jersey, authorized to wear gold free-fall jump wings; UDT-21, UDT-22, Roosey Roads, Puerto Rico, and Little Creek, VA; TAD UDT-11 *Apollo* 11 recovery team; PCS orders SEAL Team One, July 30, 1969.

After a moment, Flanagan sat down and began to laugh. The others looked on in confusion. "Well, looks like the brass doesn't hate us after all. This doc's no 'cherry.' He's already been in country once before." He then proceeded to read my record out loud to the rest of the platoon.

When he finished, Bohannan walked up, gave me a Coke, and slapped me on the back with enough force to rattle my teeth. "Doc, don't ever give me cause to hurt you again." He grabbed me in a bear hug calculated to break ribs. "Welcome to Alpha Platoon. Now get your gear off the truck and get changed. You look like you are sweating bullets!"

I gladly ran to do as he ordered, feeling that the ice had thawed. Now I had nothing to prove, except to myself.

But not all the guys of Alpha Platoon were satisfied by my past record. That evening, after getting my gear stowed away and checking in with the base doctor, I headed for the bar I had spotted on the way in. It was a little place called the Hi-Ho Club. The décor was early negligence, but it had booze and a couple of pool tables, so I thought I could make it home. Some of the guys from my platoon were already there. Wayne Bohannan greeted me warmly and started introducing me around. Ensign Bill Moody, second in command of the platoon and in charge of the second squad, was tall, slim, and very fit. He had a square jaw and a slight cleft chin that gave him a face reminiscent of a classic superhero from the comics. He was just leaving the bar to go finish some paperwork, but it was obvious as he shook my hand, that this SEAL would rather be out in the field than in any office.

"Sometimes I think Mr. Moody don't believe Hell Week is over," Boh admitted when he had left. "He loves to get us all out of racks at 0500. Says it keeps us sharp."

A muscular man with dark, gentle eyes came over to introduce himself as Frank Richardson. "But you can call me 'Preacher.'"

"Yeah, Preacher here not only watches our backs, he keeps a close eye on our souls as well. But don't kid yourself; he can bring down the wrath of God when it's necessary!"

Preacher looked somewhat self-conscious at that description, but gave me a genuinely warm smile and firm handshake. I got the definite impression that this wasn't really where he wanted to be.

A short stocky bulldog of a man in a buzz cut stuck his head in the door and Boh took the opportunity to introduce me to Dave Langlois, Alpha Squad's sixty-gunner. He had the face of an innocent kid, but the heart of a banjo-playing redneck. He definitely looked like a man who would have no trouble at all humping a heavy M-60 machine gun. He was followed closely by Jonah Benanti, his Bravo squad counterpart, who was wearing sunshades like some kind of rock star.

"I don't think he ever takes those off except to sleep," Boh joked. "And maybe not even then. You'll like him. He's also a Midwest boy. A good 'wop,' as you call 'em."

The fair-haired guy who had yelled at me earlier was Jim Ritter. His earlier animosity had been replaced by an apologetic smile. "Sorry about this afternoon, Doc. We thought you were a cherry—or that you were like Doc Curl."

X.T. Cossee, whose long nose, protruding ears, and curly dark hair gave him an exotic Middle Eastern look, concurred. "Yeah. We didn't realize they'd sent us a *real* medic."

This sentiment was repeated often as I was introduced to John Mitchell, Terry Jenkins, Mike Kearns, and Jim Loeding. None of them seemed to have high opinions of corpsmen. I was beginning to realize that my predecessor had not been a typical corpsman, at least not the corpsmen *I* knew, and that I may have had Doc Curl to thank for my chilly reception.

"So Boh, what *did* happen to your first corpsman?"

"We really don't like to talk about it much."

"Well, I would really like to know what kind of an act I have to follow."

Boh's dark eyes reflected storm clouds for a moment. "He got busted for pot, but I know he was also doing harder stuff. They're probably going to drum him out of the Teams, and probably out of the service entirely."

Now I understood the depths of the platoon's resentment. Drugs might have been commonplace in the rest of the service, but anything that altered our ability to think fast and move faster was a serious liability for SEALs. And anyone who did drugs was a liability to his teammates—especially if they depended on him for their life. Alcohol was usually the closest thing to a drug most SEALs would risk, and even then only when not in a combat situation.

"So we are stuck with a damn pecker-checker after all." The surly voice came from a dark-haired guy of medium height and build shooting pool on the far table. "Well, I hope he's on someone else's squad, 'cause I don't want to go into the bush with a nonqual dick-smith who thinks he's a SEAL. Better we take care of ourselves than risk our lives taking care of him."

"Ric Schroeder. Radioman," Boh supplied. "Ignore him."

"So what's his problem?"

"He thinks that anyone who didn't go through BUD/S and Hell Week isn't really a SEAL and doesn't belong here. Doc Curl did a lot to prove him right."

"Hey, I would have gone if they'd have let me."

"Doesn't matter. Unfortunately, there's a lot of guys that feel that way. If you didn't go through it, you're not an operator until you prove you are." He lowered his voice. "It don't help that Ric almost didn't make it through himself."

I wondered how many of the guys still felt that way. I was fairly sure I could have gotten through BUD/S. Joe Kazmar had said as much. But to these guys, actions were what mattered. I was going to have to work really hard to prove myself as an operator.

"I wonder how long until this one craps out. Do you think it will be before or after one of us gets hurt?" Schroeder continued.

"So you good for a game?" I asked, indicating the open pool table. I wanted to do something to keep myself from taking the loudmouth Schroeder apart.

"Sure. Loser buys the beer."

I tried to concentrate on my game and ignore Mr. Schroeder, but he kept putting out a load of garbage calculated to make Mother Theresa boil. *This is one of the guys I'm going to have at my back in the bush?* My grip tightened on my pool cue until my knuckles were white. I kept playing, but started to miss shots. Apparently my lack of reaction got to Schroeder. He came up close behind me to be certain I heard him.

"This bar's only for *real* SEALs. Jesus Christ, don't we have enough to contend with without having to baby-sit?"

That was the last straw. I had had enough. I slammed the butt of my pool cue backward, nailing Ric right in the crotch. As he went down I spun around and got a good grip on his head, holding him in place with two fistfuls of brown hair.

"Do you really want your pretty face smashed on my knee?" I asked pleasantly. "Or is that—" I edged my foot toward his groin and had the satisfaction of seeing him flinch—"*real* enough for you?"

From his awkward kneeling position, his face only inches away from my knee, Ric indicated in a very small, breathy voice that he did not think my continuing along those lines was a very good idea.

I released him and turned to see the rest of the guys trying to suppress their laughter.

"You're all right, Doc," Boh said, thumping me again.

After a moment, Ric climbed up off the floor and shook my hand.

"I guess I was wrong, Doc," he wheezed. "With moves like that, you've definitely got a head start on becoming an operator."

Despite our rocky beginning, Ric Schroeder and I grew to be very close over the next several weeks of training. We discovered we had a lot in common. Like me, he was an Illinois boy who had been raised Catholic and was still trying to recover from it. Ric was only four years older than I was, but he knew everything. He had a quick smile, a quick tongue, and a quicker left hook.

During training it was normal for the radioman and the corpsman to spend time together, because we were the ones who had to deal with specialized equipment above and beyond the usual ordinance carried by the rest of the team. But Ric became more than a comrade in arms; he became my new big brother.

We were split up into two squads, with Ric, Boh, and myself assigned to Alpha Squad under Lt. Flanagan. "Radical Dick," they called him. I soon learned why when he started screaming orders at us during an exercise. I actually enjoyed the challenge of the training, and could hold my own in most things—at least until we got to the firing range. I could sneak and track and do PT with the best of them, but on the range I couldn't hit the broad side of a barn. Ric tried to help me, but my improvement was slight, even with his coaching.

But the LT had a solution. He and the instructors ended up issuing me a Stoner M-63A as my primary weapon. The powerful little machine gun gave me much more firepower than the weapons normally carried by a corpsman. And if any targets came into range, I didn't have to have good aim. I just had to pull the trigger and hose them down with bullets.

By the time we returned from Niland to San Diego around the first of September, I was still the new guy, and probably would be until we hit combat, but now I felt more like their little brother. I hadn't been there at the beginning, but they wouldn't dream of going without me.

9

Off to Vietnam. Again.

IT was late in September when I actually received my orders to deploy to Vietnam. Two months earlier, the Johnson administration had begun the process that would later be called *Vietnamization,* by replacing General William Westmoreland with General Creighton Abrams. Johnson's administration was still suffering from the lessons learned during TET, so they directed General Abrams to scale down American military operations and increase the efforts to prepare the Army of the Republic of Vietnam (ARVN), to take primary responsibility for the ground war.

Abrams' tactics differed significantly from those of Westmoreland. He preferred small unit patrols to large unit search-and-destroy sweeps. Despite the change in personnel and tactics, political unrest was still very strong, and the August Democratic Convention had been beset with clashes between antiwar protesters and police and national guardsmen.

I was mostly oblivious to the protests and changes in the political wind. It took all my focus to concentrate on my preparations for deployment. I tried not to think about the fact that I had joined the SEALs to escape from the Marines and Vietnam, and here I was headed right back to the killing fields. I told myself that this time would be different.

This time I was part of a team of serious operators. Unfortunately, I was also newly married and facing a lengthy separation.

I didn't really think about it that morning as I shipped Vicki off on the early-bird flight to Chicago. She was going to be staying with her parents in Lake Forest for the duration of my tour. She had wanted to visit them for a long time, and I knew she would be fine there. But I could tell by the way she looked at me that she was worried for me—worried and trying like hell not to show it. I knew I would be fine, too. I just had no idea how to reassure her. So we both pretended that everything was perfectly normal, as if we were both just going off for a weekend visit. I didn't even go in to see her off. That would have made it all into a big deal.

It wasn't until I got back to our apartment and faced the empty rooms that the full impact of our separation hit me. I would not see Vicki for several months, and I would not be home again for at least six months. With her gone, the apartment no longer seemed like home. Just walls and a floor with my duffel sitting forlornly in the middle of the living room. She had spent much more time in it than I had, so the rooms were permanently connected to her in my mind. We had sublet our apartment for the duration, and the couple who rented it were due to move in the next day. All of our personal stuff was already gone.

I focused my mind on the task ahead, gathered my duffel and climbed downstairs to wait for Ric to pick me up. I got as far as the garage before I realized I couldn't leave without saying goodbye to the real love of my life.

She was sitting up on blocks, her green paint job gleaming in the light from the window—my precious 1959 Corvette with her new 1969 Chevy Camaro Z-28 engine that I had installed myself. I lovingly stroked the sleek lines of her fender, then kissed her and covered her with a nice, clean parachute I had liberated from the discards. I missed my wife, but I was really going to miss that car!

Ric picked me up thirty minutes later in his favorite ride, a beat-up Chevy van. We had been home from Niland for nearly a month, but it seemed like days. On the way to the Team area, Ric took an unexpected detour by Sal's Liquor Store. As we pulled in to the well-worn parking area, I cocked an inquisitive eyebrow in his direction. I knew we were having a send-off party that evening, but I didn't think *we* had to supply the booze.

He grinned. "You don't expect us to go to war without the essentials of wartime survival, do you?"

I allowed that I hadn't really thought about it. Ric's specialty was enjoying liberty to the fullest, and apparently preparing for relaxation in a strange country was no exception. I happily helped him load bottles of tequila, jugs of wine, several dozen cases of beer, and some other necessities into the back of the van.

"So just how do you plan to get all this stuff in country? The MPs are bound to confiscate it before we ever leave the tarmac, and we will have wasted a hell of a lot of good booze." *Not to mention the cash.*

"Gee, Doc, don't you trust me? You should know by now that I always have a plan." Ric had that familiar evil glint in his eye. I decided not to press him further.

Once we reached the Team area, we began the daylong task of packing our gear. Unlike the rest of the platoon's stuff, which was mainly ordnance and survival gear that was designed to withstand almost any hardship, our equipment was very delicate, requiring special care and packing. Neither Ric's radio equipment nor my medical supplies took kindly to water, dust, or rough handling. We used the standard-issue, large Conex boxes and carefully wrapped everything to keep it as safe and secure as possible for the long trip. Each box was painstakingly packed and carefully stenciled with the unit designation.

When we finished with our gear, Ric asked me to help him find one more container. Not sure what he was planning, I picked out a new gray Conex and brought it over to our work area. Together we labeled it to match the others: SEAL TEAM ONE—ALPHA PLATOON.

"Okay, let's get the rest of our 'survival gear.'"

"You mean the stuff we picked up this morning?"

"That'd be it."

"Okay." I started unloading our precious cargo of booze from the back of the van. "But I still don't see how you're going to keep the MPs from confiscating everything when they look in this case."

"That's 'cause they're not going to look in it." I gave him a puzzled look; he returned an evil grin. "Get me that spray can and you'll see."

I grabbed a can of spray paint we had used to mark all the boxes. He pulled out another set of stencils he had stashed below his seat in the van, and below SEAL TEAM ONE he quickly added: TOP SECRET. MUST HAVE AUTHORIZED CLEARANCE TO OPEN! in large letters across the box.

We stood back to survey his handiwork. "Trust me, there is no MP I've ever met brave enough to open a box full of top-secret SEAL equipment."

I had to agree. Our stash was as safe as we could make it.

With the most important items of our survival gear thus secured, we carefully loaded all our boxes on the trucks for transport across the island to NAS North Island for our flight the next morning. The chores done, we headed off to the Trade Winds bar for our send-off party.

The Trade Winds was a real high-class joint, located off the beaten path and perfumed with the smell of dirty mop buckets and aging puke. Okay, it was a dump, but it was *our* dump. There was an unspoken rule that the Trade Winds was reserved for Frogs and SEALs. Other sailors entered at their own risk. They rarely did so twice. The bar's owner was an old gal I only knew as Lisa. No one knew who really worked there. Most nights would find SEAL team members doing duty behind the bar.

Tonight was no exception. Ric and I arrived to find two SEALs, Gary Shaddock and Gary Gallagher serving the drinks. The rest of the platoon arrived right behind us and seemed very glad to see me.

Preacher Richardson slapped me on the back and steered me right up to the bar. "Hey, Doc, as the new guy, you get the honor of buying the first keg."

"Does the new guy always buy the first round?" I pulled some cash out and laid it on the bar.

"No," admitted Gallagher as he quickly took my money. "But since you're the one with all the extra pay, it's only fair that you get to buy."

I had not realized that the rest of the guys knew about the difference in my pay scale. As enlisted men, each of the other members of the platoon received, in addition to their regular pay, $55 a month jump pay and $55 a month demolitions or "demo" pay. I was an enlisted member of the platoon, but as a corpsman the same international military protocols that kept me from attending BUD/S also contained agreements concerning what medics were and were not supposed to do. One of the things a medic was not supposed to do was blow things up. Because of this, I was not allowed to collect demo pay for blowing things up. Like them, I received the regular $55 a month jump pay, but since the Navy couldn't pay me the demo pay, they paid me for diving. Standard dive pay however, was $75 a month, $20 more than the rest of the guys were making. No wonder I was popular. My teammates were not about to begrudge me my good fortune, but they were determined to relieve me of as much of it as possible in the name of team spirit. Or maybe that should be *spirits*.

We spent the bulk of the evening in the time-honored tradition of military parties everywhere—drinking heavily while swapping war stories. Most of these stories could be summarized as the old guys telling the new guys to keep their heads down and their powder dry. After several hours of stories and many more beers, I felt the need to be alone with my thoughts so I went out to the van to lie down. I was twenty years old and going back to 'Nam as a qualified SEAL operator, but I couldn't get the images of my last tour out of my head.

Ric must have understood, because he came out to the van a few minutes later.

"Hey, Doc, had enough already?"

"Yeah. Just wanted to think for a bit."

He paused, I could tell he understood. Ric always understood.

"Yeah. Let's go home."

To Ric, "home" was a small alley cottage that more closely resembled a converted garage than a home. It was a classic bachelor pad with touches that made it classic Ric. An old parachute hung draped across the ceiling of the main room, rigged with twinkling Christmas lights shining through from above. He said it made him feel more as if he was outdoors. A clothing-covered lump along one wall appeared to be a sofa, and the larger furry lump lying on it could only be Ric's German shepard, King. The smell of burning incense and the lingering scent of stale pot wafted through the air. Along with King, Ric shared his cozy hut with Sheila, a cute blond hippie from California. She emerged from the kitchen dressed in one of Ric's blue and gold T-shirts and welcomed me warmly. Sheila loved SEALs and Frogmen. As she pressed her warm curves against me in a very nice hug, I decided I liked having a fan.

She released me to welcome Ric home even more enthusiastically, and then went back to the refrigerator to grab a beer. I was still admiring the way the T-shirt clung to her shape when I realized the shirt was all she was wearing. She bent over to get the beer off the lower shelf of the fridge and greeted me with a lovely full moon. Ric came up behind her and gently slapped her on the ass, interrupting my appreciation. He grabbed her by the arm and the two of them disappeared into his bedroom.

"Goodnight, Doc! Help yourself to the refrigerator!"

That figures, I thought. *He gets nice, warm, sexy Sheila and leaves me with the dog and the refrigerator. Some friend.*

I surveyed the room looking for a place to bed down. There was only the large cloth-covered lump I hoped was a sofa—complete with snoring German shepard—and the floor. I decided to try my luck with the sofa.

"Well, King, looks like it's just you and me," I said as I shoved him over enough to make a spot to sleep. He yawned obligingly, and then made another, more obnoxious noise from his south end. I wrinkled my nose, trying not to breathe. From the stench, he must have had a couple of burritos for dinner.

Despite his personal habits, King was a great dog. He was originally trained to work with the SEALs, but we couldn't use him in the Mekong Delta. The terrain of our planned operations area was very swampy and thick with jungle vegetation. An environment not suitable for man or beast, which is why the Viet Cong felt so safe there. After all, no soft American would *dare* try coming after them in the infamous U-Minh forest. I slept fitfully, dreaming of Sheila's ass and King's breath.

I awakened to the rattle of King's dog collar as he climbed off the couch—and my legs—to push open the back screen door. As it slammed shut, I winced and groggily eyed my watch. 0530. We were due at NAS North Island by 0700 to board a noon flight to Hawaii on the first leg of the long trip to Saigon. I got up. Slowly. My legs tingled furiously as the circulation returned. Then the tingle hit bottom and bounced back to the top of my head in the form of a first-class hangover. I began to regret having quite so many beers the night before. A shower and shave helped considerably, if only because I didn't smell like German shepherd anymore. Donning a clean set of jungle cammies, I neatly packed the rest of my stuff in the parachute bag that would serve as my personal suitcase until we got to our final destination in Vietnam. Ric emerged as I finished, neatly dressed in his own cammies, and looking as if his night had been much more restful than mine.

It was typical beautiful late-summer day in Coronado. The sun rose over the newly opened San Diego to Coronado Bridge, setting it afire. Everything seemed peaceful, almost surreal, or perhaps I was just absorbed in my own thoughts. I barely noticed the trip to the airfield until we were all gathered together on the tarmac, trying to figure out which plane was ours.

"Yep, you'll be flying that C-130 with the VR-21 Squadron," an older member of the ground crew said directing us to our plane. "And VR sure don't stand for Very Reliable," he added under his breath. Completely reassured, we took our gear to the huge plane and began the loading process.

10

The Little Plane That Couldn't

THE interior of the aircraft was set up as if for a parachute jump, with all the "seats" backed up against the bulkhead, facing into the wide center aisle. The "seats" however, were nothing more than cargo netting, strung so that someone could pretend to sit on it with at least some degree of comfort. We strapped down all the boxes and footlockers in the center aisle. By the time we finished, the aisle that had seemed so wide when we boarded was stacked deck to overhead—and almost bulkhead to bulkhead—with equipment, leaving very little walking room. Once the gear was secure, we each made ourselves a little nest in the netting. We couldn't really move around and chat in such cramped quarters, and the drone of the engines prevented idle conversation, so that most of us spent the next twelve hours catnapping across the Pacific.

By the time we reached NAS Barbers Point, Hawaii, I had to admit that the warning we'd received about the squadron seemed uncomfortably accurate. Our plane landed awkwardly while sputtering some sort of black, burnt-smelling oil all over itself. The pilot, an otherwise clean-cut guy, displayed an amazing command of the more colorful parts of the English language, making some extremely rude and imaginative comments that seemed directed at his plane, then angrily red-tagged it as out of commission.

I was just glad the thing had actually made Hawaii. It would have been terribly wasteful to go down in the Pacific before even reaching 'Nam. Since we obviously weren't traveling any farther in that plane for a while, we all decided we might as well force ourselves to go on liberty.

We were all still in cammies, so those of us who were enlisted guys went over to the club on base while the officers went to see when—or if—we would be continuing our journey. It was a beautiful warm night with a tropical breeze blowing in from the shore, we were stuck on Hawaii, and about to show the rest of the Navy how SEALs took liberty. There were worse fates.

We entered the club with Dave Langlois in the lead. "SEALs on deck. Get ready to learn how real men party!" he bellowed in his deep baritone.

"Too late! We've already taught them all they need to know!" a bellow answered from across the room.

In surprise I turned toward the sound to discover the members of SEALs Platoon Bravo holding court on the far wall of the clubroom.

"Hey Buck, what are you sorry excuses for SEALs doing here?" Boh asked as we joined them.

"Probably the same thing you are," the big man retorted. "Buying a drink."

"Well, then you're in luck," Ric quipped. "We'll buy if you spill." He gestured the barkeep over, to the cheers of Bravo Platoon's enthusiastic approval. "Tell us how it is in country. What was your area of operations?"

Buck picked up his glass with the promised drink and took a deep appreciative swallow. "Well . . . we were in the Rung Sat Special Zone, also known as the Forest of Assassins, south of Saigon. We based out of Binh Thuy, primarily working the Na Thrang area . . ."

I grabbed a drink and eagerly pulled a chair up close. All the guys were doing the same. This was our chance to get the straight skinny on Charlie from some of our own. It turned out that Bravo Platoon was on their way back to Coronado after completing their six-month tour. As the booze flowed and the tales followed, we discovered that some of them had gone down to help the platoons in Ca Mau, which was to be our AO.

"You're going to Ca Mau? You lucky SOBs." Lenny Horst, Bravo Platoon's sixty-gunner and resident crazy man, chugged back his whiskey and looked genuinely jealous.

"Why? What's so great about it? It's just a mud hole, isn't it?" I asked.

"Son," Lenny began, looking at me. There couldn't have been more than two or three years difference in our ages, I was twenty and he was maybe twenty-two or -three, but time in country as a SEAL had given him the right. "There's never been a more hairy, swampy, God-forsaken place than the Ca Mau peninsula. Mud, more mud, and sucking muck everywhere. It gets in your clothes, your teeth, up your ass. There's no solid ground. You can never get dry, and there's VC in every bog and behind every bush. The whole damn place is a nest of fuckin' VC!" He flashed his teeth in a gleeful grin. "It's God's gift to SEALs!"

"Lenny may have a screw loose, but what he says is truth!" a black fellow with the nickname Killer B quipped.

I sat riveted to my chair as they gave us a first-hand account of the conditions we would be facing. According to them, the place was an ideal playground for SEALs because it was one of the Viet Cong's favorite haunts. The conditions were brutal, but we had known about the swamp. We had spent weeks training in the Tijuana mud slews and practicing small-unit tactics in the All-American canal basin in Niland. We were ready, but we wanted as much detailed information as we could get. There was no such thing as too much intel when you were going into Charlie's country.

Hours later, as the party wound down, the subject turned back to the unusual circumstances that had brought us together.

"So you never did tell us why you guys are here," Mitchell commented. "I thought you were supposed to be back in Coronado by now."

"We were." Buck drained his glass and slammed it onto the table. "But nobody told that to the fuckin' plane. It blew a gasket or a valve or something and we've been stuck here for two days waiting from them to get the goddamned part. Personally, I'm about ready to swim home." They were all furious about the delay. Who could blame them? They were going home.

"Well, you could take ours," Ric offered, "but it's broke-down too."

"Shit! Don't they have any planes that actually work?"

"We're just glad the damn thing didn't drop us in the drink!"

In my inebriated state, it occurred to me that our plane probably had a different part broken than theirs.

"Wait! Why don't we just get the part you need off our plane? Our plane is already broke, so they aren't likely to notice one more missing part. Then you can go home. After all, its not like we're in any particular fuckin' hurry to go get shot at. We'll get the part—put it on your plane—and then we'll wait for the new parts while sunbathin' on the beaches!"

My idea met with enthusiastic approval from everyone except Ric.

"Right, Doc. Like any of us water rats know anything about airplanes!"

"I think I could tell a broken part if I saw it. I did a pretty damn good job on my Corvette."

Hoots of agreement came from all the armchair mechanics in the group.

"I don't think that's such a good idea. What if you get the wrong part and the thing blows up or something? I think we should just complain to our boss about the lousy airline service!" A roar of laughter greeted that suggestion.

Lenny Horst stood up. Unlike the rest of us, he seemed perfectly sober. "Okay. I'll make a few calls and see what I can do." His expression was deadly serious. Several of his guys got very quiet as he walked away from the table.

"I still think I would be able to get the right part." I sulked.

"In your state, you'll be lucky if you can find the runway, much less the plane!" Ric chortled while pouring me another drink.

I had to agree with him. "Good idea though," I groused.

The club was closing when Lenny returned. He had a satisfied expression on his face as he walked up to his guys and announced that he had called the President. Our guys laughed.

"I wouldn't put it past you, you crazy sonofabitch!" Buck groaned.

Killer B agreed. "Yeah sure, Lenny. Go and piss off the President for us."

It was a long walk to our bunks, especially in our post-party condition. On most bases lodging for SEALs was usually placed as far away from the rest of the base as possible. Barbers Point was no exception. Our assigned space in the temporary SEAL barracks was situated in nearly complete isolation across the street from the main runway. For some reason, the Navy wanted SEALs kept as far away from the general base population as possible.

At about 0600 the next morning, I awoke to a ruckus outside the barracks.

"The plane! The plane! We've got a plane!"

I got up and joined the rest of our guys as we ran onto the runway to see what was going on. There, sitting proudly on the tarmac, was a shiny blue and white 737 with UNITED STATES OF AMERICA emblazoned on its side. We raced over to the aircraft to discover Lenny carefully inspecting the outside of "his" plane with the Air Force pilots like a proud papa. Everyone stood around laughing and shaking their heads. He'd really done it. He'd called the President, and even more amazing, the President had actually given him a plane.

Security was crawling all over the place. Shore Patrol had posted guards at the new plane, our plane, and even Lenny's broken one. We weren't wearing any insignia, so no one knew who we were. Acting as if we owned the joint, since Lenny obviously did, Ric and I went up to one of the security chiefs and asked him about all the extra guards.

"Well, sir," the young man began, not quite sure of our rank, but treating us as VIP's since we were obviously with Lenny, "there's a lot of top secret SEAL stuff on these planes, so the commander ordered a guard detail on them to protect our national interests."

Somehow Ric and I managed to keep a straight face until we got out of sight.

A few minutes later we overheard one of the shore patrol talking to Lt. Flanagan.

"So what is all this secret SEAL stuff, anyway? There are nearly three planes full of it!"

"Well, Private," Flanagan began, drawing close to the patrol officer with a very serious expression on his face, "if I tell you, I'll have to kill you." He calmly turned and walked away without so much as a grimace. The look on the private's face was priceless. I'm just glad the kid didn't ask Lenny the same question.

A few hours later, we managed to pull Lenny aside while his guys were loading the plane.

"So how did you do it? Did you really call the President?"

"Sure. He said I could always call on him, so I did."

"When did he say that?" I was incredulous.

"Well, about a year ago, when I was in Washington to receive the Presidential Unit Citation for SEAL Team One. A bunch of us went up to be part of the ceremony. President Johnson was very grateful for all our service and dedication. I distinctly remembered him telling us not to hesitate to call on his administration if ever we needed anything."

"So?"

"So I called him. It was 8:00 AM there. I told the switchboard I was a top secret Navy SEAL and had to make contact with the Oval Office. They put me through to the President's secretary. I told her that I had met the President last year and he had said I should call. So I asked if he had a minute to talk. About a minute later LBJ himself picked up the phone. I'm sure he was having the call traced, to make sure I was real. But he's real cool, y'know. He says 'How's it going Lenny? Are you SEALs okay?'" Lenny mimicked LBJ's vocal style so well we cracked up laughing.

"So I told him, no, we were definitely not okay. We had been to Vietnam and fought for our country, and now when it's time to go home we're stranded on an island because of those wrecks the Navy calls planes. I told him that it's not fair that the SEALs have to hopscotch the Pacific just to get home. Sometimes it takes more than a week for our guys to get back.

"I told him even draftees flew nonstop from Saigon to San Francisco in twelve hours—first class all the way. Why couldn't we have the same treatment?" Lenny's look of righteous indignation was almost comical.

"And?"

"And he said he'd look into it, and said goodbye. And the rest of the story is sitting over there." He gestured to the shiny aircraft on the runway. "Now if you will excuse me, I have a plane to catch."

I heard the rest of the story a month later.

Approximately seven hours after it arrived, the Air Force jet with Lenny's platoon on board landed at North Island. As was his custom with all returning platoons, Captain Schiable, the CO of SEAL Team One, met the plane and took Lenny aside. Everyone there assumed he was giving Lenny a stern lecture about ignoring the chain of command. According to Lenny, all he did was congratulate him on his improvisation.

11

Are We There Yet?

WHILE Lenny Horst and the rest of his platoon flew home in the lap of luxury, our aircrew struggled to scrounge enough parts to get our bucket of bolts into the air. They finally managed to get it—and us—off the ground. Ten hours later the jury-rigging failed and we were forced to make an emergency landing on Wake Island.

How thrilling, I thought as I climbed out of our crippled plane, *here we are, halfway to Vietnam, and we've almost gone down twice.* I noticed that there seemed to be an awful lot of oil all over the outside of the plane. *This surely can't be a good sign.* While I stood there marveling at the quantity of black goop that decorated the fuselage and cowling, the pilot climbed somewhat shakily out of the cockpit. When he reached the tarmac, he raised his arms toward the sky, then knelt down and kissed the ground. It was nice to know our pilot was such a religious fellow.

Wake Island is a little spit of a place in the Western Pacific surrounded by beautiful deep blue water, blue sky, and pristine white sandy beaches. But while the island itself was a paradise, our accommodations were a little rough. The only available sleeping quarters were those in a Japanese prison guard barracks left over from World War II. It came complete with Japanese instructions on the walls. The wounds of World War II weren't even twenty-five years old yet and many of us had lost family on one of these desolate islands to the Japs. The irony of sleeping in our old enemies' beds while on the way to another war resonated strongly with all of us. The next day, almost like magic, the crew fixed the problem, wiped all the excess oil and grease off the outside of the plane, and announced that it was in condition to fly again. Despite their assurances, I couldn't help but notice the loud cough, the puff of black smoke, and the grinding of metal on metal that accompanied the engine start. I held on tightly to my netting as we taxied down the runway and lifted cleanly into the air. I was just starting to relax when I heard a muffled boom.

"What was that?"

"One of the tires exploded," a member of the aircrew answered. "But it's okay. We're flying over the water, so we won't be needing that tire anyway."

"We've got a ten-hour flight to Guam," Ric assured me. "That should be plenty of time for them to figure out what to do." I glanced at his face. He was trying to reassure himself as well as me. It wasn't working.

I started looking around for a good place to curl up and die when I had a brilliant thought. SEALs have parachutes! I scrambled out of my seat and scooted over to Mr. Flanagan.

"LT, where are our parachutes stowed?"

"Parachutes?"

"We have parachutes, don't we, sir?"

"Doc, shut the fuck up and go find a place to sit. Why in hell would we need our parachutes in the swamps of Vietnam?"

Just then, one of the crewmen came by and patted me on the shoulder.

"Don't worry, kid. This shit happens all the time. As soon as we figure out which tire we blew, we'll be able to figure out how to remedy the situation."

"I went back to my net-seat near the cockpit and tried to relax. Hours passed and I just laid there trying to imagine how they were going to change that tire while we were in midair. The crew didn't seem concerned at all. About an hour out of Guam, I heard our pilot radio the tower declaring an emergency landing. He came on the speaker to assure us that was the way he usually landed on Guam.

The crew announced they were going to need help adjusting the plane depending on which tire was gone. I expected someone to use some kind of special equipment or hang someone under the plane to make that determination. Instead, I watched in horror as they flipped a coin and declared it was the left tire that had the blowout. We then proceeded to help them slide all storage containers and gear to the right side of the aircraft.

"Okay, boys," the pilot announced in an amazingly calm voice, "we're coming up on final approach, so I need you all to move over to the right side of the plane and strap yourselves in."

We quickly complied.

"Okay. We're coming in, so put your heads down between your legs—and kiss your ass goodbye."

I heard Preacher's muffled voice say, "Last rites, anyone?" Nobody laughed.

The pilot was good. First the right wheel touched down. Apparently the aircrew's guess was correct, because we were rolling, not crashing. I felt the plane hover on the one wheel for what seemed like forever before the nose gently dropped and I felt the front wheel kiss the runway. Then, just before reaching the end of the tarmac, the flat left tire hit the ground, screeching and smoking, and we skidded to a stop.

The perfume of burning rubber never smelled as good to me as it did then. We quickly exited the plane and surveyed the damage. Within an hour they had replaced the tire, and the plane taxied toward the repair hangar.

The naval base at Guam was a major staging area for supplies going to Vietnam. Since Ric and I specialized in "procurement" for our platoon, I borrowed the first unattended jeep I could find, and grabbed Ric and Boh for a tour of the base. Over at medical supply, I was able to trade one of our now famous K-Bar knives for two cases of "medicinal" brandy. We disguised the brandy in an empty case of serum albumin, a blood expander we used as an I.V. in the field.

Over at the Communication Center, Ric pulled the duty radioman aside to talk radioman talk while Boh and I explored the back rooms. We found, and liberated, a very nice dual-speaker ghetto blaster with a built-in cassette player, a real state-of-the-art beauty, still in its original box. I pointed out that the radio portion would be of limited use, since our area of operations was out in the boonies, but Boh managed to come up with a nice long whip antenna that we could jury-rig to our newfound radio. With it in place, we figured we should be able to get Armed Forces Radio out of Saigon from almost any place in Vietnam. To Ric's credit, he had the radioman so involved in sharing stories that the poor boy never even noticed Boh and me leave—much less the fact that we were carrying a suspicious box and a long, thin package that looked a lot like his new whip antenna.

After a little more sightseeing, we met up with the rest of the platoon for chow. I noticed that everyone seemed very laid back and quiet. I knew we were all thinking about tomorrow. After a week of hopscotching across the Pacific, we had finally reached our last stop before going into the country. If the plane held together long enough. After dinner, Boh suggested that we all go to the base theater to watch the movie. Ironically, the movie playing that day was *Oliver*, a story about a bunch of young orphans pickpocketing their way through merry old London a hundred years ago. While some of the boys' on-screen activities reminded me of Ric, Boh, and myself as we scrounged the day's booty, most of the movie was a welcome distraction from thoughts of going into Vietnam the next day.

I spent most of the night tossing and turning in yet another unfamiliar barracks, falling asleep just in time to be rudely awakened by Mr. Moody, hollering at the top of his lungs in his best drill instructor's voice.

"All right you lazy louts, hit the deck! I let you sleep in till 0600. You've all had it nice and soft just sittin' around on your asses all day until you're not fit to be called SEALs. I intend to remedy that! Out front in ten for PT."

Ten minutes later, Mr. Moody led us through some stretching exercises and then took us on a brisk five-mile run around the base. The workout turned out to be just what I needed. The balmy early morning tropical breeze began to warm up, and the tedium of the past week trickled out with the sweat. My spirit began to pick up as the blood in my heart started to race.

After the run, I felt giddy. I could tell by the silly grin most of the guys wore that it had helped them, too. A quick shower and shave, followed by some fruit and toast, left me ready and anxious to get going. The whole platoon seemed to glow with energy, alive and vibrant, like a well-tuned machine ready to go to work.

We boarded the plane, careful to stow and secure everything properly, then set about unpacking our weapons from the cases where they had been stored, untouched, since leaving Coronado. The next stop was The Republic of South Vietnam, Tan Son Nhut Airport, Saigon. We had no idea what to expect once we arrived—but whatever it was, we intended to be ready for it.

The flight seemed shorter than the eight hours it took, probably because I was so busy getting my weapons and gear ready for combat. I loaded six ammo pouches with 150 rounds each of linked 556 caliber bullets with a tracer every third round. My Stoner was capable of firing up to 1,000 rounds per minute, so even that much ammo wouldn't last long. I also holstered the Smith & Wesson Mark 22, 9mm "Hush Puppy" parabellum pistol I always carried as a personal backup. With the suppressor attached and the slide locked closed, I could fire it in almost complete silence. Plus the subsonic parabellum round had been specially designed with a slower velocity than the normal 9mm rounds to avoid making the usual telltale "crack." It was called a Hush Puppy because its original purpose was to silence enemy guard dogs without alerting anyone nearby. I never called it by its nickname around King. I was convinced Ric's dog would be offended if he knew we had a weapon originally designed to take out his cousins.

I strapped additional live ammo rounds and a number of hand grenades to my web gear, and put it on to check the fit. It had been specially adjusted to handle the extra weight of the additional live rounds and grenades. For the finishing touch I pulled my K-Bar from its sheath on my left shoulder and used my whetstone to hone its already sharpened edge until it was razor fine. To test the edge, I shaved a swath of hair off my arm. My arm looked silly, but I was perfectly happy with the results.

When I completed my preparations, the sun was starting to sink in the western sky. Looking out of the window, I could see a brown haze on the horizon, indicating we were coming up on the coast of Vietnam. A few moments later, the plane began its slow descent. I immediately noticed a change in temperature. The air grew steadily warmer and more humid. My hands became moist and clammy, and not just from the heat. A quick glance at Mr. Flanagan's face confirmed he shared my suspicions. We might be in for an unfriendly reception if the VC decided they wanted to ace some SEALs before we got the chance to do damage to them.

Unlike the regular soldiers, who came and went by the hundreds every day, SEALs traveled in smaller groups and much less often. It was rare for a whole platoon of SEALs to come in at once. We knew this made us a target, since the VC hated SEALs more than any other group of soldiers. It wouldn't take a whole lot of intelligence to figure out that we were coming. And even less to figure out which plane carried SEALs—they only had to look for the plane that was crashing instead of landing.

There was a large bounty on SEALs all over Vietnam. The Viet Cong had once ruled the night, using the cover of darkness to hide their activities, but the SEALs changed all that, striking terror into the minds of the enemy by making the darkness their own. The "men with green faces," as they called us, were feared and hated because the SEALs had proven they could challenge and beat the VC in their own backyard.

It seemed somehow fitting that our wheels—all three of them this time—touched down just as the sun was setting. The aircrew began to lower the back gate of the aircraft while the plane taxied over to the Military Assistance Command Vietnam (MACV) center. As the gate opened, I could feel the stored heat of the day bouncing off the tarmac like a blast furnace. The smell of Vietnam, an unmistakable combination of rotting vegetation, refuse, diesel fuel, and dirt, assaulted my nose. Looking toward the slowly opening portal at the rear of the plane, I had a momentary flash of Dante's descent into hell.

As the plane shuddered to a halt Mr. Flanagan took his place at the door. He really had his game face on—eyes fierce, jaw set, and weapons at the ready.

"Move off the plane and stay together! Keep your eyes open for anything suspicious!"

Hell, it was a foreign country. Everything and everyone looked suspicious. I clutched my weapons in expectation of an ambush, and noticed that everyone else was doing the same. We emerged into an uncompromising landscape of hot, dusty tarmac, sandbags, and barbed wire. As well as aircraft of all types from Phantoms and Air force 707s to Hueys and big bellied C-130 transports like ours, all involved in the business of bringing men and supplies into war and taking them back out again. And lots and lots of Vietnamese. There were Vietnamese people everywhere, but no way to know the good guys from the bad, even *with* a program. Any of them could have been Viet Cong, but they all looked alike to us.

"Why don't we just shoot everyone and go home?" John Mitchell suggested, "then let God sort it out."

After a few minutes went by with nothing happening, we relaxed a little, took a moment to get our bearings, and waited for the Naval Intelligence Liaison Officer to arrive to escort us to our new home for the next six months.

12

Welcome to Vietnam—Now Go Home

IT took several hours to unload all our gear and stage our equipment to be trucked over to the Special Operations Group compound, not far from the airport. Once everything was loaded, our convoy of several trucks and a few jeeps and vans rolled out of the airport and into the crowded bedlam of the streets of Saigon. As soon as we reached the gates of the airport, the noise and stench of the overcrowded city inundated us. A large escort of Saigon police and south Vietnamese army regulars met our convoy at the gates. But these soldiers were not there to escort us, they were all trying to sell us something or buy something from us. Surrounding our jeeps, they clamored for our attention, waving merchandise and yelling.

"GI Number One. We have what you want. Only few dollar."

I knew that most of the Vietnamese soldiers in Saigon were there for no other reason than to avoid actually having to fight in the war. It was a cushy job. I had learned from my first tour that most of them avoided work of any kind. They used their uniforms to facilitate their con games and graft. We called them Saigon Cowboys, because their version of being a soldier or policeman was like children playing at cowboys and indians, complete with the childish tactic of changing sides whenever they got bored.

As the American MPs led us away, attempting to force a path through the crowd, the pretend warriors became even more insistent.

"Just for you, GI. Anything you need, I get. American GI Number One."

Disgusted, we all kind of rolled our eyes at each other, and made little pistols out of our fingers while we pretended to shoot at these "Toy Soldiers." They wanted to play cowboy? We could play, too.

This infuriated them. They started yelling back, "You GI is Number Ten. VC kill you. Go Home GI."

After a few rounds of insults I had enough of the Vietnamese welcoming committee. Looking over at the rest of the guys I could tell they felt the same.

"Go home GI. VC kill you. Kill you easy."

That was too much. As if on cue, we all moved as one to grab our weapons, snatching them from where they rested next to us on the seats, locked and loaded. We pointed the barrels skyward, with the stocks resting on our thighs, but it didn't matter where we pointed them. These South Vietnamese regular military weren't regular soldiers. Faced with two jeeploads of angry SEALs glaring down at them with very real weapons at the ready, the Saigon Cowboys scattered like ants, jumping on their little motor scooters in twos and threes to race into the crowd. They hesitated long enough to flip us the finger and cuss us out only when they had reached the safety of the alleys.

"Hey Boh," I yelled to be heard above the din of the city, "are these the people we're supposed to help?" I waved in the general direction of the last retreating scooter. Boh answered with a series of rude hand gestures that clearly indicated just how helpful he planned to be.

I couldn't believe we had come ten thousand miles to give aid to these little bastards and prevent the communists from taking their grubby lives. At that moment it was very easy for me to understand why so many people were reluctant to help the South Vietnamese. Most of them, especially here in Saigon, appeared to be completely ungrateful to the soldiers who were fighting their war for them. I was amazed at how many perfectly healthy, nonmilitary Vietnamese men my age were running around Saigon. Rather than join up to defend their country, they all seemed to be dedicated to taking advantage of the U.S. servicemen every time they turned around. I had seen some of the same nameless faces hanging around Saigon when I left from my first tour, and at this point I would have gladly put a bullet in the head of any one of those chickenshit Vietnamese for getting in my face.

It didn't take long to reach Military Assistance Command Vietnam–Special Observation Group Headquarters, known as MACV-SOG. We pulled through the heavily guarded gates into a large compound surrounded by high barbed-wire fences and fortified with manned guard towers at every corner. Even though the compound was in the edge of the supposedly "safe" capital city, it was also the home of Special Observation Group, with ties to the Green Berets, Navy SEALs, and the CIA, and these guys weren't taking any chances.

We unloaded our gear from the trucks, in preparation for the next leg of our journey, and then Boh checked us into overnight quarters in one of the wings of the main building. After spending a week getting here, I was relieved, and perhaps even happy, to finally be in country. I could tell that the rest of the guys were, too. That night was very hot and very humid, the normal night sounds regularly interrupted by sounds of artillery fire from a nearby firebase, and I slept through it all like a baby in its mother's arms.

The next morning, after chow, we gathered in the yard to await transportation to our next stop, the Binh Thuy Naval Base near Can Tho, deep in the interior wilderness of the Mekong River delta. We had been told our transportation would be along at any moment. As we sat around waiting, I spotted familiar face. It was Frank Thornton, whom I had last seen in June, when Vicki and I were preparing to leave for Coronado. He looked a little different, decked out in his jungle cammies and boonie hat, but no amount of camo could completely cover the handsome face and devilish gleam I knew so well.

"Frank! I thought I left you at Little Creek!"

"Greg!" He greeted me warmly. "Good to see you, too."

"So how did you beat me here?"

He laughed. "Well, brains and cunning will beat out youthful exuberance every time. Seriously though, just after you left I got orders to come back in country to be a PRU advisor."

With Frank's experience and track record, that wasn't surprising. One of the most important jobs carried out by the Special Forces, and especially experienced SEALs, was to advise and coordinate the Provincial Reconnaissance Units (PRU) in support of South Vietnam. These units consisted of Vietnamese, Chinese mercenaries, Viet Cong who had defected under the Chieu Hoi program, former North Vietnamese Army regulars and even the rugged Montagnards who were the primitive native people of the highlands. It was up to PRU advisors like Frank to turn these groups into an effective force for gathering intelligence and, in some cases, actual fighting operations.

Frank's PRUs were heavily involved in the CIA-sponsored Phoenix Program, aimed at identifying the Viet Cong political leaders using data collected from local sources. The information could then be used to identify and capture suspected VC chiefs.

"I'm here to check on some intel gathered by SEALs from Team Two, Ninth Platoon."

"Well if you've got a minute, I'd love for you to come meet the rest of the guys." I really wanted Boh and Ric to meet Frank.

"Your West Coast buddies? No. Thanks just the same. The West Coast hotshots usually have no use for old East Coast fogies like me."

Unfortunately, I knew he was right. Being a child of both Teams, I always had trouble understanding the artificial barriers that prevented Teams One and Two from working more closely together. Two had, within its roster, a lot more experienced older men like Frank, as well as a number of former members of the East Coast UDTs, some of whom had started the Teams. These guys had a lot of experience and serious know-how that I felt would really benefit the younger West Coast SEALs. But Vietnam was supposed to be the West Coast's show and they guarded their territory with youthful fervor. As a result, any unsolicited advice from the more experienced East Coast SEALs usually fell on jealous, ungrateful, or deaf ears. I had escaped that particular trap only because I was still young and wet behind the ears—and my platoon was so glad to discover they weren't being stuck with a "cherry" Doc, that they completely overlooked the fact that I originally came off the East Coast.

"So how's Lee?"

"Probably glad I'm out of her hair. Lee may be my wife, but I'm in love with this place." He stared out at the distant land beyond the compound for a moment. "I really love this place." He glanced at me, embarrassed. "I think maybe Lee's a little jealous." His gaze drifted to the jungle line again.

If Frank, old warhorse that he was, had fallen in love with Vietnam, I knew I was going to be in for an exciting tour over the next six months.

"So any advice for a young upstart from an old fart?" I kidded, breaking him out of his reverie.

"Well," he put one hand on my shoulder to draw me close, "I'm sure you already know about the SEAL secret Saigon headquarters?"

"Secret headquarters?"

"Yeah," he added in a confidential whisper. "Whenever SEALs are in Saigon, we meet at our secret headquarters—the bar on top of the Presidential Hotel. I may be there myself later tonight."

I tried to maintain the same conspiratorial tone. "Thanks, I'll keep that in mind. We're supposed to leave today, but I might catch you next time."

He waved an affirmative and left for his meeting. I went back over to join the guys while we waited for our transport.

Several hours later, we still waited. Boh and Mr. Flanagan left us to find out what was going on. I asked Ric for his assessment of the situation. "I thought we were supposed to leave this morning."

"Yeah, but this base is run by the Army. And one thing that don't usually mix well is the Army and SEALs."

Apparently he was right, because Boh and the LT reappeared a little after noon, and their disgusted expressions indicated that their dealings with the Army had not gone well.

"Okay, boys," Mr. Flanagan announced, "the Army seems to be interested in one thing—giving us a bullshit runaround rather than transportation." He made certain he spoke loud enough for any nearby Army types to hear him. "So, since they are not inclined to assist us as promised, we'll take care of it ourselves tomorrow. So, until 0800 tomorrow, everyone is on liberty."

We all hooted like crazy men and ran to our quarters to change. Moments later, all ten of us were dressed to party in Levi's and sports shirts, shirttails flapping. We left almost all military trappings behind, including our dog tags, and crammed into two jeeps. Our tires squealed as we headed out, loaded with American money and a hell of a thirst. We were ready to take the city by storm—or at least give it our SEAL of approval.

13

Good Night, Saigon

THE only thing between us and a night on the town was the locked gate of the SOG compound. The Army seemed as determined to keep the good guys in as to keep the bad guys out. As we drove up to the gate, a skinny Army sergeant with beady little eyes stepped up to confront Boh, who sat in the driver's seat of the front jeep. The sergeant did not seem happy to see us.

"I need to see your pass." He squinted at us with an air of self-importance.

We looked at each other. Pass? What pass?

"No one is allowed to leave the compound without a pass!" the sergeant insisted, irritation in his voice.

Boh looked straight at the guard and smiled a predatory smile. "Pass?" he asked in his heavy southern drawl. "We don't need no stinkin' pass."

The sergeant puffed up like a cock rooster, but before he could reply, Boh stopped him.

"Men, show him why he should open the fucking gate right now." With that we all lifted our shirttails to reveal the only military gear we still carried—our pistols. The unmistakable grip of a military-issue handgun protruded menacingly from each of our waistbands.

"Don't you know the CIA when you see them?" Boh continued. "Now if you-all will be so kind as to open the fuckin' gate, we won't have no trouble here."

The guard grudgingly complied, but as we passed him I heard him cussing and mumbling—something about Navy guys and their parentage.

I remembered the secret Frank had shared with me: "Hey Boh, why don't we stop by the Presidential Hotel for a drink. I hear there may be other SEALs there."

Boh gave me a look as if I had just figured out how to count to ten. "No shit, Doc, really?"

When we arrived at the Presidential, I discovered that Boh, who was on his second tour and well-acquainted with all the best SEAL hangouts, not only knew about the "secret" SEAL headquarters, he had already reserved a few crash rooms for us. He even made certain they were near the bar so we wouldn't have too far to fall.

The bar itself was nothing fancy by American standards, but it had everything we needed: comfortable furniture, a good view of the city from its eighth-floor veranda, friendly bar girls, and a jukebox loaded with American tunes. Most importantly, it had plenty of booze.

By sunset, I had imbibed enough of the local libation that the discomfort of the week's events had faded. But not quite enough for me to think that the girls were actually pretty. The jukebox screamed full blast, belting out "Lucy in the Sky." I wandered to the bar to collect another bottle, passing some dumb shit who was making sport out of chewing on his beer glass. A couple of the boys discovered the little tropical lizards that lived in most of the old buildings. Rather than eat the munchies set out on the bar, they were grabbing the lizards off the walls and swallowing them whole.

The bar girls were friendly and attentive, but I wasn't desperate enough yet to give them a second look. They all looked and smelled the same, and neither was particularly appetizing. Most of us preferred the lizards, except for my buddy Ric. His only requirements seemed to be that his dates be female and breathing. He collected two of the girls, one for each arm, and escorted them off to a dim corner of the bar. When I passed him a few moments later, he had a girl on each knee and was using his face to evaluate which of them had the more bountiful chest.

Sometime during the evening the room began to blur. I decided to head downstairs, but the top step refused to hold still. I stumbled down a half flight of stairs, landing in a heap. I don't know how long I stayed there, trying to decide if it was worth the effort to get up, before Jonah Benanti took pity on me. I dimly remember him, sunglasses and all, picking me up like a sack of wheat and carrying me to one of our rooms. He laid me on a cot in the corner and covered me with a poncho liner before returning to the party. I got the feeling that was definitely more than he would have done for old Doc Curl.

An insistent, pounding headache forced me awake a little later. When I moved, my stomach roiled with pain and nausea, threatening to rebel. I knew I needed some pain pills. Fortunately for me, I was the corpsman, so I had plenty in my bag. I started to get up to get them, only to have my head explode and my stomach turn inside out. I could only collapse in a puking heap while my stomach emptied itself.

When I could finally move again, I crawled slowly to my bag and took out one of my handy-dandy survival kits, consisting of one Darvon for pain, a Vitamin B-1 and B-12, three All-Purpose Capsules (APCs), and an Alka-Seltzer to swallow them all with. I issued similar kits to all the guys, because you never knew when a hangover repair kit might save your life. Within ten or fifteen minutes, my stomach started to settle and my head cleared. A quick look at my watch gave the time as 4:30 AM. Now that I could think and even move again without losing my cookies, I needed some air. I got up, carefully, and walked out on the open veranda that ran along one side of the bar. The city below was almost quiet—though like most cities, it never truly slept.

A warm, moist breeze blew in, gradually picking up strength. Big puffy clouds started to gather over the hills. I lit up a smoke and watched as the clouds glowed with sudden bursts of illumination. The sound of distant thunder rolled across the landscape after each flash. I couldn't tell for certain if it was lightning from a distant storm or artillery fire. Back home in Illinois, I used to count the time delay between the light flashes and the thunder to discover how far away the strikes were falling. I waited for another flash and counted under my breath until I heard the thunder. By my count the storm—or the war—was about fifteen miles away.

That didn't bother me. I felt oddly safe standing there eight floors above Saigon. It was as if I was in a world somehow separated from both the city and the war, where only I existed. If either storm or war came in my direction, I would be safe, outside it all.

It began to rain a little after 5:00 AM and by 6:00 AM, the rain had intensified into a monsoonal downpour that scoured the city, drenching the unprotected rooftop veranda. One by one, the rest of the guys stumbled out onto the veranda to join me, some of them stark-ass naked. The rain became our communal shower as we stood there, letting the water pour over us, washing the booze and crap off our bodies eight stories above the sleeping city.

The rains in Vietnam usually lasted for a long time, so there was no reason to attempt to dry off. We just pulled our Levi's and shirts on over our wet bodies and headed for the jeeps. It was far preferable to be soggy all day than to have to endure the scorching heat that seemed to be the only other choice of weather in this country. The storm showed no sign of abating as we drove through the quiet streets back to SOG, but the pouring rain helped cover up the foul smells of the streets even as it washed away some of the grime, cleansing the city much as it had cleansed us.

Mr. Flanagan was waiting for us. As we drove into the compound, he began shouting orders at us—in his cheerful morning way.

"I hope you had a good time because now it's time to actually work! Get into cammies and get your gear. We're moving out in half an hour."

He and Mr. Moody had already succeeded in getting our big Conex boxes and footlockers trucked to Binh Thuy. We were scheduled to follow in a Marine Corps Sea Knight CH-46 helicopter as soon as the weather broke. The Sea Knight was a huge helo with a large cylindrical body. It had an unmistakable profile, equipped with two rotors, one forward, one elevated and at the rear, and could carry heavy loads or an entire platoon of men.

I changed quickly and took my parachute bag, which SEALs use instead of seabags, grabbed my Stoner and the rest of my weapons, and raced over to the helo pad. The two members of the Sea Knight's Army aircrew were hanging around their massive chopper, trying to use its bulk to help them stay a little bit dry while they finished their preflight refreshments. I nodded a greeting to them as I set my Stoner down and prepared to put the rest of my gear on board the helo. Both crewmen immediately wanted to know what kind of a gun it was. Since Stoners were only in common usage among the SEAL Teams, these guys had never seen one. They were even more amazed when they found out that I was a corpsman.

"They let a corpsman carry a weapon like that?" I could tell they were a little jealous.

"That way I don't have to be a good shot. I just have to fire in the general direction of the target." I picked it up so they could get a closer look. "This baby can shoot one thousand rounds per minute, so even a corpsman like me can hit something."

"One thousand rounds a minute? No way. You're full of shit."

"No, really." I noticed he had just finished drinking a canned cola. "Toss your can onto the dirt and I'll show you."

He tossed the can onto the ground and I brought the Stoner up and hit the can with a fifteen-round, three-second blast. The remains of the can rained to earth in metal shards. Before we could admire my handiwork, however, a deafening wail filled the air as all of the SOG sirens started screaming. The entire facility scrambled to full-alert status, sounding general quarters. Army soldiers appeared from everywhere, racing to their designated defensive positions. For a split second, I wondered if we were under attack. Then I realized the truth. I ducked into the back of the Sea Knight with the two crewmen and quickly hid my weapon. I was so used to Niland, where I could just fire whenever I wanted to, that I had forgotten we were in a war zone where they take shooting—any shooting—very seriously.

After a couple of minutes passed with no further weapons fire, the "all clear" sounded and the rest of the platoon headed toward the chopper.

As he climbed onboard, Ric winked at me. "You might want to clean your weapon when we get to Binh Thuy."

I laughed and pretended I didn't know what he meant. The first thing SEALs do after a weapon has been fired is to clean it. This comes before anything, including chow or a shower. We settled in to the belly of the helo to wait for the weather to clear, and talked about everything except the recent alert.

Around midday, the weather cleared. Mr. Flanagan and the pilots joined us on the Sea Knight, maps in hand. It was finally time to go. But just before takeoff, Mr. Flanagan turned and yelled to me, "Doc, you sure you have enough ammo left for the flight?"

I grinned and gave him a thumb's-up affirmative. He just rolled his eyes and shook his head. Then he turned to take his seat up front between the pilots.

As we lifted off the pad and headed south across the Mekong Delta, I looked out for a last sight of Vietnam's version of civilization. I saw vapor rising from the rooftops and streets below as the hot sun quickly heated the puddles of rainwater into steam. It was a totally different world out there.

Before the heat in the chopper could get oppressive, we began to climb. At higher altitudes, the air temperature cooled a bit, and I found myself dozing off. *Funny, I never realized getting closer to the war would make you sleepy. Works better than a pill.*

I jerked awake as the motors on the helo began to throttle back. We had started our descent into the Can Tho area. Peering out of the chopper, I could see the green-brown swath of the Bassac River cutting through the rice paddies and thick forest growth below. The Bassac River was a major trade and travel route through the delta area. Running from Cambodia to the South China Sea, it paralleled the Mekong River, farther to the north, for which the delta was named. Both the rivers fed into numerous smaller rivers and tributaries throughout the region. These rivers and their tributaries formed the primary roads and highways for most of the locals. They were also major routes used for smuggling weapons and supply shipments by the Viet Cong. It was the Navy—specifically the river craft or Brown Water Navy—whose job was to ensure that Viet Cong shipping suffered major shipping delays—preferably permanent ones.

It seemed that all the rivers in 'Nam—or at least all the rivers I had seen—were green-brown, brown, or darker brown. This murky coloration had given the Brown Water Navy operating in the Mekong Delta its nickname. Despite being compared to mud, the officers, crew, and support teams who manned the Navy's fighting river fleet were all very proud of their nickname and their service. They felt the name set them apart from the regular Navy men, who sailed on the much safer blue waters of the open ocean. The Brown Water men sailed on dirty water and did the dirty jobs—and did them well. It was the Brown Water Navy that worked hand-in-hand with the SEAL Teams, sharing our risks and enabling many of our triumphs.

The chopper dipped slightly as Binh Thuy Navy Base came into view. It didn't look like much, just a cluster of buildings set into a large clearing on the bank of the muddy river. The base extended into the water with several large docking areas, each clustered with a gathering of small- and medium-size boats. The base's compliment of watercraft consisted mostly of PBR craft, short for Patrol Boat River, and Swift Boats. It was also home to our Boat Support Units, or BSUs, and Hal-3, the Seawolf helicopter group that supported SEAL Team ops.

We landed to find that most of our gear was being loaded into a Mike boat for the trip to our new home. In order to reach Nam Can, the boat and our gear had to sail down the delta to Soc Trang, then travel south in the China Sea to Ca Mau, before going up the Cua Lon River to Nam Can. We were scheduled to meet it there. But we would be taking the airborne shortcut. In order to arrive at the same time as our waterborne gear, we had to give the Mike boat two-days head start.

We had only been on the ground long enough to unload our equipment when I spotted a native in casual clothing poking around our gear. No one else seemed to have noticed him. I could only see him from the back, but before I could approach him, he walked over to one of the ARVN soldiers and began speaking to him in Vietnamese. I watched as the soldier nodded and moved off. The man went back to looking at our boxes. I came up behind the man, very quietly, and asked loudly, in stumbling Vietnamese, what he was doing there. Even if he didn't completely understand me, my sudden appearance should have shaken him out of his sandals.

Instead of jumping, the man calmly answered in perfect Midwestern American English, "Just checking to see how much shit you SEALs brought down this time." He turned around to look me up and down. "And you need to work on your vocabulary, son."

I realized I was staring into the face of a very round-eyed Caucasian man wearing a big grin. "Don't worry. I have clearance." He stuck out his hand, "Name's Jim Gorman."

After closing my gaping mouth, I shook his hand and introduced myself. It was the beginning of a beautiful friendship. Jim was one of the most unusual men I ever met. He was a boat-support crew member, and had been in country for almost two years. With no real family back in the States, he made the Vietnamese people his family, totally immersing himself into the native culture. He spoke fluent Vietnamese, dressed Vietnamese, and ate Vietnamese. Whenever he was near the Binh Thuy area, he even lived with the locals in Can Tho, staying in their hooches after curfew at night. He had a real Vietnamese girlfriend—not a bar girl—and often stayed with her and her family. I realized very quickly that Jim could be invaluable in helping me to gain the skills I would need to do my job well. As our squad's prisoner handler, I had to have a good basic understanding of Vietnamese. He agreed to help me with my language skills, and we arranged to spend time together as often as possible. I think it pleased him that I wanted to learn more about "his" people.

The guys and I spent the next two days getting to know Jim as well as the chopper pilots and boat support crews assigned to Detachment Golf and to our new home, the SEAFLOAT command down on the Cua Lon River. One of the BSU crew members we hit it off with was Lt. Elmo Zumwalt, Jr. He was a great guy, despite the fact that he also happened to be Admiral Zumwalt's son. We felt it was always important to get to know the guys who might be pulling our asses out of the fire in the future.

14

Indian Country

I did not get to spend nearly as much time with Jim and Elmo and the other BSU guys as I would have liked. After two short days it was time to leave on the final leg of our journey. This time, two UH-1 Huey slicks sat on the pads waiting for us, one for each squad. From now on, most airborne insertions or extractions would be done from these versatile flying platforms. The slicks had no doors and were armed with miniguns on the front and an M-60 machine gun in each doorway. The Sea Knight that brought us sat on a larger nearby pad, its huge, double-rotored body dwarfing the smaller Hueys.

We loaded all our remaining equipment—anything and everything that hadn't already gone on the Mike boat—onto the Sea Knight. There was plenty of cargo space left on the huge helicopter, and I wondered briefly why we were using the Hueys at all. Then the Sea Knight lifted off the pad and hovered over the dock while the ground crew scurried below attaching cables. I watched as our SEAL Tactical Assault Boat lifted out of its dock to hang suspended beneath the belly of the helo. The Sea Knight was big and powerful, but it could not hold our gear, our boat, and all of us.

This was no drill. The next stop would be Old Nam Can, in the heart of Indian Country. There we would land and offload our gear, before going on to our floating base by boat. In accordance with Mr. Flanagan's orders, we all wore full field gear and carried our weapons in case the landing zone was "hot." We mounted the slicks according to squads. Our squad, with Mr. Flanagan, climbed into the first helo. Mr. Moody and his squad took the other. I quickly found a spot on the diamond-patterned aluminum floor near the open door and sat down. Boh lounged in the edge of the far door, his feet hanging out above the helo's skid, looking as if he had been born to ride a slick. Langlois, Ritter, and Richardson all crammed in the middle, their backs against the bulkhead, while Ric scooted in beside me, a big grin on his face.

Mr. Flanagan took a moment to make certain we were all aboard and ready before he nodded and took his place near the two pilots. Last to board, the door gunner hopped in beside me, smiled encouragingly, then strapped himself in and adjusted his pintel-mounted M-60.

This was it. We were finally going to the war. I didn't really believe it until we lifted off. As soon as we reached a few hundred feet, we were immediately surrounded by Seawolf gunships, our lethal escorts for the forty-five-minute flight. All our flights up until this moment had been in solitary vehicles, whether plane or helicopter. This was completely different. The wind whipped through the open door onto my face as I watched the ground shrink away below me. On either side the Seawolves, bristling with weaponry, paced us. Two protected our flank while another flew point. A quick glance out the door confirmed that the other Huey, the Sea Knight, and the rest of the escorts held formation behind us. I could not help feeling a little excited, heading into the unknown with this squadron of powerful machinery flying formation around us. The helicopter was the one thing that we had that Charlie could not match or copy. He could shoot our birds down, but he could not join us in the air, nor could he match the sudden mobility that these rotor-driven platforms gave us.

We reached the Cua Lon River at a point far down the Cau Mau peninsula near where it juts out between the South China Sea and the

Gulf of Siam, and altered course to follow the river to our landing zone at Old Nam Can. At this point so near the sea, the river was over two miles wide, which made it appear from the air like a vast greenish-brown lake. Only a little over a year before, thousands of peasants had called Old Nam Can home. But during TET, the VC had overrun the area, causing the peasants to move out, abandoning their hooches and scattering into the jungles and swamps. The only people remaining in the area were certain to be bad guys.

We approached the ruins of the town from the river. As we neared the site, the Seawolf gunships broke formation and accelerated, flying in ahead of us. The sight and sound of those predatory choppers swooping down, bristling with weaponry, was guaranteed to scare any lurking VC into hiding. Our slicks followed, descending into the landing zone under the protective watch of the Seawolves. I couldn't see much from the air except a large clearing with the remains of some native huts in it, edged by an increasingly dense line of vegetation beginning about five hundred yards back from the water's edge.

I tensed in preparation for action, my weapon at the ready. The second our slick touched down, Ric, Boh, Ritter, Langlois, Richardson, and I quickly jumped out, staying low to miss the rotors and to make ourselves smaller targets. We formed a protective perimeter around the LZ, each man taking a sector to make certain we were covered in all directions, just as we had practiced hundreds of times. Mr. Moody's squad did the same and the Hueys returned to the air as dust and dried grasses whipped around us in a whirlwind created by the rotor wash. A few minutes later the CH-46 Sea Knight descended to hover low over the river, releasing our boat to drop into the water just off shore. I glanced out at the river long enough to see a second boat approach ours to retrieve it, but most of my focus was toward the brush line and any possible enemies who might be in hiding there.

The Sea Knight, freed of its dangling cargo, continued into the LZ to touch down near us. Half the men of each squad dashed aboard to assist the aircrew as they quickly offloaded the remainder of our gear. The rest of us kept a watchful eye to be certain no bad guys could sneak up on us while they worked. Once the Sea Knight was unloaded, it lifted off immediately, heading back to Binh Thuy, followed closely by the Seawolves.

Once the choppers were gone it got quiet real fast. The only sound was the gentle wind in the bushes and the quiet splashing from the boats on the river. We were so green we were hunching down and using hand signals to communicate as if we had been sneaking through the jungle all night to get here—despite the fact that no one in the vicinity could have missed our grand, and very noisy, entrance.

"All right, that's enough! Everyone gather round!" Mr. Flanagan shattered the silence as he calmly lit up a Pall Mall. We straightened and lowered our weapons—to be greeted by a sudden burst of applause from the riverbank. We were so focused on the tree line that we had missed an entire SEAL platoon, standing on the riverbank, casually observing our performance. They were obviously the platoon we were relieving, and had come to escort us back to base.

"Great insertion tactics guys!" one shouted as they approached us. "Except that there ain't no one here but us. We've already seen to that!" I noticed at least half of them weren't even carrying weapons, and none of them were in web gear. I felt completely overdressed.

"I give 'em eight points for ability and execution," a second one called out.

"Yeah, but a perfect ten for stupidity!" a third hooted. They all laughed and pointed. I was glad we could at least provide comic relief for our SEAL brothers. When they finally finished laughing at us, they came over and offered us ice-cold beer and warm, sweaty handshakes. Despite their initial reaction, they were very happy to welcome us as their replacements.

I had just begun to relax, following their lead, when the bushes parted to reveal a small group of armed men in black pajamas. I started to raise my gun, thinking that the other platoon had been mistaken about the absence of an enemy presence, but noticed that the other platoon was not at all alarmed. I looked more closely, and noticed a rugged-looking older white man in among those black pajamas. The man, in his forties, was almost as short as the Vietnamese who accompanied him, though he had a more muscular build than that of his native companions. His tiger-stripe cammies were neat but well-worn, and his skin appeared weathered from long exposure to the sun.

"Who is that?" I asked no one in particular, gesturing toward the lucky bastard I had almost shot.

"That's Frank Flynn; he's one of the original West Coast SEALs." One of the outgoing platoon members filled me in. "He's in charge of all the Kit Carsons in our area." The Kit Carsons were all former VC who had defected under the *Chieu Hoi* or Open Arms program and were now working for the South as scouts. Like the historical Kit Carson who was their namesake, it was their job to lead the way and provide information that would keep their units safe while operating in the Indian Country that was the operational area of the Viet Cong. "It's Frank's job to match up his guys with the different platoons to ensure the best combination. He's been in and out of 'Nam on at least three or four tours by now, to the point he's become a regular fixture around here. I understand he always comes in to meet the new platoons and see what he can beg, borrow, or steal for his scouts. He'll probably be going out with you on your first few ops just to make certain you know what you're supposed to be doing. He did that with us, and it was a big help."

I stepped up to introduce myself to Frank, and included a list of the medical supplies I had brought as well as the ones I could lay my hands on. "I'll be happy to do what I can for you and your guys while I'm here." I knew that the secret to successful operations often depended on the Kit Carsons' intimate knowledge of the area and of the VC. Most of them had originally been forced to join the Viet Cong, and had suffered great privations until their defection to the South. Providing better health care for the Kit Carsons and their families was one way to keep them loyal. Survival, especially for their families, usually mattered much more to them than politics. "Get me a list of what you need the most and I'll get what I can to you right away."

Frank gave me a dazzling smile and grabbed my hand in a powerful grip. "Doc, you just made yourself a friend for life."

He spoke to his scouts in part English, part French, and part

Vietnamese. I couldn't understand all of it, but I heard him refer to me as *Bac Si,* which means doctor in Vietnamese. Upon hearing this, their eyes lit up, and they raced over to meet me and shake my hand—or shake me down, I'm not entirely sure which. The Vietnamese didn't have corpsmen, but anyone with medical knowledge was the equivalent of a doctor to them, and doctors were as rare as they were badly needed. I got the impression that I was being adopted right then and there.

While we discussed the supplies he needed, I learned that there were hundreds of Kit Carsons working with Frank, and that each of them usually brought their entire extended family to live with them when they left the VC. They had established a refugee camp several miles downriver in an area that had become known as either the Annex, or New Nam Can. Frank said there were over one thousand people living there, with more arriving in the village each day. They had no doctors or medical supplies other than their folk remedies and midwives. I agreed to make house calls on the village whenever I could manage.

Frank and his Kit Carsons helped us load our equipment into the boats waiting to carry it out to the base. At this point the Cua Lon River was almost two miles wide with very strong tidal currents. Our base was located in the exact center of the river, its perimeter protected by the swift running river itself. As we neared SEAFLOAT, I realized it was nothing like the other bases I had seen so far in Vietnam. I had been told SEAFLOAT was built on a barge, but that description lacked accuracy. It was actually constructed of a *lot* of barges, both large and small, lashed together in what appeared to be an almost haphazard fashion, and anchored securely to the riverbed. From the air I could see an armory, a fuel depot, and even a sizable section with helicopter landing pads.

Once on board this conglomerate base, the outgoing platoon met us and escorted us to the area that would become our hooch, or living area. It consisted of a separate barge with a wood frame building sitting on it. The building was screened in, rather than walled, with a corrugated sheet-metal roof. It was wired for electricity, and the members of the outgoing platoon assured us that the power even worked. Occasionally. I was glad we had lots of batteries for the ghetto blaster.

The inside of the building was maybe twenty by forty feet with the bunks at one end, a little open space, then the officer quarters that would be used by Mr. Flanagan and Mr. Moody. Each bunk had its own mosquito netting. The barge next to ours contained more wood and metal buildings housing the showers, the shitters, a prisoner area, a briefing room, and some sleeping quarters designed to house the Vietnamese Navy as well as some of our scouts and guides. This part of SEAFLOAT was designed to hold two SEAL platoons on offset rotations. The other platoon was housed on another platform adjacent to ours. The members of that platoon were out on an operation when we arrived.

We helped the outgoing platoon remove the last of their stuff and clean the place up in preparation for our occupancy. Then we said our goodbyes as they left to begin their long journey home. I picked out a bunk for myself and Ric took the one above it.

After stowing our personal stuff, we took a tour of the rest of the base. It was more like a man-made island than any kind of ship. In addition to the mess halls, armory, and fuel depots, SEAFLOAT contained a large number of additional sleeping quarters to house the various units that worked for and from the base. Most of the Patrol Boat River (PBR) and Swift Boat crews had quarters aboard, plus extra quarters for our boat support unit guys whenever they were down on SEAFLOAT.

The layout of the barges was actually designed to allow maximum protected docking area for the various watercraft that were the primary means of transport in this area. There were no roads in our entire area of operations. There was water, swamp, jungle, rice paddies, and an occasional footpath. To travel anywhere the natives had to walk, swim, or travel by boat. The trails were dangerous and winding, the water muddy and full of leeches, so boating won out as the number one method of transport. The large numbers of canals, rivers, and tributaries in the delta region formed a natural network of "water roads" that the natives used much as we use highways. Most people and goods traveled primarily by boat. That included SEALs.

Since SEAFLOAT was anchored in the middle of a large river, the only way on or off was by air or water, so there were a lot of boats. In addition to the very light and maneuverable STAB, or SEAL Tactical Assault Boat we brought with us, I saw a number of deep-water, fifty-foot, propeller-driven, Swift Boats, and smaller thirty-two-foot fiberglass PBRs, all docked and ready to go.

There was even a native sampan, for use on missions where it was important to "blend in" with the local river traffic—though I noticed that the sampan was outfitted with some very American twin Briggs & Stratton motors. At first I thought the motors were added by the boat crew chiefs to give our guys extra speed. I was informed that they actually came from the VC. Apparently such items were the "in thing" for the up-and-coming VC chieftain.

The guys were satisfied with the tour, but there was one crucial area I still needed to check out—sick bay. I found it easily enough. Just like on navy ships, the sick bay was located right behind the officer quarters amidships. I opened the door—and gagged on the stench. Far from the clean and sterile place I expected, the room looked and smelled like the Vietnamese had cooked a dog and shit him back out all in the same room. I was furious. Someone obviously used the room for something besides medical procedures. Looking around the room at the filth and disarray I felt sick. I couldn't treat wounded men effectively in this squalor! I demanded to see the base doctor or chief corpsman, only to be told SEAFLOAT didn't currently have either one. I was assured that a new corpsman from the fleet had been ordered and was scheduled to arrive the next day.

I was waiting at the helo pad the next afternoon when Gary Smith arrived and introduced himself as the new Corpsman. He and I hit it off immediately. He was a broad-built, dark-haired, New England boy, but lacked the usual stuffed-upper-crust attitude that I associated with the place. Gary did not feel he could have made it as a SEAL, but he greatly admired those who had. More importantly, he agreed with me completely on the radical changes needed to make sick bay useable. We began by making the place off-limits to nonmedical personnel or patients. But cleaning and limiting access would be only the beginning. There were not nearly enough medical supplies on hand for a place as big as

SEAFLOAT, and none on order. Gary tried to requisition some new supplies the day he arrived, but was told the order was not likely to be filled. There were no extra medical supplies available for our use. I just prayed we would not have to treat any injuries before we managed to solve the supply problem and get sick bay up to par and functional.

15

Time to Earn Our Pay

UNFORTUNATELY, SEAL missions could not be delayed just because sick bay wasn't in order. As a matter of fact, the officers began preparing for our first action while we were still unpacking our gear. While I tried to figure out what to do about sick bay, they were poring over intelligence reports and planning our first operation against the enemy.

Of course, we were also anxious to get to work. We had been trained to do a job and we wanted a chance to do it. Most of us spent those first evenings listening to the war stories from SEAFLOAT's second SEAL platoon. Commanded by a tall, strong-featured blond named Dave Nicholas, they had been there since early June and had just finished their fifth month in country. They knew the lay of the land and we listened attentively to every word.

Usually the break-in op, the first operation assigned to a new platoon, was something fairly simple, often involving assistance from the more experienced platoon. The officers had acquired some hot intelligence on VC movements. Based on this intel, they decided that our break-in op would be a joint exercise with the other platoon in a "Hammer and Anvil" ambush, and called a warning order to announce the mission.

Hammer and Anvil? I had never even heard of this type of ambush, much less studied it as I had many others. I felt a little nervous about doing something we had not practiced back in Niland. I looked around the room and saw similar consternation reflected on the faces of most of our platoon.

It was to be a daylight ambush at the intersection of a canal and a large river inlet. The canal was known to have a lot of VC traffic. There would be three squads involved. One would insert by boat a few kilometers up the canal, the second would insert by chopper a few kilometers up the inlet. They would both drive the VC toward the third squad—ours—which was to be quietly sitting in ambush at the intersection of the two waterways, waiting for the VC to come to us. We were to insert first by boat, so that we would be in position before the other squads began to "beat the bushes" and drive the enemy into range of our guns.

The officers presented the details on the mission plan the next morning during the final patrol order briefing. The tin-topped room was very hot and crowded, with two complete platoons, plus the officers and support staff, stuffed into a space designed for half that number. Despite the discomfort, I paid very close attention to the officers and chiefs as they told us exactly what our jobs would be. Ric Schroeder, John Mitchell, Wayne Bohannon, Dave Langlois, and I, along with a couple guys I didn't know from Lt. Nicholas' platoon, were to be inserted as the shooters on the ambush. We would be accompanied by two of Frank Flynn's Kit Carson scouts, also armed, plus a former VC as a guide. Mr. Nicholas would lead one of the two chase squads. Boh was to lead ours. Frank Flynn was going along with one of the chase squads since each squad would contain two of his Kit Carsons.

As I listened, my heart began to race and butterflies had a field day swooping around in my stomach. Sweat dripped down my back, beaded on my palms, but not from the heat. This would be my first real operation as a SEAL, and it involved something we had never done.

My nervousness must have showed, because Roger Hayden, a mountain of a guy from the other platoon, leaned over to give me a reassuring pat on the back. "Don't worry, Doc. We won't send more than a couple dozen Charlies in your direction. This will be a piece of cake."

"What about friendlies?" Mitch asked. "How do we tell them from the VC?"

"Where you are going there *are* no 'friendlies.'" The briefing officer assured us, "Any Vietnamese you see in there are definitely Viet Cong. It is a free-fire zone."

"Is everyone clear on the objective and your jobs?" Lt. Nicholas asked. When he received nods all around, he continued. "You've got one hour to get ready. Good luck."

This was it. I had no time to sit around brooding about my concerns. We were operating on fresh intel and had to take advantage of it right away. I tried to put my worries aside as I quickly donned my jungle cammies and slathered my face, hands, and forearms with plenty of camo cream. Once I was certain I could do a fair job of impersonating a bush, I tied my bandana around my head to keep the sweat out of my eyes. Double-checking my weapons, ammo, and web gear I made certain there was nothing shiny on any of it that might catch the sun and give us away to the enemy. It was all nice and dull. I then checked all my medical gear, pulling out Syrettes of morphine and passing one to everyone in the squad—just in case. I put a few extra in my shirt pocket. Boh came over to double-check my gear. His elaborate camo job enhanced his already fierce expression. He too looked like a bush. A very dangerous bush. Once he had inspected everyone's gear and makeup, he ordered us outside.

"Okay guys!" he yelled "You're all gorgeous. Now, get out back and test-fire your weapons."

Test-firing before leaving for an operation enabled us to be sure our weapons were in good working order *before* our lives depended on them. No matter how rushed the schedule might be, we always tried to make time for this important procedure, if only to be certain we had actually put our weapons back together correctly after we had last cleaned them. This attention to detail is probably why the SEALs had good luck with weapons like my Stoner, when the rest of the military tended to avoid using any gun complicated enough to jam if not carefully maintained, even if it was an otherwise-superior piece of ordnance.

Test-fire completed, we boarded our SEAL Tactical Assault Boat (STAB) for the quick run up the river to our insertion point. The squad-sized STAB was our own personal lightweight water-jet boat, ideal for all sorts of sports like darting up small, narrow canals at the equivalent of fifty miles per hour while chasing down the VC. It was also good for fast beer runs, trips to the beach, or getting downriver quickly to help our buddies when they were pinned by enemy fire.

The first chase squad climbed into their larger PBR for the trip up the canal. The PBR, while larger and slower than the STAB, was still quite small and fast. It was only thirty-two feet long and its water-jet Jacuzzi-style propulsion gave it a top speed of around thirty-five knots as well as the ability to turn completely around within its own length. I loved the PBR because it was basically a modified pleasure boat design with a reinforced fiberglass hull and special ceramic armor. Like the STAB, the PBR could get into small rivers and shallow tributaries quietly and quickly, but unlike the STAB, the PBR had a separate four-man boat crew, and boasted some serious onboard weaponry. Most of us preferred the PBRs to most other boats because they came heavily armed with twin .50 caliber machine guns up front and twin 60s along each side. Plus they had Honeywell grenade launchers on each side, my favorite crew-served weapons. If an insertion or extraction suddenly turned hot, the PBR's weaponry and speed could mean the difference between life and death for the squad. With the PBR it was possible to get in fast, do some serious damage, turn around in your tracks, and get back out again before the enemy realized you had ever been there. I hoped that none of those weapons would be needed this time around, especially since our STAB didn't have any.

As both boats pulled away from SEAFLOAT's dock, I could see the army slick landing to pick up the third squad. It was fast, but noisy—perfect for an operation like this where we wanted the enemy to hear them coming.

After a fast forty-minute ride down the river, we quickly and quietly pulled in to the mangrove-covered shoreline at the corner of the canal and the river. As we slid between the mangroves, I could hear the slick and PBR noisily heading for their respective insertion points. I was first off the boat, scrambling into the brush for about ten meters before I knelt up, covering the area where we were to set up ambush. Boh was next in, followed by Ric, our radioman, then the rest of the squad.

Boh immediately had Ric contact the other two squads to let them know we were in and set up for action. Then the two of them moved to the center of our zone and settled in to a crouch behind an old fallen stump. Mitch and Dave took the left flank behind some bushes while Frank and the other two guys from the other platoon set themselves to cover our rear. The two Kit Carsons, the guide, and I were still attempting to maneuver ourselves into positions on the right, closest to the canal, when I heard the PBR start to move up the canal. We were having some difficulty finding a good spot because the area had been defoliated with Agent Orange some time ago. The remaining barren branches allowed good visibility, but also resulted in a serious lack of cover for my position. The roar of the boat engine gave us a few minutes to move some logs and branches into place to create a quick blind that would conceal us from anyone running up the canal bank in our direction.

It was about 2:00 PM when we settled in for the wait. After only a few minutes, I discovered that my mouth and throat were so parched, I felt as if I was spitting cotton balls. I wasn't hot, but I was sweating profusely. It felt as if every hair on my body was standing up. I was scared to death. My eyes must have looked like saucers as I alternated staring into the jungle and up the canal, expecting Charlie to materialize at any moment.

Finally the thirst was too much. I had to have a drink. I rolled over to grab my canteen, rattling the brush. At the sound of my movement, Ric looked over at me and put his finger on his lips to shush me. I quietly flipped him off in answer. He grinned and gave me a thumbs-up as I took a big swig of water.

Replacing my canteen, I realized that all sounds of helos or PBRs had ceased. I rolled back into position and carefully searched for any sign of movement. There was nothing yet.

As we waited, I could hear the occasional sounds of a sampan motor on the river interspersed with distant shouting. I even heard sporadic gunfire—single shots from an old rifle, which I knew was a VC warning other VC of our presence. A little while later, I heard someone beating out a signal on a hollow log off in the distance.

Our guide smiled at the sound and turned to one of the scouts, "VC think green face may come tonight."

I told him to shush. He looked at me as if I was nuts. After all, yesterday he was a VC himself. He probably knew all the bad guys around here personally. A few minutes later he pulled out a cigarette and started to light it. *Just what we need! Damn Indian's sending smoke signals to tell the VC right where we are!* I grabbed it out of his hand. He looked at me with fury in his slanted black eyes. For a split second, I thought he was going to reach for one of the Kit Carsons' weapons. I raised my Stoner threateningly to make certain he knew I could get him first.

One of the Kit Carsons quickly tried to diffuse the situation, "Okay *Bac Si.* Cigarette same. Same VC."

I shook my head no and the guide mumbled something under his breath. Guides didn't get weapons until they proved themselves reliable and trustworthy, and this guy was already on my shit list.

Everything was fairly quiet for about an hour and a half. Then, one of the scouts indicated that he saw something coming up the canal bank, but signaled that he wasn't sure what it was.

"VC," the guide announced in a loud whisper. "VC come now!"

Peeking through the bushes, I got a good look at a guy wearing black pajamas, carrying a rifle, and sneaking through the brush. Another one followed close behind. I started to pass the signal down, but before I could move both scouts began firing their M-16s on full automatic. Afraid the VC would begin shooting back; I raised my Stoner and began to lay down a base of fire. As I swept the brush with quick bursts, I suddenly caught a glimpse of a tall blond waving his hands to cease fire—and then he was gone.

My gut turned to ice as I realized the worst possible scenario had occurred—a SEAL squad had walked in on a SEAL ambush. I immediately raised my weapon, screaming, "Cease fire! Cease fire!"

The firing stopped abruptly. Men began running and shouting. Screaming seemed to be coming from everywhere at once. "Doc! Doc! Doc!" someone yelled. I ignored everything else and raced over to the spot where I had seen the unmistakable blond profile of Lt. Dave Nicholas disappear.

He was lying on his back in the brush where he had fallen. I dropped down beside him, trying to find a pulse or respiration. There was none, but there was very little loss of blood. I wasn't sure where he was hit, so I started giving him CPR. After a few quick breaths I checked again for a pulse. Nothing.

"Ric, get over here and help me." Ric was there in an instant, pressing on Lt. Nicholas's chest to try and get his heart started while I continued mouth-to-mouth. In between breaths, I grabbed the radio and called for an immediate Medivac Helicopter Dust Off. Turning back to my patient, I discovered one of Nicholas's men preparing to give him a Syrette of morphine.

"Please don't give him morphine. I am trying to see if there is still a life here left to save." The man backed off and I continued to attempt resuscitation. "What about the Kit Carsons?" I gasped between breaths. I remembered that they had both been in front of the column.

"They're both dead," a voice stated.

"Mitch," I called to John Mitchell, "come take over for me for a minute." Mitch moved in and took over giving mouth-to-mouth. I knew Mitch knew what to do because I had started giving him some first aid training so he could act as the medic for Mr. Moody's squad.

I scooted over to where the scouts had fallen, hoping to find a life to save. Frank Flynn and the surviving Kit Carsons moved away to give me room, but it was too late. Both scouts had died in the first M-16 bursts.

I rushed back to Nicholas and told Ric to move and let me try. This time, as I started to compress his chest, I felt something give and knew immediately where he had been hit. I quickly unbuttoned his cammie top and cut open his T-shirt. There was a single hole about the size of a dime in the center of his blood-soaked chest. His sternum felt shattered. My mind told me that he was dead, but my heart wouldn't let him go.

I was still working on him frantically when I felt the wind from the Dust Off helo's rotors as it hovered over the canal. I was so focused on Mr. Nicholas that I didn't even notice when eight guys lifted the two of us up over their heads to pass us to the chopper. I continued to work even as the outstretched arms of the medics grabbed us both to pull us on board the helo. As we lifted off, one of the medics took over my patient for me and the other tossed out a couple of body bags for the two dead scouts.

With nothing left to do, I just slumped, dazed, on the deck next to Mr. Nicholas. I realized I was probably suffering from heat exhaustion and shock, but all I could think was that it was happening again. More body bags. My first operation as a SEAL corpsman had ended in casualties. Not only was I unable to save anyone, but I might have been partially responsible for their deaths.

A medic handed me a canteen to wash out my mouth and clean my face after giving CPR for so long. The other medic finished thoroughly checking Mr. Nicholas. He patted me on the shoulder, shaking his head. "Nothing you could do," he assured me. "He probably died instantly."

Somehow that news didn't really help.

As we landed on the SEAFLOAT helo pad, I told the crew to clear the pad and go get Doc from sick bay with a body bag. Gary arrived a few minutes later with a couple chiefs, and some other SEAL officers. They helped me put Mr. Nicholas in the body bag and remove his personal effects. We then placed him in the walk-in cooler behind the kitchen until his remains could be flown up to Saigon the next day. As I worked, I tried to focus on the job rather than the young officer who would never see another sunset.

A little while after I finished with Nicholas, the PBR arrived, bearing the two dead Kit Carson scouts, already in their body bags. I met the PBR at the dock and helped Flynn move the bodies. We took them to one of his boats, so he could take them upriver to their village where their families would properly take care of their remains.

"Doc," he said after we had placed the scouts gently in his boat, "that was a good thing you did out there."

"I didn't do nothing." I bitterly gestured toward the bags. "They're dead. What did I do but help get them killed?"

"You left a white American officer on the ground to help them." He put a steadying hand on my shoulder. "You may not think that matters, but it matters a helluva lot to the ones that are still alive. These people are used to being treated badly by everyone. The VC just wanted them as cannon fodder. The South doesn't trust their change of heart. And the U.S. soldiers often treat them like animals or trash. You treated them like people. They won't forget that. And, neither will I."

"I was just trying to do my job."

"Yeah. And that's why it matters. You were just doing your job."

16

That They Not Die in Vain

I didn't really understand what he meant at the time, and I didn't really care. I felt empty inside as we filed into the mess hall for the mission debriefing. All of the SEALs and support group involved with the operation were gathered there. Tension hung heavy in the air, with everyone full of anger and looking for an outlet. Before the debriefing could even get under way, fingers were being pointed everywhere and confusion was the general order while everyone tried to understand what had gone wrong and decide who to blame.

I understood it all too well. It had been an accident, plain and simple. Somebody was in the wrong place at the wrong time. Our scouts blamed the dead scouts. They also blamed the guide for pointing out the dead scouts as VC. Others blamed Mr. Nicholas for not knowing where he was and moving his people into our ambush. Some said our squad was not where it was supposed to be.

Maybe our platoon, which was very green, should not have been operating with Nicholas's platoon. Maybe his men had become a little complacent with their safety procedures after so much time in country. Maybe it was a combination of both. Any number of scenarios would fit. All I could do was try to see that it didn't happen again—at least not to any of our guys.

Within a couple of days of that first disastrous operation, Lt. Commander Dave Schiable, the commanding officer of SEAL Team One, and Admiral Zumwalt arrived at SEAFLOAT for an inquiry into the Nicholas death. I thought it was fitting that his death would not go unnoticed. I also was determined to make certain that he did not die in vain.

With Uncle Dave, as we referred to him, and Admiral Zumwalt inspecting the base, I realized their presence provided me with an important opportunity. This was my chance to present my case for more medical supplies directly to the CO and admiral.

I caught them seated in the mess hall together, along with the Admiral's aide. After making certain I was not interrupting anything important, I pulled up a chair and quickly described the terrible state of the medical supplies on the base. I also strongly hinted that disasters like the one that killed Nicholas might happen again, but that, even if the injured lived to reach base, we would still not be able to save them with our current state of medical readiness. In my own mind I knew that all the medical tools in the world would not have helped Mr. Nicholas, but this way his death might help someone else.

My timing was good because they had both seen sick bay. Even though Gary and I had been working on it, it was still a disaster. And no amount of cleaning would put nonexistent medical supplies on the shelves. Both officers agreed we could not adequately handle many casualties with what we had. They promised that they would see what they could do.

I went on to tell them about Frank Flynn's needs for his scouts and their families, and how the VC pilfered what few medicines they had at the Annex. The admiral's aide told me to fill out a requisition form and he would process it through proper channels.

Before I could go on, Uncle Dave kicked me in the shin under the table and winked at me. "Thanks for your input, Doc. Go back to your platoon now and I'll see you all later."

I got the message, but I had to make one last attempt to get the one thing we really needed. Before excusing myself, I looked over at Admiral Zumwalt.

"I sure enjoyed meeting your son, sir. I'll bet you're real proud of him." I had just learned that Lt. Elmo Zumwalt Jr., whom I had befriended while at Binh Thuy, had just had his Swift Boat transferred down to SEAFLOAT. "It will be a real pleasure working with a professional of his caliber down here." I could tell I had his attention. "It seems like the base is expanding every day as more Swift Boats like Elmo's and more guys like us come on board. It sure is a shame that with all these people, we don't even have a doctor." I stood up. Admiral Zumwalt was staring at me with a peculiar intensity. "Now if you'll excuse me, sirs, I'll get back to my platoon now." I beat a hasty retreat, deliberately avoiding eye contact with Schiable.

Uncle Dave came over to meet with "his" SEALs in our hooch that night. He didn't point the finger at anybody, but as the CO he was shouldering the responsibility for our error. He told us that even the best trained men make mistakes, and then went on to make some suggestions.

"From now on, all scouts and guides will be required to wear a red neckerchief. If they aren't wearing their red scarves, they must be VC." There, no more mistaken identity. "Unless it is unavoidable, do not separate your men in the field so that one group must ever advance toward another group. No more Hammer and Anvil tactics." Then he turned his attention to me.

"McPartlin?"

"Yes, sir?" Now I was going to get chewed for the stunt in the mess.

"You got that shopping list of medical supplies drawn up?"

"I can have it ready for the Admiral's aide by morning, sir."

"Screw the Admiral's aide. Give it directly to me as soon as you have it ready."

"Thank you, sir!"

He turned his attention back to the platoon at large. "And I want you all to stand down a few days and review your procedures before going out on another operation."

Since we were not on duty, I decided to spend the next few days helping Gary square away sick bay. The first step was to remove everything that didn't belong there and scrub down everything that was left. It took most of the first day to get the garbage out and scrub the floor, walls, and shelves.

While wiping down the last of the shelves, I heard someone come in behind me. Assuming it was Gary bringing in more supplies, I kept cleaning.

"I see you've finally found a task worthy of your talents!"

I instantly recognized Dick Wolfe's deep baritone. Without turning to look, I heaved my wet sponge in the direction of the voice, only to have it come sailing back to strike me soggily in the shoulder.

"I'm gone for ten days on R & R and you guys show up and everything turns to shit!"

"Gee Dick, nice to see you, too." I stepped over and clapped him on the shoulder—with the wet sponge still in hand. Just then Gary returned, and I introduced Gary as the new SEAFLOAT corpsman. "And this is my old buddy Dick Wolfe, corpsman for the other SEAL platoon."

"I'm also one of the lead petty officers," Dick added, brushing off Gary's welcoming handshake, "and I want to know what you think you two are doing to my interrogation room! How am I supposed to get good intel if I don't have a place to interrogate prisoners?"

"And how are we supposed to handle casualties if you've taken over sick bay for interrogations?" I chided. Dick had definitely become a tough operator since I had last seen him, especially if interrogations were that important to him. But I couldn't let him forget that he was also a corpsman. "Where do you keep your medical supplies? We certainly didn't find any in here. It looks like your guys used this room as a catch-all for everything *except* medicine."

"I keep everything in a footlocker under my bunk. My guys are tough. They need me more as a soldier than a medic. As leading petty officer, I have better things to do than tend their boo-boos, so I taught them all how to put on their own Band-Aids. They know better than to bother me unless they lose a limb or an eye or something serious. Until you got here we didn't *need* sick bay. You sure stirred up a hell of a hornet's nest by killing Mr. Nicholas."

A quick glance at his face reassured me that he didn't mean me personally. It was his lieutenant that had been killed, so it would have been very easy for him to hold a grudge against those of us who were there when it happened. But Dick was bigger than that, inside as well as out.

"It shouldn't have happened," I granted. "But it does prove that we need to have better medical equipment in case things go wrong. This is a war, after all."

"Well, apparently the brass agrees with you. When I left Binh Thuy on the mail chopper, there was a shitload of medical supplies sitting out on the tarmac, all earmarked to go to Solid Anchor."

"Solid Anchor?" Gary looked a little confused.

"Yeah, the Navy's name for SEAFLOAT this week." Dick explained, "The brass likes to keep everyone guessing by changing the name of their little commands every once in a while. I also heard a rumor that we might be getting a doctor out of Saigon or off one of those hospital ships. It could happen in the next couple of days."

Gary and I couldn't help but smile at each other. A doctor! My plea had been heard. It meant that Dave Nicholas did not die in vain. Perhaps because of him, others would live.

17

Is There a Doctor in the House?

I was lounging on the beach, enjoying the sun and watching a golden-haired goddess in a string bikini walk by. As I watched, the goddess glided over to my hammock. She smiled, slowly bending down toward me, her crimson-colored lips parting as she yelled, "Wake up, McPartlin!" in a deep baritone voice. Her delicate hands suddenly transformed into two big beefy mitts that reached out to grab me roughly by the shoulders. In a moment, the beach at Coronado vanished. The blond beauty vanished. And I found myself staring up into Dick Wolfe's much uglier red-bearded face.

"McPartlin, you have got to see this!" The idyllic image of sand and sky shattered as Dick dragged me out of the cozy little nest I had made for myself in the shade between the sandbags. For a moment I had been in paradise—Coronado's version of paradise, anyway—but I came fully awake to find myself on the back of our barge, still in Vietnam.

"Damn it, Wolfe. I had a good dream going down—and you weren't supposed to be in it." I pushed him away and stood up, still trying to clear the sleep-fog from my brain. "What's so important?"

"Quick, the new doctor is here. You have got to get a load of this!"

The new doctor! I threw on a T-shirt, put on my flip-flops, and rushed over to sick bay with Wolfe. We entered to find a skinny young officer standing in the middle of the room, dressed in helmet and flak jacket, apparently giving orders to Gary, who was standing stiffly in front of him. I couldn't hear what the officer, obviously our new doctor, was saying, but Gary looked uncomfortable.

"I'm HM2 McPartlin, Alpha Platoon, SEAL Team One," I interrupted, stepping up and offering my hand.

Wolfe followed suit, introducing himself as a corpsman as well. "You must be our new doctor."

"Oh, good." The young man ignored my outstretched hand while giving Dick and me an imperious look. "I see I have two more corpsmen. Run out to the flight deck and get the rest of my gear. And see if you can find a cold soda while you're at it."

Wolfe and I just looked at each other for a moment in disbelief. Then we crossed our fingers, "Aye-aye, sir," gave a quick salute, and left. As soon as we were out of hearing range, we both began laughing our asses off.

"That guy probably went straight from his residency to take the two-week officers course," I snorted. "Straight out of school and thinks he's God."

"Yeah, and probably finished at the bottom of his class. He would have to be a real loser to draw this shit job."

A couple hours later, Wolfe and I popped our heads back into sick bay. The doctor was there, still wearing his helmet and flak jacket. Gary had apparently escaped.

"Hey, where is my gear?" he demanded.

Wolfe looked at me, I looked at him, and we both shrugged our shoulders like the Marx brothers.

"I thought I told you to bring my gear here."

"Gee, Dick, did you hear him say 'please'?" I asked, looking at Dick with exaggerated concern.

"No. Greg, did *you* hear a 'please'?" Dick responded.

"No, I sure did not."

We turned to the doctor in unison, smiled, and waved, "Bye-bye,

Doctor!" then calmly turned and walked away, ignoring the angry yells that followed us.

The good doctor immediately went whining to the SEAFLOAT "Black Shoe" Commander, to tell him he thought he was going to have a problem with a couple of *his* corpsmen. He told the CO that *his* corpsmen were not obeying his orders. Wrong move on his part. Fortunately, the CO was not impressed. When the word came back to us a few hours later, Dick decided to have a chat with the young man. I followed at a safe distance, curious to see what Dick would do, and prepared to render first aid to the geek if necessary. Dick found the doctor in sick bay, *still* in his helmet and flak jacket. Without waiting for an invitation he walked in, grabbed the little guy with both hands, lifted him like a sack of grain and deposited him on his butt on the examining table.

"Doc, we need to get a few things straight about how things work around here."

The fellow's face was white as he looked up at Wolfe, who towered over him despite his elevated seat. I stayed out of sight, letting Dick have his little talk in apparent privacy.

"I understand you bitched to the CO about us, 'cause we wouldn't be your lackeys."

The doctor said nothing, and was damned by his silence.

"Well, you need to understand this: We are not *your* corpsmen. You are *our* doctor. We requested a doctor, and they sent you out here to fill our order. The only reason you are here is to insure that we get all the supplies we need and to help us take care of the local civilians. *We* will take care of our own people ourselves." As he spoke, Dick leaned in over the poor doctor, forcing the young man to bend backward, almost lying on the table, to avoid him. "If we need you, we will *ask* for your help. You are to stay out of our way until and unless we do so. Do you understand?"

The doctor gave a jerky little nod.

"Good. I'm so glad we had this chat." Dick gave him a pat on the back, nearly knocking him off the table, and turned to leave. He stopped at the door to look back at the young man, still sitting on the table. "You know, Vietnam is a very dangerous place. Anything can happen here. With the enemy all around us, it's really not a good idea to piss off the only two SEALs on the base who also happen to be corpsmen." The doctor's eyes were very large as they followed Dick's retreating back. I ducked back out of sight before he could see me. One SEAL up the ass was enough medicine for the day.

The next morning, I chose a spot next to the doctor at the mess table. He was easy to spot, still wearing the flak jacket, with the helmet sitting beside him on the table. As I moved the helmet to set down my tray, I half expected more abuse. But instead of insults, he actually smiled a little.

"So, what did you say your name was?"

"Why? Are you going to put me on report for not getting your bags?"

"No, man," he shook his head emphatically, "I'm sorry about that. I just didn't realize you and Wolfe were Navy SEALs."

"So what? That shouldn't matter. Out here you need to lose that bullshit officer attitude and lighten up." The doctor was at least six years my senior, with college and med school behind him, and I was telling him to lighten up while in the middle of a war zone. It seemed perfectly natural to me.

"Can I be honest with you?"

I nodded encouragingly.

"This place scares the shit out of me." He picked up the helmet I had moved and held it protectively in his lap. "I've only been in country about a week, and that was all spent out in the South China Sea, on the hospital ship *Repose*. Out there, all you hear are the stories of how many doctors and medics get shot up every day. Yesterday, coming here on the helicopter, was the first time I ever saw the shore. I had never seen any Vietnamese people at all before we landed."

I realize that his behavior at our first meeting may have been the result of stress from the trip. Now that he had had a chance to settle, he just seemed like any other scared kid. Perhaps there was hope for him.

"Well, just relax. We're pretty safe out here. And don't wear that flak jacket or helmet anymore. You won't need it—unless we go to general quarters."

He looked unwilling to believe me, gripping his helmet even more tightly.

"Well, if you insist on keeping that, I don't suppose you have another helmet or flak jacket that I can borrow? Because I don't remember ever getting either one. And if I did, I don't have a clue where they are." He grinned, and released his hold on the helmet. "Name's Greg McPartlin, from Lake Forest, Illinois. You can call me Greg." I stuck out my hand.

"Dr. Marshall Franklin." He shook my hand this time. "You can call me *Doctor* Franklin." He emphasized the title.

So much for the change in attitude. "Well, then, Goodbye *Marshall.*" I excused myself, collecting my plate. As I stood up, I noticed that Tong and Zung, two of our Vietnamese scouts, were seated just beyond the screen in the other room. Leaning over, I pointed them out to the doctor. "You see those little slanty-eyed bastards right outside? Well, yesterday they were VC. Do you have any idea how much bounty the VC would place on a real American doctor?"

His eyes got big as he whipped around to stare at the scouts. As I headed to the chow hall door I saw Wolfe walking in the other door.

"Hey Wolfe! Go introduce yourself to *Doktor* Marshall Franklin," I yelled, stressing the title with Germanic intensity. I looked over at the scouts, who had been watching, and pointed at Marshall. "*Bac Si,* Number ten. You don't tell VC, okay?" The scouts laughed at the joke. Both Tong and Zung had lost their families to the VC. They were loyal and fierce little fighters who hated the VC more than any American ever could. Tong was very slim and wiry, and looked more Mexican than Vietnamese. His father was a doctor in Hanoi, but he hated commies. We were probably his fourth or fifth platoon. He knew the ways of the SEALs, spoke good English, and was always right up at the front of the patrol with the point man. We may have just acquired an MD, but to scouts like Tong, I was the real doctor.

As a result, it didn't surprise me to find Tong and another Kit

Carson I knew named Nhut, right up front at our hooch the next morning, looking for a doctor. Jim Gorman, my friend from boat support and mentor in Vietnamese was with them. As always, he looked and acted more Vietnamese than American, despite his citizenship papers, and often spent more time at the Annex village than at the base. He had become both translator and unofficial liaison between many of the scouts and the base. Most of the time he insisted on speaking to me in Vietnamese, which really pissed me off, but really helped my language skills.

"*Bac Si.* Come quick. Need help at Annex." Tong spoke urgently. "Nhut's wife big trouble. Cursed. Baby cursed."

I looked over at Nhut, but he just stood there, unable to speak, looking stricken and desperate. At my questioning look, Gorman filled in the details—in English this time.

"The midwife at the Annex told them Nhut's wife is going to die because the baby is cursed."

"What do you mean 'cursed'?"

"The baby's backwards."

In an American hospital, a breeched baby only created minor complications. Out here, among these people, it was usually a death sentence for both mother and child.

"Let's go. Now!" I grabbed a full field medical kit, a couple IVs, some drugs, and oxygen and we raced down to the dock and grabbed one of our high-speed SEAL Tactical Assault Boats for the run over to the Annex village.

Nhut's tiny hut was crowded with villagers, all gathered around the straining mother. I pushed through the crowd to check out Nhut's wife. The midwife, an old wise-faced *mama-san,* held the young woman's shoulders tightly as I knelt at her side.

"Baby dead," she stated, matter-of-factly. "Baby cursed."

I ignored her and began to check out my patient. The frail young woman was only semiconscious and in real bad shape. Her arm was so thin that it took a moment to find a good vein, but I got a glucose IV going as fast as I could. I started her on oxygen immediately, and checked all her vital signs again. They were beginning to improve as the glucose and oxygen kicked in. Before I could check on the baby, I needed silence.

"Everybody out. *Di di mau!*" I ordered everyone out but the midwife, then moved to check on the baby's position. The mother had fully dilated. I could feel the baby's bottom locked tightly in her cervix. I adjusted my position and placed my stethoscope on her abdomen, looking for a heartbeat. At first I heard nothing, but kept moving the stethoscope around her lower abdomen until I picked up a faint fetal heartbeat.

"Baby alive still," I announced.

"No. Baby dead," the midwife insisted. "Baby dead!"

I reached over and placed the earpieces of the stethoscope in her ears and held the scope over the baby's heart. The *mama-san*'s eyes got wide as she heard the unmistakable sound of life. Her face lit up in a broken smile, marred by the fact that half her teeth were missing and the rest were black from years of chewing beechnut.

I yelled to Jim to get a stretcher. We had to get the mother to SEAFLOAT if there was any chance of saving her or her baby. Jim and Nhut brought the stretcher, and we gently loaded her on the STAB and raced toward SEAFLOAT. While the little speedboat flew over the water, I started a second IV of saline solution. By the time we arrived at SEAFLOAT, the mother's vitals were improving.

I was relieved to see Dr. Franklin and Gary both in sick bay as we entered with our patient.

"Doc Franklin, we got a problem here." I placed the stretcher on the table, still keeping track of the girl's vitals while Jim escorted Nhut out of sick bay. "She's breach, and she's been in labor a long time."

Franklin just stood there, staring at the woman as if he had never seen a Vietnamese girl before.

"Dr. Franklin!"

"Well, what do you expect me to do about it?"

"You have to do a C-section. I still have a fetal heartbeat."

"But she's Vietnamese! She doesn't belong here."

"Doc. I don't care if she's *Pekinese!* Right now she needs your help. She doesn't have much time."

"Then send her to a Vietnamese hospital. Let her own people deal with it. She's not my problem."

I couldn't believe what I was hearing. "But the nearest Vietnamese hospital is at least three days away by sampan! Both of them will be dead long before they ever get there. We are her only chance. Now are you going to help or not?"

Dr. Franklin just glared at me, then turned and stormed out of sick bay. At that moment, I was glad Wolfe was out on an operation. I knew that if he had been there, the doctor would have found himself in desperate need of his own services. I wanted to hurt him myself, but right now the young mother needed me more. I looked over at Gary, who was glaring after the doctor with a look of undisguised fury.

"Well, looks like it's just us."

"Have you ever done a C-section before?"

"Not by myself," I admitted, "but I've assisted. And I *have* delivered babies. How about you?"

"Nope. But I'm willing to learn."

"Let's do it."

18

Bring One In, Take One Out

WE shut the blinds on sick bay and turned on the operating room light. Gary cleaned and prepped the mother while I added a little nitrous oxide to her O_2 and a little morphine to her IV. She went out so fast that for a second I was afraid I had killed her. A quick check verified that her vitals were okay, if not very strong. We didn't have much time. I quickly poured alcohol on my hands and threw on some gloves. Gary laid out battle dressings in an empty ammo box to receive the baby, and set the makeshift bassinet on a table nearby. Grabbing a slightly curved scalpel blade, I snapped it onto the handle in preparation for opening the woman's belly while Gary watched her vitals.

I started to make my incision, pressing gently with the sharp scalpel, but the blade slid off the woman's thick, leathery skin, leaving only a scratch instead of the expected cut. I had no idea these people's hides could be so tough. I tried again, with more force. It took a surprising amount of pressure from the knife on her pelvic area just to make a cut. I finally managed a clean incision through all the layers of skin and was rewarded by a warm gush of blood and fluids bursting from her pressurized uterus. Using my finger, I reached in and moved the baby's tiny head a little to one side while I cut the hole larger with my other hand.

Once the opening was large enough, I maneuvered the baby's head to the opening and gently pulled the baby out. It was a boy. I knew Nhut would be thrilled. Once he was free of his mother, I cut the baby's umbilical cord and carried him over to Gary's makeshift bassinet. Laying him down on the battle dressings I began to aspirate the embryonic fluids and mucus from his mouth, throat, and nose. Once the air passages were clear, I held him upside down and patted him on his back to make him take his first crucial breath. He seemed to hang there, motionless, forever—though it was probably only seconds. Then the little guy started to squirm and gasp for air, his body turning from a blue gray color to a pretty pink as he took his first breaths and started to scream. I wanted to cry right along with him.

Gary, busy helping the mother, looked over and smiled. I grinned back, and set about cleaning our new baby while half crying, half singing to the baby: "Don't you become a new VC that will someday shoot me."

Once he was clean, I wrapped the baby tightly in a clean, dry towel and opened the door to invite Nhut in to see his new son. The word of the birthing had already begun to spread around SEAFLOAT, and a big crowd gathered outside of sick bay. The gathering naturally attracted the attention of the CO, who came in to see what was going on. A moment later, probably drawn by news that the CO was in sick bay, Dr. Franklin rushed in.

"Why wasn't I informed of what's going on here?"

Gary glared at him.

I just smiled, still holding the baby. "Oh, good. You are just in time to close, Doctor. Would you be so kind as to check on the condition of Nhut's wife?"

With the CO standing right there, Franklin didn't dare refuse. He quickly put on gloves and began to check the mother. But the CO's presence did nothing to stop his mouth.

"Where did you people learn your sterile technique? A barn? This incision is all wrong. We're going to have to flush out the uterus with more saline before we can close. It will be a miracle if this woman doesn't get peritonitis from your ham-handed procedure."

I felt my face getting flushed as I grew angrier at every word he uttered. Boiling inside with fury, I gently laid the baby in Nhut's arms and walked over to the table to check on the mother's breathing.

"You never should have tried this under these conditions. What did you think you were doing?"

That was enough! I ripped my gloves off, throwing them on the floor. "You sonofa . . ."

Before I could begin to dress down the mealymouthed motherfucker, I was interrupted by the arrival of the chaplain. He stepped calmly into the room, wearing his stole and carrying holy water. Everything I wanted to say froze in my throat as the chaplain moved past me to the mother. Apparently oblivious to the loud voices raised moments before, he began to baptize the baby and mother.

"Let us pray."

I ducked my head as he began to pray out loud, only partially listening as I fought to control my temper.

". . . and so, dear Lord, I ask you to bestow your mercy and blessings on this family. And please pull Dr. Franklin's head out of his ass and help him to save this new baby and its mother. Amen."

"Amen!" I repeated enthusiastically.

The chaplain's prayer must have worked, because Dr. Franklin completed his work without saying another word. Gary and I made up a little area in sick bay for Nhut and his family, so that his wife could rest for a few days to get her strength back. They were very grateful for the help, but when I went in to check on them around 6:00 AM, they had already gone, leaving the room spotless. Gorman said their whole family had come to get them before dawn to take them back to their village.

The next day, the commander of the Vietnamese Navy on SEAFLOAT, along with the local Vietnamese officials, presented Gary and me with the Vietnamese Life Saving Medal. Two days later, Dr. Franklin was ordered back to the hospital ship *Repose,* where he no longer had to worry about treating Vietnamese peasants or wearing his flak jacket.

Gary and I decided SEAFLOAT could make do without a doctor. If Marshall Franklin was an example of the best the Navy could send us, we figured our patients were better off with just us corpsmen. I still wanted to be a doctor, but only so long as I was never like him. But I was still a SEAL corpsman, and as such was required to operate in an environment far outside of the safe haven of Dr. Franklin's sick bay. Our few days' break ended about the time Nhut's baby was born, and our platoon resumed operations in the U-Minh.

During our first month, we settled into a routine with the two squads of our platoon operating on alternate nights. Our squad would go out one night, and Mr. Moody's the next. If we didn't have any fresh intelligence on which to base an operation, then the op that night was geared to gather fresh intel. In order to avoid establishing any sort of predictable pattern, we varied the time, direction, and means of transportation for each op. Most of these first operations were pretty much the same type of search-and-destroy missions I had learned while among the Marines, except that we were hunting and ambushing VC instead of letting them hunt and ambush us.

A typical op involved one squad and one Kit Carson setting up an ambush on a well-traveled VC canal or jungle trail. Depending on the purpose of the op, we would wait for our prey to come into the ambush, and either capture or kill them. Most of these operations took place in designated free-fire zones well after curfew. All the natives knew about the curfew, and had been warned that anyone moving around after dark was considered fair game, to be shot on sight. Occasionally a stubborn old fisherman or peasant wood chopper worked late, ignoring the curfew. Unfortunately these independent and enterprising souls usually ended up getting their asses blown away.

One night, during that first month, our squad was involved in setting up an ambush on a canal known to be a regular VC route. The secret to the success of this type of ambush was dependent upon our ability to blend in perfectly with our surroundings—usually for hours at a time—so the enemy never suspected we were there until the trap was sprung. We all put on our camo paint, to make sure that our white faces would not glow in the dark and give us away, and wore headbands or hats to keep our hair and the sweat out of our eyes. The other squad came by, beers in hand, to critique our makeup jobs and generally harass us. Of course, we made a point of doing the same to them when it was their turn to operate.

As always, Lt. Flanagan had the best camo job. It looked as if he had hired a makeup artist to paint his face. But when we climbed on the STAB for the ride to our insertion point, he wrecked it by sticking a pack of Pall Malls into the sweatband of his hat. The red Pall Mall logo on its white box looked just like a little red target stuck right to the LT's head. In the dimming light, the little four-cigarette C-ration pack glowed.

"*Dai-uy,* you've got a nice bull's-eye on your head there," Boh commented.

"I'm trying to keep them dry."

"They won't be dry if you get blood all over them."

We inserted into the area just after sunset, and spent most of the night hidden along the edge of the canal, half in and half out of the muddy water. There was no moon that night, and the darkness covered everything like a thick blanket.

I held my place in the mud, weapon in hand, trying to remain perfectly quiet as we waited. Hours passed and the tide rose, soaking me up past my waist until I was so frozen I didn't think I could move if I had to. After a while, we heard voices in the distance, and the sounds of someone paddling a sampan, but I couldn't see anything. The sounds continued, on and off for several hours, but never close enough to be certain of the source. Sitting there blind and cold, my imagination began to run wild until I was sure there were dozens of VC sneaking up on us through the darkness.

As I tried to calm my fears, I smelled the presence of something moving very near my position. I couldn't see anything, but I felt them. I knew someone was there. I signaled Ric, who popped a flare lighting up the canal. A sampan, which must have passed only a few feet from my position, was caught in the fiery illumination. Mr. Flanagan yelled out to the occupants of the sampan in clear Vietnamese, ordering them to surrender. Instead of raising hands in surrender, or freezing in place, one person on the boat made a quick move, as if to reach for a weapon. He had no chance. The night suddenly erupted with the deafening sound of automatic weapons fire as the entire squad unloaded on the sampan and its occupants. As the flare flickered and extinguished itself, we ceased our firing. The darkness descended once again over the canal. We listened carefully in the abrupt silence that followed, but heard only moaning coming from the other side of the canal.

After a moment, I heard Ric on the radio calling for our STAB to come up the canal from the river to extract us. They had heard the sounds of a fierce firefight and were already on their way. I could still hear someone groaning in pain on the other bank.

"Boh, lets go check out the other bank. I hear someone over there."

Boh nodded, and we prepared to swim across the canal but stopped when we heard weapons fire coming from our STAB as it came up the canal. They were firing on the far bank as they slid in to pick us up. Within seconds, we boarded the boat and turned its spotlight toward the other bank. The sampan had been reduced to kindling wood. Beyond the ruined boat, on the far shore, an old man was lying in the mud, somehow still alive. His home must have been nearby because he called to his wife from where he lay, and we heard her screaming back at him. As we watched, she came out of the bush, jumped into the canal, and began to dog-paddle toward her spouse.

Instinctively, I grabbed my med gear and started to jump out of the STAB to go to the old man's aid. Before I could jump, Tong, our scout for the op, grabbed my arm to stop me.

"No, *Bac Si*. It not your fault he out after curfew. His fault. He probably VC. All people here VC. Why else he be out so late?"

The other guys immediately agreed with Tong, and I reluctantly sat back down in the boat. As we began to back away from the bank I turned back to see that the woman had reached her spouse's side. He was no longer making any noise. The woman started screaming curses at us and shaking her fist. Tong raised her weapon and took aim at her.

"No!" I yelled, joined by the whole squad in horrified chorus. Tong lowered his weapon, obviously surprised by our vehemence. But we were not here to shoot unarmed women and peasants. This was not the job we were trained to do. On the ride back to base, we all vowed that this kind of shit was not going to happen to us again.

A couple of days later, we received an intelligence report that an old cadre-level Viet Cong chief had been killed at the canal a couple of nights earlier, in the same general direction where we had held the ambush. Mr. Flanagan insisted that the details of the report were too close to be coincidence. The man in the report had to be our guy, so I guess that made his death all right on somebody's scorecard.

If the old man had been a cadre chief, then there was probably still a lot of VC activity in his area. Mr. Flanagan decided he needed another look, if only to satisfy his curiosity. He and Tong did a flyover in a Seawolf helicopter from a fairly high altitude in order to avoid raising the suspicions of the Viet Cong on the ground. When they returned, Mr. Flanagan announced that he had seen enough from the air to believe that there was VC activity. He worked out a plan for us to go in early the next morning and set up an observation post, or OP. If we saw a lot of Viet Cong during the day, we would stay all night for an ambush. Flanagan put together a squad that consisted of most of the members of Alpha squad as well as two of Mr. Moody's men, Jonah Benanti and Glenn Harvey.

I realized that this type of operation would require us to stay awake and alert for at least fifteen hours and as many as twenty-four, while remaining perfectly still. After the patrol order was given, I handed every man in our squad the usual morphine Syrette for medical emergencies, but added four Dexamil seventy-five milligram tablets.

"These pills," I explained, "are an amphetamine. They are 'stay awake' medicine, to be used only if you can't keep your eyes open. Properly dosed, they will keep you awake and alert. If you need them, take one tablet every four hours."

The following morning, while it was still zero-dark-thirty, we slid quietly off the front of the PBR and up the muddy bank of the river to the selected site. As had become standard operating procedure, I went in first, followed by Mr. Flanagan, and Ric, our radioman. By the time first light broke in the eastern sky, we were already settled in for a long, hot, boring day. We heard coughing and smelled the smoke of cooking fires as our neighbors started their morning routine, never suspecting that we were hidden in their midst. Several times during the day, one or two armed VC walked down to the river, apparently to check things out. Some of them came so close to our position that we could have reached out and grabbed them. But we held back, hoping for the motherload later.

By nightfall, after fourteen-plus hours of sitting still in the sauna-like heat, I felt myself getting really hungry and sleepy. I popped a Dexamil and drank about half of my canteen. Back in the states, Dexamil was used as a diet pill because it not only increased metabolism, it also curbed appetite. A few minutes later I was wide awake and my stomach had stopped growling. I felt better but the heat lingered, despite the fading sun, and no breeze drifted through to help. Right after sunset the mosquitoes came out in force and began to feast on my exposed skin. I always carried a small bottle of repellant, so I quietly mixed it with some camo paint and blindly touched up my makeup.

About 2000, I heard one of the guys on my left flank rustling around and talking in loud whispers. The hair on the back of my neck stood straight out. *Here they come,* I thought, slowly turning my Stoner to the left. I strained to see what was coming, but couldn't see anything or anyone. Suddenly, the sky lit up as someone to my left popped a flare. I hit the dirt in a shooting position desperately scanning the area for targets.

"Where?" Boh yelled. "Where are they?"

Apparently he couldn't see anyone either.

"I don't see them," Mr. Flanagan called out.

Another flare lit the darkness. Still no targets, but we were now compromised. We couldn't see any VC, but now they certainly knew where *we* were. I turned to Ric, but he was already on the radio calling for an immediate extraction. The PBR sped up to the bank minutes later to pick us up. It was our standard operating procedure for the lieutenant to extract last, preceded by me, as corpsman, so I held back with Mr. Flanagan, covering our departure. As everyone else scrambled onto the boat, Mr. Flanagan touched my shoulder.

"Doc," he whispered angrily, "go check out Harvey and see what the hell his problem is."

I climbed onto the PBR and scooted over to where Harvey huddled on the deck. I noticed that he was sweating profusely and his eyes looked like two small dots. I checked his pulse, it was racing and his respirations were shallow.

"Hey, Glenn, what's up? You feelin' okay?"

It took him a few moments to focus on me. "I dunno, man. I saw VC. Lots of them. Comin' down the canal at me."

"You saw Charlie?"

"Charlie, and elephants, and all sorts of shit. And they were comin' right at me."

"Did you take any of the Dexamil I gave you?"

"Yeah, sure. I took one every hour for the past four hours, just like you said."

It was now perfectly clear what had happened. Harvey had overdosed and was suffering speed hallucinations.

"I told you to take one every four hours. And then only if you absolutely could not stay awake!"

"No man," he began shaking his head emphatically, "that's not what you said."

I didn't bother to answer him. I just set about getting him some water until we could get back to base. But he was obviously angry.

"I did what you said, you fucked-up quack! You sorry excuse for a SEAL. No wonder I never liked you! Of course, you're not really a SEAL, are you? You never had to go through Hell Week. You never had to put it all on the line. You have no business calling yourself a medic, much less a SEAL!"

I tried to ignore his raving, but the words hurt. I was sorry that he felt that way. I knew I had done my job. His attitude just reminded me once again that there would always be SEALs who would never view me as an equal. The other guys all made a point of ignoring Harvey's rant, but I wondered if any of them also felt I didn't belong there.

Once we got back to SEAFLOAT, I gave Harvey some of the medicinal brandy I had snagged in Guam to take the edge off. Most of the rest of us drank beer and played cards until our pills wore off and we could catch some shut-eye. No one talked about the op. Again something had gone wrong with communications, but at least no one got hurt this time.

19

Aiding and Addicting

OUR platoon spent most of that first month learning the ropes. We refined our standard operating procedures (SOPs) while learning how to work the area and utilize the terrain. Dick Wolfe's platoon had just finished its fifth month in country. With only one month to go on their tour, they started winding down their operations. They stopped doing any night ambushes and, for the most part, only operated in reaction to fresh intelligence. Their officers stepped back to allow the leading petty officers (LPOs) to take over the planning and execution of most of the missions.

This put Dick right in the heart of what he loved. As both corpsman and senior LPO, he planned and carried out several successful ops for his platoon while I was still getting my feet wet. We often spent time together between missions, none of it wasted. I eagerly listened as Dick shared his experiences with me. Before becoming a SEAL, he had been very active with his Marine Recon unit, learning some unusual tricks and gaining valuable field experience. The very fact he survived his tours with the Marines as a front line corpsman made him special. I got him to show me some of the unorthodox medical procedures he had picked up along the way.

"Did you know you can use a life vest to save lives miles away from any water?"

We had been talking about unusual medical uses for everyday items. I looked over at the nearest standard issue life vest, and could not immediately see how it could be useful away from water.

"Think about it. If you have a serious wound or a fracture, just wrap the vest tightly around the injury, then pull the tabs and inflate it. Presto! You have either a terrific splint or one heck of a pressure bandage."

"And even if it doesn't work, you can be certain the victim won't drown!" I laughed, surprised that something so simple had not occurred to me—or to most of the medical corps.

Dick was also the first person to tell me to ignore all I had been taught about using salt tablets to combat heat and dehydration, insisting that salt tablets could actually make dehydration worse.

"But the doctors taught us that salt tablets help prevent dehydration," I insisted.

"Yeah, and I'm telling you they're full of shit. Most of them aren't the ones trying to survive this heat while humpin' out in the bush. Our bodies need water to combat heat and dehydration, not salt. I've seen the proof. Trust me, drink lots of water and leave the salt for the cook. And give your guys extra water instead of those morphine Syrettes. Morphine belongs with you, not with any GI Clueless."

"What's wrong with passing out morphine?" I was surprised that Dick didn't agree with my drug distribution. "Shouldn't every guy have some painkiller at hand in case something happens?"

"In case of what? You're the corpsman! So long as you're alive, you'll be the one giving the shot to anyone in the squad who needs it. And if you're dead or disabled, they can damn well get it out of your pockets anyway. Let 'em carry their own bandages and first aid supplies, but keep the heavy stuff to yourself."

I could tell Dick was very passionate about this issue, but my imagination insisted on coming up with grisly scenarios in which I was lost or blown to little pieces along with all the morphine while my guys were suffering without it. "Why worry so much about protecting the drugs?"

"Because I've seen guys hoard the stuff and use it to lace their pot—or whatever else they're smoking. Before too long they're hooked. After that, they're nothin' but a liability to the unit and to their buddies. You've already had a taste of that with the Dexamil incident."

I shouldn't have been surprised that Dick knew about Harvey's OD. Dick had a way of finding out about everything.

"Your entire operation was blown by one careless guy—and that overdose was supposedly an accident! You were lucky. There were no casualties—this time. Do you really want to risk your butt with guys who are so spaced they can't tell the difference between a bush and a bullet? It's just a good idea to keep the stuff to yourself."

I could tell from the bitter edge in his voice that this knowledge had been gained through hard experience. I had seen all the movies and heard all the shit about poorly trained draftees who got hooked on drugs to escape the horrors of war. In those stories, they were running around scared to death all of the time until they either freaked out or got their butts shot off, or both. But I couldn't really imagine that happening with any of our guys. They were too well tested and well trained for that. Most of us had made it through our training because we enjoyed the rush. We didn't need drugs to get a high, we had combat. Oh sure, I knew there were a few potheads in every platoon—even ours. The shit was everywhere, it was cheap, and it was guaranteed to take your mind away from where you were and what you were doing. That was the problem. There is no room in a war zone for a drug-fuzzed mind. Survival meant staying sharp.

I was no choirboy. I did try smoking pot a few times, but I didn't like the feeling. It fogged my head while making me ravenous and silly at the same time. I usually wound up either laughing my way to the chow hall to make sandwiches, or wandering around begging guys for a few of their cookies from home. I really hated the lack of control grass induced in me. I discovered a cold Budweiser worked much better as a relaxation aid, without the dangerous side effects. Most of the guys felt the same way and avoided drugs while on SEAFLOAT. We couldn't afford to get fucked up while on duty. And so long as we were on SEAFLOAT, with the Viet Cong all around us, we were always on duty.

Dick's insistence on controlling the morphine made me wonder what else he kept on hand. He showed me what materials he felt were essential on an operation, and what materials he kept for use on base. He had a special lockbox for his more dangerous medications, which he opened for me. He said the lock was to make certain no one could get at them for recreational purposes. I was surprised to see a number of unfamiliar pre-loaded syringes in amongst the other drugs.

"What are these?" I asked, picking one from the group to read the label. "Thiopental Sodium?"

"Yeah, Sodium Pentothal."

"That's a barbiturate isn't it? A sedative?" I looked at the large number of Syrettes in the box. "Why do you need so much Sodium Pentothal?"

"Truth serum." He grinned.

"What?"

"Juice a prisoner's IV with a little of this and he'll usually start babbling his guts out."

"Isn't that dangerous?"

"Sure, if you don't know what you're doing. But with the right dosage, and the right interrogation techniques," he flexed his fingers meaningfully, "the prisoner loses his inhibitions and can be led to confess everything he knows."

"And with the wrong dose?"

"Well, give too little, and they just get sort of mellow and start babbling nonsense. Too much, and they become unconscious—or dead. I'll show you how to use it correctly."

I wasn't entirely certain it was a skill I wanted to learn. But I figured it was better to understand a drug you didn't need, than to need one you didn't understand.

"So where did you learn this stuff? I know they didn't teach you that in A-School or field medical."

"I picked it up while working with my Marine Recon unit, during my first tour. I've had to use it more, here, though." Dick took the syringe from me and carefully placed it back in his box. "My Marine buddies taught me a lot of tricks they don't teach in school."

"So do you miss 'em? Your recon buddies?"

"Naw. I saw some of them just last month."

"Last month?" I knew Dick had been on SEAFLOAT for most of the last five months. Most of the Reconners were active much farther north.

"Yeah," Dick laughed. "Where do you think I went on R&R? Not to some boring old beach in Hawaii. I flew up to Da Nang and spent my off time kicking butt with my Marine buddies. We went on several patrols against the NVA." His eyes lit up as he spoke. "Much more relaxing than the beach!"

I just shook my head. "I always thought you were a little off. Now I know you're a fucking lunatic!" There weren't many sane guys who would give up a paid vacation in Hawaii for a chance to get killed by the North Vietnamese Army. "So what are you going to do at the end of your tour? They're not going to let you go back up to Da Nang to retire."

His face fell, and I knew I had struck a nerve. He shut and locked the box, and shoved it back in place with more force than necessary.

"They've got me pegged to be a *cadre* instructor for the *Team.*"

Instructor slots were normally considered plum assignments—unless you wanted to be somewhere else. I did the math, knowing he would have to stay stateside through at least one full rotation as an instructor. "That means it will be at least a year to fifteen months before you can redeploy back here."

The morose expression on Dick's face confirmed that I had the right of it. After all his talk about drug addiction, I realized Dick was an addict himself. Vietnam was his drug, and the action of combat provided him with an incomparable high. No wonder he had stayed in country through his R&R. He wanted to get as much time in the bush as he could before he was forced to leave it all behind. I could understand his feelings. I had begun to feel a little of that high myself.

"I'll bet you'll be a great instructor!"

Slowly his grin returned. "Yeah. Those pukes will never know what hit 'em! But before that happens, I've still got time to settle some more scores with Charlie!"

Several days later Dick got his wish. It was late October and our platoon was in the hooch, winding down for the night. Dick's squad was out on an op, and expected to return soon. All the guys were playing cards or listening to music on the jam box. All except Glenn Harvey, who was laying on his rack, fidgeting and staring into space with a dopey expression on his face. It had been several days since Glenn had overdosed on Dexamil. He should have been well over it by now, but he certainly looked stoned to me. I didn't want to believe that Dick's concerns about addiction could apply to a SEAL, but it was beginning to look like Harvey was into something more than Dexamil. I wandered over to watch the card game but kept one eye on Glenn.

At 2000 hours, the word came down that a chopper flight from Binh Thuy was running very late. There had been no contact from the helo since it left base. No contact could mean a broken radio, but the fact that they were also late almost certainly meant the bird was down. And everything between Binh Thuy and SEAFLOAT was Indian Country. If anyone was still alive, that person would need help to stay that way. We knew we were the only ones capable of rescuing them in the dark, even before the LT poked his head into our hooch.

"Stand by for a possible rescue op. Consider this your warning order. Alpha squad will lead. Mr. Moody's squad will back us up."

"What's the situation, LT?" Ric asked as he pushed back from the game.

"We're pretty sure the bird is down. They're trying to make contact with any survivors and confirm the location. We're go the instant they get confirmation." Mr. Flanagan ducked back out of the door and headed back to the radio room, leaving us to prepare for action.

I looked back at Harvey. He was giggling as he got off his rack and started to get his gear together. He definitely had no business going out tonight. As part of Mr. Moody's backup squad, his presence was not essential to the mission.

"Glenn." I walked over and touched him on the shoulder to get his attention. His eyes were a little glassy and dilated, confirming my suspicions. "I think you might want to sit this one out." I was careful to speak only to him. No need to embarrass him in front of the whole platoon.

"Why?" He rounded on me. "Because some wannabe SEAL says so?"

"No," I answered him calmly, "because your corpsman says so." I leaned in close and whispered dangerously, "Do I need to make this official?" He had to know that anything official would mean involving Lt. Flanagan. Mr. Flanagan didn't mind us getting a little buzz off the booze every now and then, but he had zero tolerance for anyone having anything to do with drugs. He had gotten rid of my predecessor primarily because he was too lax with the drugs. I had no intention of following that example. Nor did I want to see a fellow SEAL, even one like Glenn Harvey, suffer Flanagan's wrath. If the LT saw Glenn in his current state, Flanagan would probably court-martial Harvey right on the spot, and then insist on shooting Glenn himself. I really didn't want that, and I hoped there were still enough brain cells functioning in Harvey's addled head for him to realize that he didn't either.

"Fuck you!" Glenn shot me the bird. But he returned to his rack, tossing gear out of his way before he threw himself down on it.

Satisfied that he wouldn't push the issue, I headed out the door to get medical supplies for the rescue op. Boh, who had apparently been watching from across the room, followed me out and pulled me aside.

"So, what's up with Glenn?"

"I told him he needed to sit this one out. He wasn't real happy about it."

"Because of that Dexamil thing the other night?"

"No. Because of whatever he's on right now. I think he's got his own stash."

"Harvey?"

I could tell Boh didn't believe it.

"Doc, Glenn's always been kinda goofy, but I don't think . . ."

"Boh, that guy is way too goofy to go out in the field tonight. And I don't mean like the Disney dog either. Maybe he hasn't been a problem before, but trust me on this, he's taken too much of something. He's gone beyond booze or weed. And I for one do not want him anywhere near my back—especially with a loaded weapon. I'm beginning to think that Dexamil OD on the last op may not have been as much of an accident as we thought."

As I spoke I watched Boh's expression change from one of disbelief to anger.

"I think I need to have a little face-to-face with Mr. Harvey." The chill in his voice made me very glad I was not going to be part of the discussion. Boh would never be a Rhodes scholar, but when he talked, people listened. I thought about hanging around to see what would happen, but before I could go back, Ric came out after his own supplies which were stored in our Conex box next to mine.

"I thought you were going after the gear?"

"I am." I fell in step with Ric.

"So what's eatin' Boh?" He gestured at our LPO's retreating back.

"I think Boh's the one who'll be doing the eatin'," I commented. "Someone's tail is about to be royally chewed."

Ric looked confused, but I decided not to enlighten him as we opened the box and gathered our supplies. I got a couple of cans of serum albumin. If the helo was down, there would probably be casualties. Rick gathered fresh batteries for his radio.

When we returned to our hooch, I noticed that Glenn Harvey was very quiet and withdrawn—and very, very sober. There was definitely a hunk gone from his posterior.

"So what did you say to him?" I asked Boh, quietly.

"I simply explained that he could be a SEAL, or he could be a doper, but he couldn't be both. Then I explained the Wayne Bohannon Addict Recovery Program to him in grim detail." Boh grinned dangerously. "Seems things happen in the bush, and I can't always tell the difference between a VC and a doper."

Boh's little pep talk seemed to work. I never saw Harvey stoned again.

20

In a Blaze of Glory

"HEADS up!" The LT caught our attention. "A fly-by spotted some wreckage at the mouth of the river. They think there may be survivors."

We immediately grabbed our gear and weapons and loaded into the PBR. The river flew by below us like black tar broken only by the spray from our boat. We were quiet and focused. I knew the survivors' best chance was if we could sneak in and get them out before Charlie found them. Any hope of a silent extraction was dashed when we heard the sound of rifle fire off in the distance.

"It's Wolfe." Ric was on the radio. "His team was near the area, returning from their op when they heard about the sighting. They're on the scene and taking fire. But Dick says it's nothing he can't handle."

Just then we heard the unmistakable sound of twin 50s opening up, their staccato fury ripping through the night. The rifle fire abruptly ceased. Moments later it began again. For the rest of the ride we all listened to the dance being played out in the darkness ahead. The insulting crack of sporadic rifle fire was answered by the fierce retort from the PBR's machine guns as David and Goliath did battle over ownership of the fallen bird.

As we finally neared the canal, I strained to see any sign of the fallen chopper, but could only make out the dim outline of the shore and the tree line. We still didn't know if anyone survived. We were ordered to hang back to protect the flank while Wolfe's squad kept the enemy pinned down in hiding. Downed helos made valuable targets for the VC—especially if they still contained useable weaponry and equipment. If Charlie could get his hands on a U.S. soldier or two in the bargain—well, that was icing on the cake. And Charlie didn't really care if they were alive or dead.

It was almost first light when we saw the red streak of a pencil flare. A call for help. That meant someone was alive. We could do nothing but listen as Wolfe's squad cautiously approached the canal. In the predawn, the two pilots and both door gunners stood by the wreckage of their Army slick. Everyone had survived the crash. Now it was Wolfe's job to make certain they stayed alive. Those flyboys are okay in the air, but they get a little nervous on the ground—especially when surrounded by VC. The sun had come up just enough that I could barely make out the ghostly shadow of the downed bird resting amid broken trees in the mud just short of the canal. We listened as the squad quickly inserted and formed a protective perimeter while Doc Wolfe checked out the survivors. Except for being a little bit shaky, everyone was apparently okay. The helo had autorotated to the ground after engine failure. The pilots tried to guide it to the edge of the canal, but overshot their target a little and crashed down through some old, dead jungle foliage into the mud.

The squad gathered up the flyboys and escorted them to their PBR. We knew the VC would be right behind them. After several long, tense moments, we finally heard the PBR motors start. About fifteen minutes later the triumphant squad pulled up alongside us with their grateful cargo, but before we could begin the run back to base, Wolfe held up his hand for silence and turned to look expectantly back toward the crash site. As if on cue, a huge explosion shattered the dawn. A fireball bloomed through the brush, rising to light up the sky over the wreck. In its glow I could see that Dick was grinning from ear to ear.

"Guess Charlie found the chopper!" Flanagan commented.

"And the presents we left just for them!" Dick laughed.

While the pilots and door gunners were being escorted back to the PBR, Doc Wolfe and a couple of his men had booby-trapped the downed helo using C-4 and some incendiary grenades with instantaneous fuses. There would be no souvenirs for Charlie tonight!

Once back at SEAFLOAT, I escorted the slick's crew into sick bay to inspect their wounds. Out here, even the smallest scratch tended to get infected. I gave them all iodine and some sterile water to wash up their nicks and scratches. They were lucky, no one needed stitches though they were all a little bruised and sore. I gave them some Darvon tablets and sent them to the mess to await their ride back to Can Tho. Wolfe stopped in briefly to check on them.

"Hey," one young man said as he grabbed Wolfe's hand. "If it hadn't been for you guys, we would probably be needing body bags instead of Band-Aids."

Dick actually looked embarrassed. I understood his reaction. This time *we* saved *them,* but just as often the Army flyboys were the ones pulling SEAL asses out of the fire. More important, to us anyway, was the fact that these brave soldiers, with whom we worked so closely, were all volunteers. They actually chose to insert and extract SEALS on many of our operations, despite the fact that we usually overstayed our welcome and were often only a few steps ahead of hot lead as we raced to get the hell out of the LZ.

A military helicopter was no piece of cake to fly, especially in a hot landing zone. It was even worse for a green flight crew straight out of training. For some reason flight school didn't offer a course on dodging bullets. You could only learn that by doing it. Most new pilots were understandably apprehensive once they realized the VC were determined to turn their bird into Swiss cheese. They would often come in too high or too fast to drop us off.

"Hey there! We're SEALs, not goddamn eagles," someone would yell. "If we could fly we wouldn't need you! Put it down easy and slow. If we break a leg falling out of your bird, you'll have done Charlie's job for him!"

The pilots who survived usually learned and became quite skilled at maneuvering their helos into some very tight spots. Some of them could even swoop down and drop their passenger right on top of a sleeping VC in his hooch. For the VC, it was a hell of a wake-up call.

One of the best of these chopper jocks was on SEAFLOAT when Kilo Platoon acquired some very exciting intel for an operation. Still high from his successful rescue op of a week before, Dick was itching for another solid operation before he had to give it up to go home.

"This may be our last big op before we ship back to the world." Dick's excitement was contagious as I helped him pack for the mission. "John's put a lot of work into planning this one." John was the other leading petty officer for Kilo Platoon. "He's gathered some very hot intel on a midday meeting of some very high VC honchos and their North Vietnamese advisors. They're meeting in a rinky-dink village that just happens to be in our area of operation." He grinned fiercely. "We're gonna swoop in and snatch some high-level gook brass and kick some ass. Shake up their afternoon tea." He laughed. "We may have to go back to the world, but before we leave, these suckers are gonna know we've been here!"

"Go out with a blaze of glory, huh?"

"You got that straight!"

The predatory gleam in Wolfe's eyes made me wish I was going with him.

All of Alpha Platoon and the rest of Kilo gathered on the helo pad to see Wolfe's squad off. We must have made an odd sight, Wolfe's squad was loaded for bear and all decked out in their cammies and web gear, and there we were, wearing nothing but our bathing suits and T-shirts.

"Happy hunting!"

"Bring back a gook for me!"

"Don't forget to be home in time for dinner!"

Dick laughed and waved as the helicopters bearing his squad lifted gracefully off the pad. I reflected that Dick always seemed happiest when he was going into battle.

With nothing to do, I went to sick bay, turned the fan on full blast, and stretched out on the examining table for a siesta. I had barely gotten to sleep when I heard some yelling from the radio room next to sick bay. I could hear guys starting to run around. I quickly rubbed the sleep out of my eyes and stepped out of sick bay to see what was going on.

"Doc!" One of Kilo's junior officers, Barnes I think, grabbed me in the hall. "Get your gear! One of the choppers went down! Wolfe is down!"

I don't think I really heard the words that came out of his mouth as much as I felt them—like knives in my gut. I spun around and ran back into sick bay. Everything seemed to be moving in slow motion as I grabbed a full medical bag and raced for the helo pad. I had no weapons or web gear, just my medical bag. I jumped aboard a Seawolf helo with Barnes right behind me. I was still wearing only a bathing suit, a blue and gold T-shirt, and coral booties. There was no time to change. I was a corpsman now, not a shooter. It was up to the other guys to cover me. After taking a moment to reload the guns on the helo, we were off to the crash site.

As we neared the area, I saw other gunships in the air, circling the downed helo. There were a few small lightweight OV-10 Black Pony fixed-wing spotter aircraft, as well as a flight of heavily armed Marine A-4 Skyhawk jets circling high overhead, prepared to provide close-in air support in case it got too hairy. As we arrived on the site, I saw the downed helo, lying sideways on a pile of splinters of shattered bamboo and thatch. The chopper looked as though it had crashed right through the roof of the targeted hooch.

Barnes and I didn't wait for our Seawolf to touch down. We both jumped out while it was still a good eight feet off the deck. As soon as I hit the ground Lt. Prouty, who had been in charge of the op, ran over to meet us, one arm held at an awkward angle.

"What happened?" Barnes asked, yelling to be heard over the rotor wash from our helo. I knew from Dick's description that the plan had been for the Slick to swoop down and hover right above the hooch at the time of the meeting so that the squad could jump right through the bamboo ceiling and surprise the targets. Wolfe's job, as corpsman, was to insert first by jumping clear of the hooch and set up a position to guard the rear escape in case the targets evaded the rest of the squad.

"The pilot lost control . . ." the LT managed. He was obviously in pain and attempting to appear calm. "Caught a skid on the roof as we were inserting. He tried to power up and break free, but the minute he applied power we flipped right over and dropped the bird right through the roof."

Apparently the weight changes created as the squad jumped out of the helo caused too much variation for the pilot to control that close to the hooch. But where was Wolfe?

I ran over to the downed helicopter to find that the other platoon had gotten all the wounded out. They had bandaged them up pretty well—just as Doc Wolfe had showed them. But Wolfe was not with them. One of the door gunners had been thrown out and badly burned. I tended to him and prepared him for Medivac. There were four or five dead guys lying sprawled under the wreckage in the hooch. They turned out to be the targeted VC. *When all else fails, drop a helicopter on 'em,* I thought, my brain trying hard to avoid the panic I was beginning to feel.

I turned back to the wounded and noticed the other door gunner, very pale and obviously in shock. I recognized him as the gunner manning Wolfe's side of the chopper.

"Are you okay?" I asked.

He nodded, but he looked terrible. "Wolfe. The doc . . . I saw it hit him. As we were falling—the blade—it hit him"

"Where is he? Where is Doc Wolfe? Do you know?"

He pointed to the bushes a few meters away.

Dick's best friend from his platoon joined me as I went into the bushes in the direction the door gunner had indicated. We pushed branches and grass aside as we searched. Then I caught a glimpse of camo-print fabric through the brush.

"There he is."

He was lying facedown in the dirt. Part of his head was gone. When the chopper flipped, the rotor blade must have hit him as he tried to jump clear. He must have been bending over at the time because the blade had taken the back of his head completely off, killing him instantly. The impact from the spinning rotor had thrown him several meters into the bushes. The remains of his head looked like he had on some sort of macabre face mask, with no eyes or mouth.

When I saw him all the strength drained out of my legs. I just collapsed to my knees beside him.

"Aw, Dick, look what they did to you." I found myself talking to him as if he were a child with a splinter in his finger. "Geez, Dick. Just look at this mess." I gently picked up all the pieces of his skull I could find and placed them in the empty cavity of his head. He just lay there while I worked; facedown, his head turned slightly to the right, as if he was listening to my baby talk. His best friend helped me remove his web gear. I tied his camo shirt up over his head to cover the damage. Then we gently carried him out to the landing zone.

Lt. Prouty had suffered a separated shoulder in the crash. He waited for treatment until we brought Dick out of the bushes. I dimly remember popping his shoulder back in place and putting his arm in a sling. If he said anything to me, I don't remember it. The Medivac choppers touched down and we put Dick on the second one. I climbed in beside him. As we lifted off, I looked over at him, lying there on the floor of the helo while the breeze ruffled the thick red hairs on his white bear-like chest, the wad of camo-cloth covering his head.

I turned away to check on the condition of the wounded survivors. They were all doing well, so I turned to adjust Lt. Prouty's sling. While retying the sling, I looked over at Wolfe and that was when it hit me that his chest wasn't moving. He wasn't breathing. He wasn't alive. This could not be happening! He was supposed to be going home in a couple of weeks. I had just talked to him an hour ago. The body on the deck couldn't be Dick Wolfe. I spent the rest of the trip in a daze.

Once we landed at SEAFLOAT, I helped the wounded off the helo. All of Kilo Platoon was there. I asked everyone to remain off the helo pad and give us some room as the Chaplain, Mr. Flanagan, and Gary came out to meet us.

The pilots shut down the helo and stepped out for a smoke. For them, this was a routine Medivac. The Chaplain placed his stole around his shoulders and began the last rites. I could not focus on the words as I removed the contents from Dick's pockets. I handed Dick's morphine syrettes and medical supplies to Gary who, as SEAFLOAT corpsman, would see they were stowed safely. I gave his Rolex watch and weapons to Mr. Flanagan. I then carefully took his hipboots off and fastened an ID tag to his big toe. Gary and I then slid him into the body bag, with his shirt still pulled over his head, and I zipped it from his head to his chest, covering the damage the rotor had done. The rest of his body looked perfectly normal—as if he were sleeping.

I had put many men in body bags, but this was different. It wasn't supposed to happen to Dick. He was invincible.

Mr. Flanagan nodded to the men waiting beyond the pad. All the members of both platoons, Wolfe's and mine, came forward to the helo to pay their respects. A couple of his men knelt and held his hand while the chaplain prayed.

Once the prayer was over, one of the guys reached up and began to unzip the bag, another reached in to lift up the shirt to see what had happened to him.

"Hey!" I started to protest, pushing their hands away.

"Doc." The chaplain gently pulled me away from the body. "Doc, don't worry about it. Sometimes the only way some people have to accept that someone is really gone is by seeing all the horror of that death for themselves."

Before I could protest, Mr. Flanagan took me aside. He must have known what I was feeling. "C'mon Doc, lets go have a beer and leave Wolfe with his platoon. You have a whole platoon of your own that's looking up to you to be strong."

Even though there were only a few years between us, he comforted me like a parent.

"Sure. No problem, sir. Nothing a couple of six-packs won't gloss over."

So much for Dick's blaze of glory. I joined the LT, spending the rest of the day drowning my sorrows and starting Wolfe's wake a little early.

The next day, Gary pulled me aside to make certain I had taken something for my hangover.

"You know, if you're short a corpsman for an operation, I'll go." I shook my head. Gary didn't have the qualifications or training to survive in the bush—especially on SEAL ops.

"Look, I know I can never be another Wolfe. I wouldn't even try.

But I'm a good corpsman. All I'm saying is that I know you're short a medic, and I'm willing—if you guys ever need me."

It was true that Gary was good. He knew a lot of hospital shit and preventative medicine that I had forgotten, and some I had never learned. He also had a lot of guts. He knew the risks and was volunteering anyway. Dick would have been proud.

"Thanks, man." I clapped him on the shoulder, then winced as it reverberated up my arm into my aching head. "I'll be sure and tell the guys about your offer."

I hoped we would never have to take him up on it.

21

Snatch and Grab

I missed Dick, but I didn't have much time for mourning. Only a few days later, Lt. Flanagan put together an intimate little operation that required my full attention.

"Doc." Flanagan found me in our hooch, lounging in my bunk, trying not to think about Wolfe. "Go find Schroeder and meet me in briefing in five minutes."

"Anyone else I should round up?"

"Nope. Just you and Ric. 0900. We got a little job to do."

That immediately piqued my interest. It was standard procedure for the corpsman and the radioman to work closely with the LT, but there had never been an operation that only involved the three of us. All our ops to date had involved an entire squad or more. Fortunately, Ric and I were used to watching out for each other since we were always first in and last out. It was procedure on all our ops for the corpsman and radioman. This way, if something disastrous were to happen during the insert or extraction, the men on the ground would at least have medical supplies and a way to call for help. Lt. Flanagan usually insisted on being extracted last on all his operations. He was not about to stay in the field without his corpsman and radioman—not that we would have let him, especially since we were working in such a friendly and safe neighborhood.

On the occasions where there was only room for one or two in the extraction vehicle, Ric would go and I would take the radio and stay with Flanagan until we could extract together. We had become a team within the team, but it had never been put to a real test.

I found Ric sitting on the deck hoarding a patch of shade. He was savoring the last of his morning coffee while trying to avoid the rising heat. Even though it was only 0900, our little outdoor steam room had already heated up, and there wasn't even a hint of a breeze.

I repeated Flanagan's summons. "Just us?"

"Seems so," I answered, "but who else does he need when he's got the best?"

Ric snorted and chugged the last of his coffee.

"Wonder if this has anything to do with last night's op? I know Mr. Moody's guys brought home some bacon."

"We'll know in a minute." Neither of us had been on the previous night's mission, but we knew the guys had nabbed a VC prisoner.

We arrived at the briefing hooch to find the shades drawn. Inside, an overfed Vietnamese man sat hunched on a stool in the center of the room. He looked pale, bathed in the glare from the single bulb hanging from the bare fixture on the ceiling. Flanagan and two of our scouts, Zung and Nhut, flanked the man. He sweated profusely. The drawn shades did nothing to cool the room, but I suspected, from the expression on the scouts' faces, that the prisoner's perspiration had other causes.

"Hey Doc," Flanagan acknowledged my arrival, "are you up for a little dress-up?" At my obvious confusion he laughed. "You, me, and Ric are going to become VC this afternoon and go meet this guy's buddies." Flanagan patted the prisoner on the back in mock affection. "Our friend here was scheduled to meet the district VC commander at sunset. He says the chief is a very important man and does not like to be kept waiting. We're going to let him keep his appointment, especially since he has graciously agreed to take the five of us with him. After all, it just wouldn't look right for him to go to such an important meeting alone." He smiled and showed his teeth. The prisoner was not smiling, but he was frantically nodding agreement to something, his gaze darting rapidly among us as if desperate to please.

"The VC certainly won't be expecting *us,*" Flanagan continued, "so we should be able to surprise the shit out of them and get the target out alive."

I grinned. This was starting to sound like fun.

"Doc," Flanagan stepped over to me, while making certain the prisoner could still overhear him, "you take charge of our friend here for the trip. And if he is lying . . ." he turned to look directly at the prisoner, ". . . make sure he doesn't come back with us."

The rest of the patrol order was simple. The six of us would dress like VC to attend the meeting. Once in, we would snatch the VC chief and extract back to base. I was nervous, but excited. This would be my first op with only two other SEALs, and it promised a lot of action. Ric and I quickly ran back to our hooch and climbed into our black pajamas. We kept native and VC clothes on hand for just this type of infiltration op. SEALs are famous for using camouflage to become invisible. Sometimes the best camouflage is to look like everyone else. Even with VC clothes on, our light-colored hair marked us as a pair of white boys in black pajamas, so we finished the disguise with large cone hats, like those worn by the peasants and farmers. With the hats in place, I thought we looked remarkably like VC.

"Hey Ric, you defecting?" Jim hooted. "When the VC decide to keep you, can I have your girl?"

"Heck with Ric's girl. I want Doc's 'Vette!" Benanti countered.

"As if either one of you assholes could handle anything that hot!" Ric quipped, leaving them to decide whether he meant the girl or the car.

Once dressed, we went to the weapons locker to gather some ordnance. In addition to our own weapons I procured an extra rifle—an old M-1 Carbine—and carefully loaded the clip with blanks. Ric and I collected the weapons, medical gear, and the radio, and carried the load to the dock to prepare our sampan for the trip.

I checked the twin Briggs & Stratton motors over to be certain the mechanics hadn't missed anything. Besides giving the boat some speed, the motors were an important part of our disguise. All self-respecting VC VIPs had two motors on their boats. So, as we were trying to look the part as best we could, we had to have two on our sampan as well. The Briggs & Strattons had originally been part of a U.S. grant to give boat motors to the peasants to win the hearts and minds of the farmers by making their toil a little easier. But somehow all the best U.S.-donated motors ended up on the enemy's boats. The more of them the U.S. Government gave to the farmers, the more VC chiefs ended up with brand-new motors. When our boat crews tried to requisition one, however, there was never one available. Our government was too busy giving them to the enemy.

This state of affairs led our SEAL predecessors to improvise. A local VC chief showed up one day with a shiny new American-made Briggs & Stratton on his sampan. So that night, the SEALs stole it. As far as our men were concerned, they were just recovering the misappropriated equipment. The sampan happened to be attached, so they brought it along as well. When the VC chief objected, they simply appropriated him along with his boat.

Now that same sampan was our undercover SEAL delivery vehicle and the VC chief worked for us.

I left Ric with the boat and went to gather our "guide" from his cell. When we returned to the dock at 1400 hours we were greeted by the rest of our squad. Boh came by, cold beer in hand, to wish us a good op.

"You guys are fucking gorgeous. Who's your tailor? Ho Chi Min? You'd fool your own mothers—if you weren't so tall."

"Beats bein' ugly," Ric snapped.

"Sure. But at least I'm charming. And don't worry about a thing. After the VC are through with you I'll take good care of Sheila. She sure is good in bed!"

Ric shot him the bird.

Despite Boh's comments, I thought we all looked very convincing in our matching black pajamas. So what if some of us were a little tall for VC? I figured anyone who looked that closely would probably not survive to talk about it.

The prisoner stared at our little cadre as if perplexed by the transformation. He watched in growing agitation as each man loaded his weapons into the sampan. In addition to our personal knives and handguns, Lt. Flanagan brought an over-and-under M-16 with a grenade launcher, Nhut and Zung carried M-16s, and Ric and I both had our Stoners. Our guide stood there and stared at all our weapons. He pointed at my Stoner and refused to get into the sampan. Apparently, he had just realized that he was the only one who was unarmed. When I told him to get in the boat, he began insisting—then begging—for me to give him a weapon, too.

"I show GI. Give gun. I shoot VC. Kill VC good. I number one friend."

After a moment or two of his whining, Flanagan shot me a look I recognized.

I appeared to deliberate while the guide continued to beg.

"Okay," I relented. "I'll give you a gun. But you do not fire until we tell you to. Understand?" I repeated the order in Vietnamese as I picked up the M-1 and held it out to him. He acted as though I had just given him a Christmas present.

"Okay. Understand. I do good. I number one scout." He grabbed the M-1 out of my hands and held it to his chest protectively. Zung and Nhut looked disgusted. If the prisoner proved trustworthy, he would never know we didn't trust him. If not, the blanks would prevent him from doing too much damage before I could take him out.

I guided our prisoner to the center of the sampan to sit in front of me, where I could keep a close eye on him. The sampan was not very wide, so we had to sit single file. Nhut took station in the bow with Lt. Flanagan behind him, then Ric with the radio, the VC, and me. Zung climbed into the stern to drive. He smiled, then fired up the twin Briggs & Stratton engines and headed the bow north up the Cua Lon River.

With the engines on full throttle, it didn't take long until we were in Indian Country. There was no obvious difference in terrain, the mangroves still crowded along the water's edge in an unbroken line of green, the water flowing past was still the same mud-brown, but I could feel a change in the air. This land belonged to Charlie. As we headed upriver, the banks gradually closed in. The Cua Lon was almost two miles wide at SEAFLOAT's anchorage, but here it was probably less than a mile from side to side.

After we had gone about six kilometers upriver, I noticed a small opening in the tree line of the left bank. As we neared it, I could see it was the mouth of a canal branching off from the main waterway. Our guest gestured to the tributary. *This way to the VC.* Zung turned into the canal and slowed the motor. I noticed that the vegetation along the banks seemed to grow thin and sickly as we passed farther down the canal. There were the same numbers of mangroves here as in the main river, but these trees were devoid of most of their greenery, the victims of defoliation by the Ranch Hands and Agent Orange. That was fine with me. The lack of live vegetation gave Charlie less cover in which to hide.

In front of me, the prisoner started breathing heavily. I watched as his gaze began darting rapidly from side to side. His hands twitched where he held the M-1. I caught Flanagan's eye and silently gave the sign for "VC now," then took my Stoner off safe. A warning shot sounded. It was fired from close by, from someone not too deep in the mangrove swamp. Two quick shots fired from farther ahead echoed in answer to the first. *Gentlemen, our presence has been noted,* I thought, but said nothing.

It was almost low tide. The bare, twisted skeletons of the denuded mangrove trees protruded from the muddy banks in a frozen rictus, looming ever closer as the banks closed in on us. Except for a few tufts of green where hardy weeds and grasses resisted the poison, everything was a shade of brown—the water, the dead trees, the swamp, and the line of the dike beyond the mangroves. Even the sky seemed stained with rust. The canal rapidly narrowed until it seemed I could touch both banks with my hands. The area was almost all swampland here. There was no turning around now. Fortunately the lack of greenery gave us pretty good visibility on both flanks.

Just before 1800, Zung turned off the engines. Everything was dead quiet for a few seconds. Then I heard, one after the other, the sounds of the jungle: bugs, birds, and, finally, bad guys. We rounded a slight bend in the canal to find a junk tied up to the bank, about thirty yards away. Two armed VC casually stood guard, their AK-47s shouldered. There were almost certainly many others out of sight. Nhut called out a greeting from his seat in the bow. The two guards, their AK-47s still shouldered, waved a friendly hello. *So far so good,* I thought.

As we approached, our prisoner suddenly shouted something to the guards in Vietnamese. I couldn't understand his words, but the mood immediately turned serious. Everything around me seemed to happen in slow motion as I watched the guards try to bring their rifles to a firing position while shouting to their unseen comrades. In front of me, the prisoner stood up in the sampan and started firing his M-1 blanks wildly. I threw off my cone hat and rolled out of the boat, Stoner in hand, careful to keep the sampan between myself and the enemy. Landing in only three feet of water, I stood up easily. From their reaction, the VC were definitely not expecting an American to come out of that boat. All 6 feet 2 inches, 190 pounds of me rose up out of the water like an avenging devil with a machine gun. Definitely more company than they bargained for.

Ric grabbed the prisoner and pulled him down out of my field of fire. Nhut and Zung were firing even as I stood, but the rocking motion of the sampan made it impossible for them to hit anything. Flanagan also fired away with his M-16, screaming at the top of his lungs. He looked like a wildman in black pajamas. Seeing him, I had no doubt how Radical Dick had earned his nickname.

More VC appeared like ants from inside the junk and out of the mangroves, firing their AK-47s at us. Unlike the rest of our team, my feet were firmly planted on hard mud as I raised my Stoner and started squeezing off rounds—several at a time until my tracers found their targets, then a quick fifteen-second burst to take them down. The burst expended my 150-round ammo drum, but it convinced the remaining VC on the bank to stop shooting and make a run for it.

Despite the unsteady footing in the boat, Ric managed to pick off two of the remaining VC as they ran into the mangroves. Lt. Flanagan and Nhut jumped onto the junk and tossed in a concussion grenade. Seconds later, the junk exploded in a blast that threw mud, wood, and shit everywhere. I ducked down behind the sampan and shielded my head with my arm from the rain of filth and debris. The grenade had apparently rolled into the bilges and the resulting explosion blew out the whole side of the junk. Once the rain subsided, I glanced up to make certain the LT and Nhut were okay. I saw them digging among the wreckage of the junk, weapons ready.

I waded ashore to begin checking bodies while Ric got on the radio and called in the Sea Wolves to cover our extraction. We had just made a lot of noise and couldn't expect the party to stay private for long.

"Doc, get in here," Lt. Flanagan yelled for me from inside the wrecked junk. I left the bodies of the dead VC and ran to the junk. Inside the wreckage of the hold, Lt. Flanagan stood over a severely wounded Vietnamese man. "I think we found our target." He picked up some bloody documents and a new Russian revolver. "He had these on him." We both knew that only someone of at least the level of a district chief would be likely to carry detailed documents and a Russian revolver.

The man was covered with blood. He had been gut-shot. Part of his lower intestines dangled out of a large gash in his abdomen, and there was a good-size chunk of wood embedded in his thigh. He was awake and obviously terrified. He screamed when I approached to check him out. Fortunately his wounds looked worse at first glance than they were.

"Nhut, tell him I am *Bac Si.*" The man visibly calmed upon hearing the Vietnamese word for doctor. "Tell him I can save his life and fly him to our hospital—or I can leave him here to die a slow and painful death. It all depends on what he can tell us."

Nhut rattled off my ultimatum. The man looked shaken.

"What can you tell us that could possibly be worth saving your miserable life?"

Before Nhut could finish the translation the LT grabbed my shoulder to get my attention.

"Doc!" Flanagan nodded toward our sampan. "It's Zung. Something's wrong."

I turned toward our boat in time to see Zung slump over in his seat. Ric pulled the sampan up beside the remains of the junk. I left the gutshot VC with Flanagan and Nhut and rushed to Zung. His blood covered the bottom of the sampan, but the only wound I could find was a small hole in his neck. A chunk of wood from the exploding junk had nicked his carotid artery. He was rapidly bleeding to death. It would be only a matter of moments before he bled out. I stuck my thumb in his neck and with my index finger on the outside of his skin, pinched off his artery.

"Ric! Call in a dust off! I need your can of serum albumen!"

Ric quickly passed me his can of serum while calling in the request on the radio. It wouldn't be enough.

"I need everyone to give me their serum cans."

Lt. Flanagan and Nhut quickly passed their cans to Ric, who set them on the floor of the boat. I grabbed my field surgical kit out of my pants pocket with my left hand, still holding the artery closed with my right. I pulled the hemostats out of the kit and inserted the hemostat clamp into Zung's neck and clamped off his carotid artery. With my right hand free, I found a good vein in his right hand and quickly started an IV of serum albumen to replace his lost blood. I then covered him with his poncho liner and laid him down to help prevent shock. There was nothing else I could do for him. His survival was in the hands of a higher power.

"Blackjack, Blackjack, this is Sky Shepherd. Please identify position." I heard the Seawolf helicopter on Ric's radio even though we could not hear them overhead yet. Ric threw out a green smoke grenade.

"Blackjack, Blackjack, I have green smoke, over," the voice cracked from the radio.

Ric confirmed, "Roger that, Sky Shepherd."

"Blackjack, get your heads down. You have company, big-time."

I looked up to see fifteen to twenty well-armed VC moving along the dike line about 150 meters out. They were headed in our direction.

I started to yell at Flanagan, still in the junk, but my words were drowned out by the sudden sound of powerful rotor engines as two gunship helos screamed by only a few feet overhead. It was the Seawolves from HAL-3 out of Binh Thuy. They flew low to the deck like bats out of hell, armed for bear—or at least Charlie. The swishing hiss of their rocket launchers and the rattle of their mini-guns were punctuated by the explosions as the rockets found their targets. At that moment, those sounds were sweeter than any rock concert had ever been. The fight was short, but definitive.

"Blackjack, Blackjack! We sent our company to hell. Medivac five minutes out. Are you ready to go home? Over."

"Standby, One." Ric turned toward the ruined junk. "Flanagan, are we done?" he yelled.

"Doc," Flanagan yelled. "Our prisoner here says he can lead us to American POWs. Can you keep him alive?"

I climbed back into the junk and looked again at the prisoner.

"If he is telling the truth, I will do all I can. If he is lying, he has seen his last sunset. Tell him that, Nhut."

Nhut spoke quickly and was answered by a panicked babble from the wounded man.

"He say he no lie. He say please help *Bac Si.*"

I left the piece of wood from the junk still embedded in his thigh because I didn't want to risk another bleeder. His guts were another problem. I stuffed his intestines back in his stomach cavity and put a large battle dressing on him, but he kept oozing abdominal fluids and blood. The dressing was not enough. If I was going to keep this guy alive, I had to stop the fluid loss. Then I remembered the trick Wolfe taught me. I took off my UDT life vest, worn under my black pajamas, and tied it around the wounded man's stomach real tight. Once it was securely fastened I pulled the CO_2 cartridge. The VC let out a gasp from the pain as the vest quickly inflated around him. He quieted when he realized that he was no longer bleeding and might just make it.

I carried the prisoner out of the junk to the sound of gunfire. The Medivac helo had arrived and was hovering about three feet over the swamp. Aboard, the Army door gunners were apparently a little spooked by all the carnage that surrounded us. They were just shooting wildly toward the tree line as if afraid that some of the bodies might get up and shoot back. I lifted our important prisoner up and held him like a baby as I slopped through the mud toward the Medivac. Ric passed me with Zung over his shoulder. He carefully deposited him in the helo, gave me a quick encouraging smile, then went back to help Lt. Flanagan. They had to gather whatever documents and weapons they could find and blow up the sampan and the junk. One of the Seawolves would extract them.

The Medivac crew helped me transfer my prisoner into the helo and climb aboard. Once we lifted off, I turned toward my two patients. The color was coming back to my prisoner's face and his breathing was easier. I turned toward Zung. He lay very still and had no color. I looked closer to find he wasn't breathing at all. I looked back at the VC chief and his makeshift pressure bandage. I sure hoped he was telling the truth. His life depended on it.

22

This Must Be Hell

THE next morning, I awakened to the smell of cooked bacon. For a moment, I had the pleasant illusion that I was home and Mom was making Sunday breakfast after mass. But it was never this hot at home. I opened my eyes and slid from under my poncho liner. Only 0600 hours and sweat was already beading up on my neck and forehead. It might be December, but it sure as hell didn't feel like it. I pulled open my mosquito netting and sat up, ducking my head to avoid hitting it on the top bunk.

"Doc." Ric's voice came from above me as his foot appeared beside my face, "move your head or I'll step on it."

Without a word, I grabbed his leg and pulled him off the bunk. He landed on the floor and immediately came after me. We must have looked like two big college kids playing grab-ass in the dorm, except this was no dorm and this was definitely not college. We were at war—right in the center of it, and I had lost a man the day before. At least wrestling with Ric kept me from thinking too much.

"Hey listen up! Alpha squad!" Boh interrupted our roughhousing. "Get some chow while you can. Report back here in half an hour." He turned to join Lt. Flanagan at his desk. As we passed them to find chow, I noticed they were examining a map. Ric and I grinned at each other. I smelled an op in the making.

It turned out that I really did smell bacon. It was not a dream. I stepped outside our hooch to find that Jonah Benanti had somehow procured some real bacon and was frying it up on a Coleman stove outside our barracks. He had about two pounds of thick-sliced succulent pork sizzling over the fire and guarded it like a pit bull with sunglasses. My mouth immediately began to water. I grabbed some bread and peanut butter and tried to look casual as I approached the stove.

Jonah was not fooled. "No way, Doc. This is my private stash. My personal pig."

"Oh yeah? When was the last time you had a tetanus shot?"

"Doc, you wouldn't . . ."

"Depends on whether I'm feeling well fed or not. And right now I'm starving for pork."

Jonah grudgingly served up several slices onto my plate.

Boh came out as I was sitting down to enjoy my meal. Before Jonah could protest he just grabbed a couple of pieces out of the frying pan and put them on his plate. Ignoring Jonah's resulting invective, Boh sat down to join me.

"Doc, we got a good op coming up this afternoon. Could be a long one. You might want to go over to sick bay and see if you need anything." I knew what he was hinting. It was one of "those" ops. Probably one that might involve a long wait or a prisoner snatch. I would need some special supplies. Each of the squad members carried whatever basic medical supplies I told them to carry—usually enough to cover personal emergency first aid in most situations. I always joked with the guys, telling them to carry the meds I suggested, or if they didn't, I might not be willing to share my really big Band-Aids if they happened to spring a leak. But I was responsible for any specialized medical supplies—especially the dangerous ones.

I nodded, wolfed down the remainder of my bacon, and got up to go to sick bay.

"Doc, the patrol order will be at 0900."

"Got it."

Gary was already in sick bay when I arrived. He was working longer and harder to cover the increasing number of sick calls on our growing base. We had put in a request for more corpsmen, not a doctor this time, but they had yet to arrive. The other SEAL platoon would be leaving in a few days, but that would not necessarily mean there would be any decrease in workload.

"Morning, Doc."

"Same to you, Doc." All medics and corpsmen are called "Doc," but it can get confusing when we're talking to each other. Gary and I often made a joke out of it.

"Got an op coming up. Would you please unlock the controlled substance locker for me?"

Gary nodded and got his keys. He knew the drill. Once the cabinet was opened, he stepped outside of sick bay to give me privacy. All controlled substances had to be constantly kept under lock and key. Not because of the SEALs or regular Navy guys, or even the scouts—but because of the South Vietnamese. There were a lot of Vietnamese brown-water sailors on and around SEAFLOAT, and those sneaky little shits would steal anything of value they could get their paws on, especially drugs. They were banned from coming anywhere near the SEAL barge. Technically, they were our allies, but there was not a SEAL on the base who would think twice about shooting the ass off of any of those little chickenshits if they got too close to SEAL country. We had a lot more respect for the VC we were killing than for the South Vietnamese we were there to protect.

Looking over the inventory in the locker, I began selecting the needed supplies. I took out a bottle of 75 mg Dexamil tablets, opened it, and took out fourteen pills. I also grabbed a box of morphine Syrettes, a couple of IV kits and some syringes. And, in case we got a prisoner, I added two vials of Sodium Pentothal.

"Doc," I called out, relocking the cabinet, "come on back in."

Gary stepped back inside as if nothing had happened. Technically, he outranked me and was a hell of a corpsman himself, but he never questioned me about the stuff I took on my ops. We had a bond, as brother corpsmen, as close in some ways as the bond I shared with my SEAL brothers.

He often accompanied me on my visits to the so-called "friendly" villages, most of which were VC controlled. He helped me pass out pHisoHex soap or birth babies. We had both become pretty good at the birthing thing since our experience with Nhut's baby. Of course these visits were not purely for humanitarian purposes. They gave us a chance to gather a lot of good intelligence. And in many cases, we even managed to win the hearts and minds of the peasant VC supporters. Of course, had any of the village chiefs ever found out the truth—that the *Bac Si* doctor who patched up their kids by day was also one of the men with green faces that haunted their nights—I would never have gotten out alive. I made a point of rarely going to the same village twice—unless the rest of the squad was at my back.

Gary knew the risk, but he went with me anyway.

"Later, Doc," I said, handing him back his keys and hefting my kit.

"Same to ya, Doc." He smiled and went back to his work.

By 0900, the sun hung high in the sky and the briefing hooch had become a hot, steamy oven. I had arrived early and was drenched with sweat by the time the rest of our squad assembled. Without thinking, I popped a couple of salt tablets in my mouth and grabbed some water—in accordance with the procedure we had been taught for dealing with heat. The rule was to take salt and avoid drinking a lot of water. Before I swallowed the salt however, I remembered Wolfe's advice. He had insisted it was better to forgo salt and stay well hydrated. His advice had been right on the money so far, so I spit out the pills and drank extra water. It seemed to help. Lt. Flanagan and an older officer entered the hut as I finished my drink.

"Doc," Flanagan came up to me, "you did a good job on that Charlie prisoner yesterday. NILO here"—he identified the older man as a Naval Intelligence Officer—"got some interesting intel from him up at the field hospital in Bin Thuy while he was conscious. The doctors were real surprised that he was alive. They really liked that life vest trick of yours." He gave me a quick pat on the back, then stepped back to allow the NILO to take the floor.

"Men, I'm not sure what we have here," the NILO started. I laughed inside as Flanagan standing behind him rolled his eyes. Dick Flanagan was not a man who joked around much, but some things were even too ridiculous for him.

The NILO, oblivious to the LT's reaction, continued. "We may or may not have the location of an American POW. That prisoner you brought us believed he saw an American captive. He gave us the location where he thought an American was being held. He said he had seen an American last year, only a couple kilometers south of the U-Minh Forest. He sighted a white man in a small rice farm village."

That piqued my curiosity. I knew the place. We had recently run an operation not far from there and had heard rumors of a round-eye male in the vicinity. It was deep in Indian Country. If we were going in, it was going to be a very long, nasty hike.

"Now the curious part," he went on, "is that there are no reports of a missing American anywhere close to this area."

In fact, that area of the U-Minh was so remote and out of touch that the peasants often mistook the few Americans they did see for left-over French forces.

"So even if he did see a white man, it is possible this guy could be a missionary, or even a Frenchman who got left behind."

"Or if we're really lucky," Flanagan interjected, "a Russian advisor. We have to plan accordingly, because there is still a remote chance the man is an American captive."

I thought it unlikely. "But if this guy was an American prisoner, he would almost certainly have been hustled north on the Ho Chi Minh Trail long ago."

"There's one more possibility," Boh pointed out. "He could be an American defector. What then? Do we have plan for that?"

Flanagan looked grim. "We'll cross that bridge when we get to it." He turned to the NILO. "Thank you sir, for coming out here to share that information. We'll take it from here." He escorted the NILO to the door. "Take five, guys, while I see our guest to his helo."

"Sir?" I caught the NILO as he was leaving. "What happened to the prisoner?"

"You were the one who treated him?"

I nodded.

"Well, after he gave us the information, he lost consciousness. I'm afraid he never woke up. The docs were amazed he lived as long as he did given the damage. You did good, son."

I nodded thanks as he left with Lt. Flanagan. At least the prisoner had given us something before he died, though that didn't make me feel any better about losing Zung. The little scout may have once been VC himself, but I had grown to respect him and trust him in the short time I had worked with him.

I returned to my seat to wait. We knew that no serious planning would take place with an outsider present. Only those actually involved in an op were allowed near our briefing room during a patrol order. More than one U.S. military mission had been compromised by people who thought they were talking privately in a base club, unaware of the innocent-looking busboy quietly sweeping the floor nearby. Lives were often lost when that same busboy reported everything to his VC handler.

"Okay, listen up." Flanagan caught our attention as he returned and closed the door behind him. "Here's the deal. It would take days for us to sneak in there on foot and we'd still not have a clue what we might find. So this is what we're going to do . . ."

As Flanagan outlined our plan, I drew a sigh of relief and lit up a smoke. We would be inserting via Army slicks. I liked flying a lot better than slogging through a mangrove swamp for hours on end. The plan involved a new kind of operation and a bit of subterfuge. One of the problems with airborne insertions was that Charlie could hear the choppers coming. He had time to hide in the bush before the birds could even land. We might find a cache of supplies, but the VC themselves—especially the high-level chiefs—usually escaped. They would wait in hiding until the Americans left, and then return to business as usual once the coast was clear.

But this time, the plan was for both squads to go in, terrorize Charlie as usual, and appear to leave. But only one squad would actually extract. The other got to stay behind to throw Charlie a surprise party.

This was to be our first "stay behind" op, so we loaded up for bear.

Mr. Moody brought in his men. Two Army slicks were ordered for 1400 to be our insertion helos. Two Seawolf gunships would fly escort. We were to come in real high and loud so they would hear us coming in plenty of time to run into the forest and hide. Once down at the LZ, both squads would storm the little cluster of thatched hooches, concentrating on making a lot of noise and shooting at the trees. Then the helos would return for an equally noisy extraction—but only one squad would actually leave the area.

At 1100, Flanagan dismissed both squads to get ready. It felt strange for all of us to be going out together. Usually, we operated with just seven or fewer SEALs at a time. While the operating squad was preparing for their mission, the other squad usually spent their time drinking beer, smoking, and harassing them. But with all of us on the line, an ominous silence replaced the usual banter. A silence broken only by the sounds of men preparing for battle: the quiet metallic clanks of ammo being loaded into magazines and the clicks of web gear being adjusted and fitted with ammo and grenades, all punctuated by occasional grunts and whispered comments.

"Anyone tired or hung over, see me by noon," I called out, breaking the mood.

"Hey Doc, when we hit the ground, stay the hell away from me!" Jonah yelled out. "They're going to shoot your ass off today."

"Not if they see yours first!"

At least we were back to the typical bantering of guys about to put their lives on the line. It felt kind of like suiting up in the college locker room before the big game. Except in this game there were no cheerleaders, no spectators, no referees—just plenty of balls. And mine were in my throat.

The brutal sun baked the corrugated metal of our hooch until the interior was sweltering. We wore only UDT swimsuits and flip-flops, but the lack of clothing didn't help. By the time my gear was ready sweat ran off my body in rivers. The other guys were looking just as good. There were fans in the room, but they only served to move the hot air around like a convection oven.

"The VC won't have to shoot us," Ric commented. "We'll be roasted well-done long before we ever get there!"

"Hey Jonah! Got any more of that bacon?" Mitch mopped his face with his bandana, then made a show of wringing it dry. "I'll bet you could fry it in here right now without a stove!"

I set my fully-rigged web gear and supplies on my bunk and pulled my Kodak camera out of my locker to add to the pile. "This must be what hell feels like." I gave my equipment one last look. "Okay. I prescribe a trip to the bar!"

"Hey! Doc's buying!"

I elbowed Ric—hard. Of course we weren't going to the bar to get alcohol, just to escape the heat. The little room we used for a bar was one of the few places on SEAFLOAT with real air-conditioning. We trooped into the small dark room, snagged some sodas, and shared banter and small talk while our body temperatures gradually dropped back down to a comfortable level. Some of the men from the other platoon offered us some beer. Since they were at the end of their tour, they were on light duty, and allowed to indulge. We declined. The beer would have to wait until we got back.

I was finally starting to feel normal when the unmistakable vibration of distant choppers' rotors throbbed through the tin roof. Our ride was on its way in. Reluctantly, I downed the last of my ice-cold Coke, and joined the rest of the guys as we headed back into the sauna to get dressed for action. By the time I geared up and trekked over to the large barge SEAFLOAT used as a helo pad, I was sweating again. The only movement in the air came from the prop wash off of the four helos as they landed. I faced toward the gust, greatful for even a brief moment of relief.

Once the birds were down, Mr. Moody and Mr. Flanagan greeted the pilots and they all headed to officer's country for their mission briefing. While they discussed logistics, we test-fired our weapons and inspected each other's gear. Satisfied with our preparations, we found some shade and had a smoke. The door gunners waited a moment, probably to be certain the fireworks from weapons testing was over, then joined us in the shade. They looked a little warm from their flight in, so Boh sent a runner for a case of pop for them.

I had my Kodak with me, but we didn't carry cameras in the field. If I wanted pictures I would have to get someone else to take them. I pulled the camera out of my pocket and hunted for a likely candidate. The door gunner from our assigned bird, a blond guy named Josh, seemed perfect.

"You know how to work one of these?"

"Yeah. I used to have one just like it."

"I want to get some pictures for my scrapbook." I handed Josh the camera. "See if you can get any good shots while we are inserting and extracting."

"Sure. You got it."

"But," I grabbed the strap, "only use this if we are *not* getting our asses shot at."

"I got it. No pictures of shot-off asses!" He grinned and tucked the camera into his pocket.

"Well, Doc, you ain't getting no pictures today," Jonah taunted, "'cause the VC are after your ass!"

Ten minutes later, Lt. Flanagan came striding onto the helo deck, flanked by the pilots. He twirled his fingers over his head to signal "let's get going." The pilots and door gunners jumped for their birds and quickly brought them to life, once again cooling the air as the propellers spun up to speed. Mr. Moody loaded his squad into the first helo, then Flanagan gave the thumbs-up and we scrambled into ours in the usual order. Mr. Flanagan climbed in to kneel between the pilots. Then Langlois, Richardson, and Ritter climbed in one side with Boh in the door. Once they were in, Ric and I loaded into the other side with me in the door, next to my new friend, Josh. Ric sat on a seat above and behind me while I sat on the floor with my legs hanging out the open door. With the whole squad aboard, the helo was crowded, so Ric grabbed the back of my web gear to make certain I wouldn't fall out when the pilot made a sharp turn.

As we lifted off, the heat receded with the ground. The rotor blast quickly dried the sweat on my face and cooled my body. I started to relax for the first time all day. Looking down I watched large areas of rice fields, forest, swamps, and jungle pass by below my dangling feet as we climbed. It really was beautiful country from the air. The many shades of green were thick and lush, a great quilted carpet broken only by the multitude of vein-like brown canals that crisscrossed the entire area.

Mr. Moody's helo flew close formation beside us, with the two Seawolves flanking both our birds on the outside. From my vantage point in the door, I could easily see John Mitchell, only twenty yards away, hanging out of the door of the other slick. It was too far to yell, especially over the rotor noise, but we had no problem communicating with each other using hand gestures—though most of our signals were punctuated by frequent use of our middle finger. Mitch loved to fly and he was making the most of his air time.

We climbed until we reached an altitude of about 2,500 feet. At that height, the air was cool and fresh. Everyone grew very quiet. Up here, away from the oppressive heat and frenzy of the war, with only the roar of the wind and chop of the rotors, it was a separate world. I tried to focus my thoughts. I started saying whatever quick prayers I could remember from Catholic school. I think all of us used that time for introspection. I looked up from my brief prayers to see Preacher Richardson watching me. Preacher just lowered his eyes, smiled, and gave me the "peace to you" sign. I found that strangely comforting coming from him. It was little things like that which proved I was working with very special people. It always amazed me that such a gentle and religious man could be a SEAL. But there was no one better to have at your back in a firefight. On this mission he functioned as backup radio man and carried a grenade launcher.

A change in engine noise signaled the beginning of our descent. Mitch and I gave each other the thumbs-up sign as we rode our respective helos down the LZ. The village that was our target area lay situated in a small clearing along the edge of a canal, with a dike and field of elephant grass to one side, and some heavy vegetation and trees on the other. According to plan, we came in high and slow, giving everyone in the village time to run and hide.

From my vantage point in the door I noticed something from the tree line. It was green tracer fire. Someone was shooting at us with AK-47s. Well, I thought, if they're firing at us, then we must be in the right place!

I started to point out the incoming rounds to Josh, but before I could say anything, one of the Seawolves broke from formation, dove toward the woods, and opened up with his mini-guns, firing on the tree line. At the rate of 3,000 rounds per minute, the gunship's 7.62mm bullets tore large chunks out of the foliage. When the mini-guns fell silent, there were no more green tracers.

Our slick dropped in fast on the far side of the dike, very close to the first hooch. Boh and I jumped from opposite sides of the helo while it was still six feet above the elephant grass. We immediately took up a perimeter to cover the helo as it landed to allow the rest of the squad to scramble out. Once we were all down, everyone in our squad moved to take up their assigned positions. Mr. Moody's squad did the same about fifty meters to our left. The helos lifted off again, while the Seawolf gunships circled protectively above, firing sporadically toward the heavy growth in our vicinity to suppress any potential enemy activity.

With the birds away, we moved in quickly and loudly, breaking every rule of stealth for which SEALs are usually known. We moved in screaming and shooting away at anything that moved and a lot more that didn't, until everyone in the village, including the dogs, ran away to hide.

Flanagan, Bo, and Ric checked out the hooches while the rest of us covered our area of fire. It only took a few moments for them to determine which hooch housed the important VC. While Mr. Moody's guys continued to shoot up the place, Flanagan called in our squad.

"This building is probably the best site for our ambush." Flanagan indicated a large bamboo and thatch hooch by the canal. "Pick your spot and get invisible, but keep eye contact with me and each other."

I scouted around the structure until I located a small rear entryway that opened over the canal. I took up a concealed position that allowed me to keep an eye on the canal and most of the area around my side of the hooch. Unfortunately, it also reeked of human excrement. A quick look confirmed that my chosen spot lay a little too close to the local bathroom. Their shitter was nothing more than a small plywood board with a hole in the middle, suspended partway over the canal. At low tide, as now, the seat hung over the muddy bank. But when the high tide caused the canal water to rise, the area would be covered with water, somewhat flushing the area and disposing of the waste right back in the water they used to bathe and wash. No wonder these poor people suffered from so much disease and dysentery.

Farther over, near the edge of the hooch, I spotted a small sampan tied up at the edge of the water. It was covered with a canvas tarp and some strategically placed branches. I quickly checked it out, carefully moving the branches aside while checking for booby traps. Peering under the canvas I discovered a cache of weapons and ammo. This was definitely the right place. I signaled Mr. Flanagan and pointed out my treasure. I think I actually saw a smile crack on his face as he grabbed Ric and radioed Mr. Moody.

"We've got a weapons cache here. We're pretty sure we've got the right hooch. We're going to set up here."

"Roger that," I heard from the radio. "We're calling in the extraction."

I returned to my hiding place and watched the rest of my squad disappear into theirs. The noise of circling helicopters grew louder as the two slicks approached the extraction site. Yellow smoke filled the air as signal grenades landed in the high elephant grass. One of the grenades ignited the grass. The additional smoke from the fire made it impossible for any prying eyes to see that only one squad was actually leaving.

As Mr. Moody's squad lifted off, the prop wash from the helo's giant blades fanned the flames and blew smoke, dust, and fire everywhere. From my vantage point, it looked as though a firestorm was descending on the village. *Hell can't be much worse than this,* I thought.

23

Purple Heart, My Ass!

IT only took a few moments for the choppers to leave the area. I listened as the rotor noise receded into the distance. Silence, like the aftermath of a nightmare, descended on the abandoned village. For a while, the only sound I could hear was the cracking of the fire. But even that faded as the fire died down. The area was swampy and the grass too damp to sustain a fire for long. I waited, perfectly still in the silence. I didn't know how long it would take the villagers to return, but I knew they would be back.

After several long minutes, I heard the sounds of returning life. At first it was just the animals: chickens venturing from cover, pigs diving into their mud wallows, and dogs barking in the distance. Then I felt my hair bristle on the back of my neck, like a dog ready to fight. The VC were returning. I couldn't see or hear anyone, but I could *feel* their presence. Despite the heat, I broke out in a cold sweat.

Then I started to hear voices: the singsong, high-pitched sound of Vietnamese, spoken in a highly agitated but excited tone. Laughing. Singing.

They don't have a clue, I thought.

They appeared out of the bush, stepping out into the open less than fifty meters away from my position. Their hats were pushed back from their dark hair and their guns were carelessly balanced on their shoulders. They hooted and slapped each other's backs like teenagers after the big win, while commenting on what fools' the Americans were. As I watched, the bushes parted to reveal a man far too large to be Vietnamese. He wore typical Viet Cong black pajamas, but a shock of long blond hair protruded from under his bush hat. He carried an AK-47 with casual ease. Here was our white boy—but he was definitely no American prisoner.

Mr. Flanagan gave the signal not to shoot. We wanted him alive.

I turned to cover the rear as four armed VC came out of the bush behind our position and approached the sampan just a few meters away from me. The hooch was between them and the rest of our squad. I signaled "Four BAD guys!" and moved into position to interdict them. Stepping out of my concealment to face them, Stoner at my shoulder, I called out to them to surrender—"Chieu Hoi! Chieu Hoi!"

Four pairs of eyes stared at me in shocked surprise as I held them at gunpoint. The two in front released their weapons and immediately started to raise their hands. But, to my amazement, the two men behind them swung their rifles up over the shoulders of the front two, using them as human shields, and took aim at me. I couldn't believe what I saw, but my reactions were instantaneous. I knew even before I moved that I was staring into four pairs of eyes that would never see anything again. Part of me couldn't believe that they were making me kill them. My finger tensed and four heads exploded as I released a short burst of deadly fire. So much for silence.

Without waiting for the bodies to hit the ground, I quickly ducked back into concealment. I could hear the rest of the squad as they opened up on the VC approaching from the front. The VC responded in kind, filling the air with flying ammunition. Bullets cut through the bamboo hooch around me like hundreds of tiny hot knifes through a sheet of butter. My heart pounded so fast I thought my chest would explode.

Mr. Flanagan yelled commands like a crazy man, now that there was no longer a need for silence, and Boh barked out orders as well, while the VC fell before us or scattered back into the jungle.

The firefight seemed to last an hour, but it was probably only about ninety seconds. Then the shooting stopped. I could hear the bloodcurdling screams of a wounded VC close by. We broke from cover and searched the area. While we checked bodies and collected documents and weapons, I prayed we were not going to find a dead American. But after searching the entire village we did not find the blond man. We couldn't find any non-Asians at all. Who was this guy? How did he get away?

During the search, the survivors who had escaped to the jungle started taking potshots at us. Flanagan called the helicopters back as the sporadic fire ricocheted around us. We didn't get the white boy, but we still had work to do. With the dying VCs' screams reverberating in our ears, we stayed low and moved fast. Ric set a charge to blow up the sampan and destroy the weapons cache. Boh placed booby traps under some of the dead bodies. I returned to the dying VC. His wounds were mortal. His lower body had been ripped to pieces. He just lay there looking at nothing and screaming until it seemed his lungs would burst from the effort. Dropping down beside him, I pulled out a morphine Syrette and injected it into his jugular vein. He quickly quieted as the morphine instantly stopped his brain and heart. Animals are put to sleep in much the same way, though I tried not to think about that. Leaving the body, I ran back to the hooch and tossed an incendiary grenade inside. A few seconds later, the hooch and a portion of the nearby jungle burst into flame. I ran for the extraction point, staying low and trying to dodge bullets.

The helos came in low and fast, with the door gunners spraying the surrounding jungle with machine gun fire. I added some covering fire of my own as the rest of the squad loaded onto the helos. Once everyone else was on board and the bird started to lift off, Mr. Flanagan and I jumped aboard.

Looking back through the smoke and fire at all the bodies that now littered the ground throughout the burning ruins of the village, I reevaluated my earlier observation. *Now* it really was hell. But perhaps the flames would at least sterilize the riverbank.

On the way back to base, I asked Josh if he had gotten any pictures.

"Well, man, I got some of your backside as you were inserting, but during the extraction I was too damn busy shooting bullets to cover your ass to shoot any pictures of it. Does that count as getting your ass shot off?"

I grinned and made a show of looking at my rear end. "Nope. Still attached. Guess we'll try again next time."

"Sure thing."

We never did find out who the white man was, but we found out who he wasn't. He definitely wasn't an American. In the final analysis, it was decided that the blond man was probably a Soviet advisor, and while we didn't capture him, we did catch the VC with their britches down. The fake extraction–ambush method worked so well that we decided to try it again a few days later.

We had received some good Intel on the location of a district-level VC province chief. Our intelligence source had provided detailed info—right down to the exact location of the chief's hooch. I discovered that we had the same slick and helo crew as on the previous stay-behind op. I gave Josh my camera and told him he had his chance to try again for pictures—so long as my ass was not getting shot.

Once again we all inserted en masse near the village and descended on the target hooch. Apparently this time they didn't hear the choppers coming. We almost caught our target on the first try. When we reached the right hooch, the chief was still inside. As soon as we entered the front door of the bamboo building, the chief *di-di-maued* right out the back door just as fast as he could go. We didn't bother to chase after him. A few other VC were not so quick on their feet. We nabbed several prisoners before they could reach the bush.

With our target gone, the platoon made a rather noisy show of gathering prisoners to leave. While Boh, Dave Langlois, our scouts Tong and Chang, and I found places to hide, the rest of the platoon threw the prisoners on board the slicks and then extracted with them. The two slicks lifted off and joined their Seawolf escort circling above. I listened as they left the area. Silence soon settled back in.

It only took about five minutes or so for the VC who had escaped to start returning from their hiding places in the bush. Most of them were talking and laughing, as if this was nothing more than a fire drill at school. They laughed about how they had once again beaten the "green faces." Certain of their safety, they held their weapons by the barrel, dangling them casually over their shoulders. We waited and watched as they went back to their hooches, relaxing as if nothing had happened—completely unaware that those same green faces were in their midst. Moments later, even the province chief returned. We waited as he greeted his door guard, settled into his hooch, and began going about his regular business.

Then our five green faces emerged from hiding and moved on the chief's hooch. Boh called back the birds, waiting just over the horizon, while Dave took out the guard on the chief's door. As one we burst into the hooch. Backed by Boh and the scouts, Dave used his sixty gun to spray down everyone else while I went after the province chief. I could hear the birds returning, and I knew that the rest of the village would hear the commotion and start coming after us any moment. It was time to leave.

I grabbed the chief, only to discover that he had been gut-shot during the short firefight. I immediately went to work on him while Dave, Boh, and the scouts gave cover. He had stopped breathing. Working quickly I rendered CPR. His pulse and breathing restored, I stopped, but not fast enough. With all the blood, mud, and sweat, I smelled bad enough on the outside. But he had to vomit in my mouth, too. His pulse was erratic and his respiration shallow, but he was breathing on his own. I started an IV with serum albumin and put a pressure bandage on the wound. At least this fellow would not need the life-vest treatment. With the prisoner patched, I grabbed the IV bottle with my teeth, hoisted him into my arms and headed for our ride. Boh moved in to help me carry the wounded VC while Dave and our scouts flanked us, providing covering fire as we escaped the village. As I ran toward the waiting helo, I could see Josh, in the door gunner seat, snapping pictures of our approach, just as I had asked.

Suddenly we started taking fire from the tree line off to the opposite side beyond the rice paddy. Apparently, not all of the VC had returned to the village. The ones still in hiding were using us for target practice. The fire originated from the tree line to my left.

Dave, who had been concentrating his fire behind us, spun to the left and began rocking and rolling into the tree line with his sixty gun. Boh and Tong, running on my left, joined him, adding the power of their M-16s. I glanced in the direction of the incoming fire just as a VC came up fast on my right side. The scout to my immediate right, Chang, opened up. The VC went down and at the same instant, I felt something strike me hard in the right shoulder. I spun around and crumpled to my knees. Fire burned in my shoulder as if someone had shoved a hot poker through it. Somehow, I managed to hold on to the IV bottle in my teeth while keeping my left around the prisoner. My right arm refused to respond. I realized I had been hit.

"Come on Doc! No time for lollygaggin'. Ride's waitin'." Boh quickly dragged me back to my feet, scooping up my patient with me. Together we managed to get the wounded prisoner and ourselves to the bird. The situation happened so fast that Josh was still snapping pictures when the attack started. He immediately dropped the camera and grabbed his machine gun to give us covering fire as we stumbled the last few yards to the slick. Dave and the scouts pulled us in. Still putting fire in the tree line, we lifted off and moved out.

Once I was certain my prisoner was stable and had not been hurt further by our fall, I checked out my own wound. Judging from the gore around the injury, I wasn't sure if I had been hit by a stray bullet or by fragments of bone from the VC who fell next to me. The damage wasn't too severe, just a clean cut through my shoulder, but it hurt like hell. I was not a happy individual.

"Well hell, man, at least I got pictures," Josh commented, once he saw I wasn't going to die. He waved the camera triumphantly.

"I told you not to take any pictures if we were getting our asses shot," I snapped.

"Hell, Doc," Boh laughed. "Near as I can tell they missed your ass completely!"

LANDING on SEAFLOAT, we were immediately ambushed by a TV news crew. Apparently, the operation was much more important than I thought. Admiral Zumwalt had come in to see the results and the camera crew had arrived with him. I gritted my teeth and pushed through the gauntlet of cameras and newsies, intent on getting my wounded prisoner to sick bay.

Gary met me near the chopper pad and helped me with my patient. The prisoner was unconscious, but breathing easily. We cleaned and redressed his wounds, replacing the battle dressing with something more substantial, and made him as comfortable as possible. He would be interrogated later. Judging from the brass outside, this guy was important.

With my charge stabilized and secure, Gary turned his attention to me.

"Now let me look at that shoulder."

"It's just a scratch." I suddenly felt self-conscious.

"Yeah, and we both know that even a scratch can get seriously infected out here. *Doc.*"

I did not miss his emphasis. He was right. As a corpsman, I did know better. It just seemed different when I was the patient.

"Go get your shower and then we will attend to that wound."

I left sick bay and ran right into one of the reporters I had dodged on the way in. I was in no mood to deal with newsies—especially those like Morley Safer who couldn't understand that a well-armed corpsman is a live corpsman. I had already survived beyond the normal life expectancy for a field corpsman in Vietnam and I wasn't about to apologize for that to anyone. If Admiral Zumwalt had not rescued him, it probably would have gotten ugly.

Once clear of the newsman, Boh took charge of my weapon so that I could go straight to the shower. I cleaned all the mud, blood, and shit off my body and scrubbed out the wound with pHisoHex soap, then headed back to sick bay. Gary was waiting for me. He pointed to a chair and I obediently sat down to allow him to check out my shoulder. He gave me something for the pain and went to work.

"You were lucky. The fragment missed the bone and went clean through. It's going to need stitches and it will definitely hurt for a while. You'll have to take it easy."

"But will I be able to play the piano?" The pain meds were starting to kick in.

Gary snorted. "Why? You couldn't play for shit *before* you were injured."

Josh came in to sick bay as Gary was cleaning and stitching my shoulder.

"You left this on the helo." Josh handed me my camera.

"Thanks."

"There may be some decent shots on it." He turned to leave, hesitating at the door to watch Gary work. "At least you'll get your Purple Heart. I hear the girls love guys with medals." He grinned and left to return to his chopper.

A Purple Heart. I hadn't even thought about it. Up to that point, no one in our platoon had been injured. We were kind of proud of that. I wasn't sure if I liked the idea of being our first casualty.

"I'm not even sure I was hit by a bullet, much less an enemy bullet."

"But you *were* wounded. A fragment of bone can do as much damage as a bullet in the right spot. If it had hit somewhere else, it could have killed you. Besides, it doesn't matter how you were wounded for the Purple Heart. I know a guy who fell off a bar stool in Saigon and broke his arm. But he got a Purple Heart." He finished sewing up my shoulder and wrapped it with a bandage. "There you go. Forty stitches. Almost good as new."

"So I can return to duty, Doc?" I grinned.

"Yeah, Doc. But I would prefer if you didn't go out on any operations right away. Give it time to heal before you let the VC have another shot at you."

"Sure, Doc. Whatever you say." We both knew I had no intention of letting a little nick in the shoulder keep me out of action.

As I left sick bay, I thought about the fact that it was people like

Mr. Safer, secure in their starched, ordered lives, who made a big deal about Purple Hearts. To them, every Purple Heart was proof that we didn't belong in this war.

Just outside, I ran into Dave Langlois and Boh, and we headed to the mess for some badly needed chow. They had finished cleaning their weapons, as well as mine, but were still covered in grime and camo paint from the op.

"How's the shoulder?" Boh said, deliberately patting me on the bandages.

"Ouch! Doc says I just might live."

"Glad to hear it, Doc. Wouldn't want to face Charlie without you." He said it as a joke, but I could tell he meant it.

We reached the mess and Dave pulled up short.

"Jesus. What happened here?" he exclaimed. The room had been transformed. There were white tablecloths on all the tables, silverware set out at the places, and I could smell steaks on the grill. Surely, this was not *our* mess hall.

"Maybe I was hurt worse than I thought, this smells like heaven!"

"Who cares? It's food," Boh said, leading us into the room.

"Good food, from the smell of it." By this point, between the meds and the stress of the long day, I was famished.

Before we got more than a few feet inside the door a guy in dress whites ran up to stop us. He was decked out like a Navy poster boy, complete with gloves and the fancy rope over his shoulder and he looked very disturbed to see us. I could almost understand his distress. The room was decorated for an elegant dinner and we definitely clashed with the décor. I wore nothing but my trunks, my flip-flops and a bandage, while Boh and Dave were still dressed from the field. Their camo uniforms were caked with mud, their faces were smeared with sweat-marred camo paint, and they stank. Just the sort of thing to add color to an admiral's reception.

"Gentlemen, would you mind waiting until after the officers have eaten?"

That was not the thing to say to three starving SEALs who had just returned from an operation.

"Yeah, we fucking do mind," Dave replied, never one to mince words.

Before things could get ugly, the cook, who knew us, beckoned us over to the chow line.

"Come on in, guys." He waved us through a side door and gave us our food. As we sat down to eat, at the nice white table, Admiral Zumwalt came in. Unlike the poster boy, he had no problem with SEALs invading his reception, and came over to see us. He greeted and made small talk with each of us. He inquired about my shoulder, deliberately avoiding any mention of my earlier run-in with the news crew.

When he got to Dave, the admiral asked him his name.

"Dave," Langlois said. "What's yours?"

Without losing a step, Zumwalt answered, "Elmo."

"Hey, good to meet you, Elmo," Dave said, shaking the admiral's hand enthusiastically. "You gonna eat lunch with us?"

We laughed, and the Admiral said that he would be eating nearby. Zumwalt had a way of making us feel as if we really mattered to him.

As we were finishing off the last of our steaks, Lt. Flanagan came over to see us. He had dressed for the reception, but the dress whites looked somehow out of place on him. He looked much more natural with camo paint on his face.

"How's the shoulder?"

"I'll live."

"We may get some important intel out of that prisoner. Good work, guys."

We nodded our thanks and Boh and Dave left for some badly needed showers. I started to follow, but Flanagan stopped me.

"Doc, I've got the paperwork to put you up for a Purple Heart."

I had been thinking about the whole medal business. Somehow it didn't seem right that a guy who falls off a bar stool in Saigon could get the same medal as someone who had their leg blown off. My little scratch certainly didn't seem to be on par with a real, serious injury from combat. So far our platoon had no official casualties. Did I really want to be the one to spoil that record? And for what? Proof that it was dangerous in the field?

"Sir, if it's all the same to you, I think I'll pass. I walked out on my own, and I'm good to go out tomorrow. I don't need a medal for that. It's my job."

Flanagan gave me a long measuring look. Then he smiled, a rare sight for him.

"I'm glad you feel that way. As far as I'm concerned, a Purple Heart is nothing but a good marksmanship medal for the other side. It was yours if you wanted it, but I'm proud that you don't."

Later, back in our hooch, we all got together and decided that we were going to try to maintain a perfect record of no Purple Hearts at all. If we could get our entire platoon through the tour with no serious injuries, considering the number of ops we handled, we would be the first SEAL platoon to manage it. That record would be far better than any medals.

"So it's agreed," I verified, "if I can patch you up—you don't need a medal. But if anyone gets wounded bad enough to require a Medivac to the hospital—then they deserve that Purple Heart!"

"Amen! No hunting medals. SEALs don't need no stinkin' medals for getting cuts and scrapes. It's what we live for!" Ric laughed and pounded me on my injured shoulder.

After I could see again through the haze of pain, I slugged him back. "Of course if you do that again you're going to earn a Purple Heart of your own—posthumously!"

24

Gimme a Break

I went out on an operation the next day, bandage and all. It was fairly uneventful, and we got back just in time to say goodbye to the other platoon as they headed back to the world. There was no word yet as to whether SEAL Team One would send another platoon to take their place. For now, at least, we were the only SEAL game in town.

As I watched the helos lift off with the remnants of his platoon, I missed Wolfe all over again. The recent operations had been particularly hairy, with a lot of shooting and a tremendous amount of pressure, and the combination of losing a friend and getting shot myself weighed on me more than I wanted to admit. I needed a break.

Fortunately, Mr. Flanagan seemed to read my mind. The next morning, he announced that he wanted to stand down the platoon for a few days to review intel and do some operation planning. Apparently, our recent prisoner had provided a lot of new and interesting information.

The choppers that had taken the other platoon off also brought in two new regular corpsmen to help Gary. This meant that he would no longer need me to help handle the daily sick calls. With the platoon standing down and extra corpsmen in sick bay, I recognized a perfect chance to escape the war for a while.

Several hours later, with everyone's shopping list in hand, I ran out to meet the mail helo and grab a ride to Binh Thuy. I was pleasantly surprised to discover my buddy Jim Gorman was also hitching a ride on the mail helo. He had gone full native and I almost didn't recognize him. He only stayed on SEAFLOAT when he had to. He greeted me in the local dialect and smiled brightly when I returned the greeting in passable Vietnamese.

I climbed aboard and settled in for the ride, but before the helo could lift off, Ric ran onto the pad waving to the pilots to hold. They hesitated, and Ric jumped aboard and settled next to me.

"Flanagan wants me to go with you!" he yelled to be heard over the rotor noise. "I'm supposed to keep you from getting into trouble!"

"*You* are going to keep *me* out of trouble?" I was incredulous.

"Isn't that a little like giving guns to the Indians?" Jim commented.

The pilots looked back at us to see if they could leave yet. Ric and I both flashed them a peace sign and smiled. They rolled their eyes and resumed takeoff. Jim just laughed. This was going to be good.

Landing at Binh Thuy was a major thrill after six weeks straight on SEAFLOAT. We went over to the Detachment Golf (DET Golf) office and checked in. We left all our gear and weapons there and changed into civilian clothes. Once that was taken care of, we went straight to the bar. Compared to the tiny little room on SEAFLOAT, the bar on this base was positively spacious.

Inside we ran into a couple of members of SEAL Team Two who had come over from Rach Gia. They introduced us to some friends of theirs, Nigel and Geoff. They were SAS men from Australia who had come down from Vung Tau. The Special Air Service was the Australian equivalent to the U.S. Navy SEALs. The Aussies were a couple of years older than most of us, which made them seasoned veterans to me. As I listened to them recount some of their exploits, I realized that they were not fighting a conventional war. Like us, they had been trained to handle anything. But where most U.S. forces had to fight the war with one hand tied behind their backs, the Aussies were apparently free to operate without regard to those limitations that made our jobs harder. They worked anywhere the bad guys were, with no worries about crossing country borders. Wherever the enemy went, they went. It sounded great to me.

"So, mates, care to join us for some laughs up at Vung Tau?"

"No, thanks." Gorman finished his beer. "I have all I want in Can Tho." He wished us well and left to find his Vietnamese loved ones and his second home.

The guys from SEAL Team Two also declined. They had to get back to their platoon. Ric and I looked at each other and grinned. We didn't have any pressing engagements for a few days. At that point, we would have been willing to go almost anywhere for a little fun, but hanging out with the Aussies in what was considered the Riviera of Southeast Asia sounded particularly sweet.

"Sure. We're game. Vung Tau it is," Ric confirmed.

"Vung Tau?" A clean-cut young fellow came over to our table. I noticed he wore aviator sunglasses even though the room was dark. "Couldn't help but overhear. I'm based out of Vung Tau. Great country up there."

"So do you always wear sunglasses in a dark bar?"

"Even at night," he quipped. "Its part of the company uniform. Name's Don Scully, CIA."

I nudged Ric. "Maybe Jonah Benanti should go CIA. He's already got part of the uniform."

We pulled up a chair for Don and ordered another round for our new friend. I realized after talking with him that he was probably in his early thirties, though he looked and acted younger. He was a helo pilot for the CIA. After a few beers, he offered to take the four of us to Vung Tau in his Air America helicopter.

VUNG Tau was the most beautiful town I had seen since arriving in Southeast Asia. During the French colonial period, it had been a resort area. The CIA had taken over an old French château that overlooked the glittering waters of the South China Sea. Don proudly introduced us to some of his company friends and showed off his home away from home. I could see why he was proud. These CIA guys lived the life of luxury. Each man had his own private room with bath, including hot water. It was a beautiful, huge compound with luxurious gardens and ponds. The main living room had been converted into a bar, complete with pool tables and pinball machines. The whole place looked like an expensive country club back home. I realized I was in the wrong branch of service.

The CIA guys were really friendly and anxious to hear about SEAL operations. As we settled in at the bar, I let Ric take center stage. Ric could tell a story better than I could, and he really knew how to embellish a good firefight. I found myself enjoying the company of the Aussie SAS men. It sounded as if they had definitely been around the block.

About 9:00 PM that night, after a lot of CIA booze, Nigel invited me to come and see their quarters.

"A Yank is always welcome. We should be able to get there in time for Mid Rats. Whaddaya say, mate?"

Sharing the traditional late-night Navy meal with my new Aussie buddies sounded good to me. I agreed, leaving Ric to carry on without me. I was a little tipsy and didn't realize until we arrived at the harbor that their base of operations was actually a ship, the *Clive Steele*. I thought it was very courteous of them to invite me to their home away from home. I didn't know at the time that they had Cinderella liberty, and had to be on board by midnight anyway.

The *Clive Steele* was completely unlike any U.S. Navy ship. I only saw the SAS section, but she looked more like a floating bar and casino than a ship of war. The impressive buffet laid out for Mid Rats reminded me more of cruise-ship fare than any military rations I had ever seen. I was not only in the wrong service—I was from the wrong country. These SAS guys really knew how to fight a war!

Nigel and Geoff immediately set me up with a couple of cans of Victorian Bitters.

"Here, mate. We've tried your piss-water excuse for beer. Now see what a real brew tastes like."

I was impressed with the full-bodied taste and quality of the Australian beer. It definitely had more character than most American brews. It also had about twice the alcohol content. We drank and sang songs, played craps, drank, ate, and drank some more. I lost count of how many beers I had. After several hours I realized I was losing the ability to walk, talk, and sing on key. Nigel noticed I was in no shape to travel.

"You look like you need a lie down, mate. I've got a hammock you can use."

"But I have to get back to Ric."

"No worries, mate. We'll get you back to the spook house by morning."

I was in no shape to argue. I passed out as soon as I reached the promised berth.

I awakened with a throbbing rumble in my head. It took me a moment to realize that the rumble was not entirely in my head. The hammock gently swayed beneath me. But I was lying perfectly still. *That's funny. The hammock was rock-steady last night.* There could be only one reason for the low rumble and the sway. *The ship was moving!* "Oh, shit!"

"Good day, mate." A perky young Aussie looked up as I rolled out of the hammock. "I didn't know you was going to Perth with us."

I brushed past him, running through the hatch and out to the deck of the ship.

The coastal mountains of Vung Tau could barely be seen as distant hills on the horizon. The morning air was crisp and clean. The usually brownish water of Vietnam was turning blue as we left the mainland behind. But I was in no mood to appreciate the beauty. The shore was moving farther and farther away, and with it any hope of rejoining Ric and the rest of the gang. And to top it off, my head pounded off-beat with the drum of the ship's engines.

"Oh, shit!" I was in trouble. Nigel had forgotten to get me off the ship before it got under way. The vise around my head tightened as the coastline receded behind us.

I ran back into the ship until I saw Geoff and some of my new friends from the night before.

"Nigel forgot to wake me. You've got to tell the captain to turn the ship around! I've got to get off!"

They looked at each other, and laughed.

"Oh, sure, mate. You can swim, right?"

"Yeah, why?"

"'Cause if the old man finds out he's got a U.S. Navy SEAL stowed away on his ship, he'll have you thrown over the gunwales and let you swim back!"

The drum pounding in my head turned into a sledgehammer. Like it or not, I was bound for Australia.

Back at the CIA compound, Ric waited in the bar growing increasingly nervous. I should have been back before morning. As the CIA guys hustled in and out he started asking them if they had seen a missing SEAL.

"Why? Did you lose one?" a tall guy quipped.

"You mean the other SEAL that was with you?" a pilot named Max replied. "He went to Australia."

"Yeah right, Max," Ric laughed. "I'm serious."

"No shit, man," the first guy insisted. "He left with those SAS guys last night and boarded their ship. No one saw him get back off. The *Clive Steele* got under way at 0600 hours for Perth."

So much for keeping the Doc out of trouble! Flanagan would probably kill me for letting him get lost like that. But Flanagan was not the only problem. If we didn't check in with someone in the next day or so, we would be listed as missing in action. Ric left the bar and began searching the compound until he found Don Scully with a group of other guys in the garden.

"Don, I need your help. Greg went with those SAS guys last night, and now he is on his way to Perth!"

"No shit? Australia?" Don held a straight face for the better part of a minute before he broke out laughing. "Hope he likes kangaroos!"

The other guys snickered. Not one of them seemed surprised. The entire CIA compound already knew about the missing SEAL and they were all getting a big kick out of it. Ric was the only one who didn't know where I was. He wasn't sure whether to be angry or glad that someone else did.

Once he stopped laughing and could talk again, Don patted Ric on the shoulder. "Let's see if we can get your friend back."

Scully led Ric over to the communications center. It only took a moment for Ric to establish radio contact with the *Clive Steele*.

"*Clive Steele*, this is *Blue Jay 3*. We believe that we may have accidentally left some equipment on board your ship. Over."

"What kind of equipment? Over."

"That would be U.S. Navy SEAL equipment. Over."

A few minutes later, the *Clive Steele* confirmed that the missing SEAL equipment was indeed on board and granted permission for a helo to land and pick it up.

BY the time the Air America helo touched down on the *Clive Steele,* we were more than a hundred miles out to sea. The water had turned a deep blue and the light ocean breeze had lost all scent of Vietnam or the war. My head had even stopped pounding. I was enjoying the ride so much I didn't really want to go back, but I knew I had no choice.

I jumped aboard the helo to find Scully piloting with Ric in the copilot's seat.

"You must be our missing SEAL equipment." Ric threw me in the back like a bad dog, then laughing, offered me a semi-cold beer.

I politely declined with a gesture of my middle finger.

We flew low, skimming over the water at an altitude of only a couple of hundred feet. After an hour of flying, I began to smell a change in the air. At almost the same moment, the coastline came into view. The water turned brown beneath us and the air grew thick with the smell of mud and rotting vegetation that was pure Vietnam.

"Well, back to the fun and sun capital of the world!"

Upon landing, the CIA quickly escorted us to the bar. As soon as I entered the room, the CIA guys waiting there hoisted their own cans of Victorian Bitters and broke into a rousing chorus of "Waltzing

Matilda." The whole thing had been a setup, a CIA plot, a little "innocent hazing" for the two young American SEALs. Everyone but Ric and I had been in on it. After a moment, I took the beer they offered and joined the party. After all, we were just a bunch of young guys having fun while carrying guns.

25

You Gotta Have Hope

IT stormed that night. I was too restless to sleep, and lay staring into the dark, listening to the rain pounding the sheet-metal roof over the room Ric and I shared at the CIA compound. I arose at first light, in time to hear the last rounds of night artillery blindly shooting into the hillside. They stopped right at sunrise. The rain slowed to a gentle cool mist and the scent from the lush gardens below our room sweetened the air. It made me wonder what the place had been like in its heyday with the French. It must have really been something! By the time Ric awakened, the rain had stopped. We had a couple more days left before we had to be back at SEAFLOAT, but no particular plans in place.

At breakfast, Ric introduced me to Max Owens, a CIA pilot he had befriended while I was on my way to Australia. Max flew a single-engine, fixed-wing, turbo-prop Porter, a French plane that could take off and land on a dime. We mentioned being at loose ends for the rest of our leave, but Max had a solution.

"I have to take some big-shot VIP brass back over to Cam Ranh Bay. There's plenty of room on the plane if you boys want to come along. This guy's been a real jerk, so I would appreciate the diversion."

"Sounds good to me!" I recognized the call to adventure when I heard it.

"Meet me on the driveway out front."

The plane sat parked just outside the main building on the driveway. I had not seen a runway, but I figured it was nearby—possibly camouflaged. Max was right about the room on the Porter, the sleek silver-and-blue plane comfortably held four with plenty of room for cargo. The VIP, however, was not impressed, and said so. I saw Max's eyes flash as the obviously well-fed VIP pompously asked if Max could find him more suitable transportation.

"No sir. This is the only flight to Cam Ranh Bay today. You can take it or leave it, but I have to get these men down there, ASAP." He winked at us when the big guy wasn't looking.

I climbed in and grabbed a seat behind Max. He started the engine and turned the plane around on the driveway to face the front gate. I started to ask him where the runway was hidden when he hit the gas. The little plane leaped forward in response and hurtled down the driveway toward the closed gate. Before I had time to say anything, Max pulled back on the stick and the little plane hopped over the front gate and leaped almost straight up between the buildings.

"What the *hell* are you doing?" The VIP up front was white as a sheet. "Are you trying to get us all killed?"

Max ignored him. Once we were safely airborne, he turned and winked at Ric as if to say, "Take that, you asshole!" This guy must have really done something to piss Max off.

Cam Ranh Bay lay a couple hundred miles up the coast. A couple hundred miles of some of the most beautiful scenery I'd seen in a long time. If I hadn't known better I would have sworn we were flying up the Gulf Coast of Florida.

After a while the VIP recovered from the takeoff enough to attempt conversation with us.

"So how long are you guys staying in Cam Rahn Bay? If you can stay a few days, you can see Bob Hope's Christmas show. I can probably get you some good seats for the show with some of the staff officers."

I caught that dangerous sparkle in Ric's eye that usually meant trouble. Ric and I were in our civilian clothes, so this fellow had no way of knowing who we were, and he was trying to kiss up, just in case.

"That's very kind of you, sir, but the company has already made plans for us."

"That's right," Max verified quickly. "Sir, I thought you knew. These men are on the advance security team for the Bob Hope show."

"Well, of course. Special security. I thought you might be." He was trying to act knowledgeable and important. "I knew you were coming. But I didn't think you would arrive on a CIA plane."

Ric threw himself into the part. "You didn't think we would want to blow our cover by coming in announced, did you? This way no one is expecting us and we have a better chance to find out just how good the security really is."

"Oh. Of course. Makes perfect sense," the large man nodded enthusiastically. I tried to keep a straight face, but it wasn't easy.

"But now that you know the truth, you have to keep it to yourself. We can't do our job if our cover gets blown before we're done. Can we count on you?" Ric's earnest expression was priceless.

"Absolutely. You can count on me. You will have my full cooperation. Anything you need during your stay on base, I'll see to it."

Ric sat back and winked at me as we prepared for landing.

We came in over the broad, white, sandy beach that framed the bay, flew over the brush and on to the tarmac runway. The landing was much more relaxed than the takeoff. We taxied to a halt near a waiting jeep. It turned out our VIP was the head supply officer of the base, a position which Ric and I felt we could possibly exploit.

As we climbed out of the plane, Max asked him where the CIA office was located.

The guy laughed. "It's the closet across the hall from my office. Don't blink or you'll miss it."

We acted as if we thought the joke was really funny and laughed as sincerely as we could manage.

Ric and I requested transportation and a driver to assess our security needs for the show, which would be arriving the next day. Mr. VIP scrambled to comply. We got a nice new jeep and a young corporal, who was probably a couple years older than I, to act as our driver and guide. Then Max joined us as we set to work, determined to play our part to the hilt.

First we checked out the dressing rooms and backstage area, plus the building that would be used as overnight housing for Bob Hope and his cast. We then checked the base perimeter. Even I could tell they were a little lax, so we suggested they build up the manpower in the guard towers. We had the MPs completely convinced Ric and I were top security experts working for the CIA and on loan to the Bob Hope show.

Our VIP friend made certain we were provided very nice rooms in the Bachelor Officers Quarters. Once word got out, we were wined and dined at the Officers Club to the wee hours. Max impressed them with his bullshit CIA exploits, and Ric and I told everyone how nice Bob Hope is and how pretty Ann-Margret is.

The following morning I was awakened by someone pounding on our door. It was 0800.

"Who is it?"

"It's Max. Hurry up and get your butts out here. I need you to meet some guys that just came in."

"What guys would that be?"

"Bob Hope's *real* advance security detail. The corporal just picked them up."

I was suddenly wide awake. So was Ric. We got dressed quickly and went outside to meet Max and the corporal at the jeep.

"They're over at my building, in the bar."

Ric dismissed the corporal and we got into the jeep and drove over to the building the CIA used. The bar there was always open. Once inside, I whipped up some Bloody Marys while Max and Ric admitted our scam to the Hollywood-type security guys. They told the real security guys everything we had done, including beefing up security in the guard towers.

"Well, it sounds like you boys have made our job easier. It'll save us some time and a few headaches."

They were great. Instead of being angry, they seemed happy that we did their job.

"Since you've done the hard part, why don't the two of you come with us when we meet Mr. Hope's plane this afternoon? As far as we're concerned, you are still part of our security team if anyone asks."

Bob Hope loved it when his security guys told him what we had done. He came over to meet us. There was no mistaking that famous profile. As soon as he entered the room, Ric introduced himself and was rewarded with a warm handshake. I followed suit, awed to be in the presence of the great man.

"Greg McPartlin, sir. I'm very pleased to meet you," I gushed.

"McPartlin . . . McPartlin. I know that name from somewhere."

"Well, sir, my brother Fred said he met you two years ago. It was at your Christmas show in Chu Lai. He was a Marine fighter pilot stationed there."

He looked closely at me for a moment. "Are you John McPartlin's boy?"

That floored me. Dad had been one of the pioneers of TV and was station manager for the second CBS affiliate in the nation out of Chicago. He had told us that Bob Hope and he had been friends years earlier when Dad was in radio. That was years ago, yet Mr. Hope still remembered.

"Yes, sir."

"Well you be sure and say hello to John for me. And keep your heads down while you're in country. They're shooting real bullets out there, and I hear the VC don't care much for SEALs!"

He knew all about the SEALs. There wasn't much Bob Hope didn't know about the military. I think he had been entertaining the troops since the Civil War. He had a very professional and friendly staff who really went out of their way to let servicemen like us feel appreciated. They even let us hang around with the rest of the security detail backstage.

The show started at around 5:00 PM. Ric and I were backstage, ogling the Playmates when Bob Hope walked by us, with the ravishing Ann-Margret on his elbow, in preparation for his entrance. Before he stepped onto the stage, he turned around, flashed that famous smile at us and said, "You two men stick around for a while. I might need you."

We weren't sure what he meant, but we didn't want to stay too long. It was only a matter of time before someone discovered our charade and, as far as we could tell, Max had ditched us. We could not spot his plane on the airstrip. Without Max, we needed another escape and evasion (E and E) strategy in the event we were busted. With all the brass at this show, that seemed a likely possibility. Ric and I started surveying our terrain, planning our E and E. The stage backed up to a mound of sand just off the beach. We could see the waters of the bay beyond. Like all good SEALs, we decided to follow our training.

"If we get busted and the MPs start coming for us, head for the water."

"Roger that," Ric said, flashing a bright smile at one of the passing dancers. "Until then, we might as well enjoy the show."

And enjoy it we did. We watched from the wings through all the songs and jokes, pretty girls dancing, and of course, Ann-Margret. After several encores, Bob Hope stepped out on the stage to give his traditional holiday greeting from the troops to the folks back home watching on TV. He said a few words, and then suddenly gestured at the two of us standing carefully hidden in the wings. "Greg and Ric, come on out here and let the folks see what the best-dressed troops are wearing these days."

We had no choice but to join him on stage. We were in civilian clothes: Hawaiian shirts, shorts, aviator sunglasses, and ball caps. We looked more like refugees from the *Road* movies than military personnel.

"I want to give special thanks to the United States Navy, for sending a couple of their elite Navy SEALs to oversee base security for us. These guys did a heckuva job."

On that note, Ric and I knew we had had it. I could see a few officers on the front rows signaling over to the MPs to detain us. Our VIP friend looked like he was about to burst a blood vessel.

Bob Hope saw what was going on and whispered to us, "Stick around, boys. Maybe we can give you a lift somewhere." Then he turned back to the audience and continued. "Thank you all. You've been a great audience! Merry Christmas!"

Ric and I escaped from the spotlight and quickly melted in with the stage crew. We helped them pack the show and load the entertainer's plane, while carefully avoiding the line of sight of anyone in uniform. The crewmen appreciated the help. They offered us a ride into Saigon.

"We should be landing at Tan Son Nhut by 2000 hours. They won't notice a few more bodies on board. We can drop you there if that will help."

We gladly accepted their offer and boarded the C-130. The front part of the huge plane resembled a regular airliner, with seating for about forty people. The back two thirds were filled with stage equipment and luggage. We took the two seats farthest from the front and slid down low, hoping no one would notice the extra passengers. The guys from Les Brown and His Band of Renown took the seats right in front of us. They noticed us sitting there and grinned. We made the "keep quiet" sign. They gave us the thumbs-up and sat down.

Bob Hope was the last to board, having to glad-hand all the brass who had come to see him off. When the door shut and we started to taxi, Mr. Hope picked up the intercom phone to address his cast.

"Congratulations, everybody, on a terrific show! You should all be proud. I know I am." Everyone but us applauded and cheered.

"By the way, did anyone see those two SEALs get on the plane?"

We sank lower in our seats, trying to use our vaunted SEAL skills to disappear into the upholstery. It might have worked, but the band members in front of us decided to help by ratting us out.

"They're back here!"

He peered in our direction until he spotted us. "There you are. Stand up, boys!"

Busted, we stood. And Bob proceeded to tell his whole cast how Ric and I had fooled the base security pretending to be with his show. Ric and I waved, and everyone turned around to give us a round of applause.

Once the applause died down, he continued. "Now, if these two knucklehead sailors can breech security so easily, you better look under your seats to make sure Charlie didn't stow away too!"

After the short hop to Saigon, we deplaned in a hurry, just in case any MPs were watching for us. We walked quickly right out the front gate and jumped on the first pedicab we could find. I told him to take us to the Presidential Hotel. The streets were packed, as usual, so it took about forty-five minutes to weave our way over to the hotel.

A couple of other SEALs were in the lobby when we arrived.

"Hey Doc! We all heard you were on your way to Australia."

"Nah! That was a couple of days ago." I flashed a big smile and put on my sunglasses. "Now I'm in the entertainment business."

26

Back to Work

I looked forward to getting back to the war—if only to catch up on some much-needed rest. After a final blurry night at the Presidential, we caught a hop on a supply chopper to Binh Thuy. We landed just in time for noon chow, then went to the Base Exchange to fill everyone's shopping lists. We picked up candy, gum, magazines, cassettes, and yes, even 8-track tapes. Once we'd finished shopping, Ric and I collected our gear from the DET Golf office. It felt kind of weird, after playing civilian for five days, to slip back into our cammies, grab our weapons, and put on our game faces to head back into the lion's den. Before we departed, we checked with the NILO to see if he had anything he wanted us to take down to SEAFLOAT.

Ric and I left the NILO's office with our weapons strung over our shoulders, and our arms laden with grocery bags for our teammates. It should have been business as usual, but something didn't feel right. I chalked it up to five days of very eventful leave and headed out to the helo pad to look for a ride. The Jolly Green Mail Helo was on the pad getting her fuel tanks topped off. This close to the holidays, the mail helo made two runs a day to SEAFLOAT, in an attempt to get as many packages as possible delivered to the men by Christmas.

Ric and I pitched in to help load the helo, remembering to leave a little room for ourselves. The pilot, a young jumpy sort named Tom, was in a big hurry to leave, and not all that happy to have passengers.

"So what's the rush? It's not a long flight," Ric finally asked.

"The sooner we leave, the sooner we can unload and get back. If we don't take off in the next thirty minutes I'll be stuck on SEAFLOAT all night. I want a fast turnaround."

"Hey, man. Don't worry. If you do get stuck down there overnight, we'll let you stay with us in the SEAL area."

My attempt at reassurance did not improve his mood. "Yeah. SEALs," he grumbled under his breath. "Might as well have a fucking target painted on the helo."

"What?"

He turned toward me, but did not meet my eyes. "You SEALs are the problem. I hear they've got a bounty on your head large enough to send every gook paddy farmer in the region out gunning for your hide. And I get to be the lucky sonofabitch to fly you home. And all I got for defense is a couple of door gunners."

For a moment, I thought he was kidding. Then I noticed how pale and nervous he was. To him, we were dangerous cargo. I sidled over to where one of the door gunners was loading his ammo.

"So, what's with him?"

The gunner, a tall black man with very little hair, had introduced himself as Anthony. At my question he looked over at the pilot and shook his head. "Boy used to fly gunships. But apparently he wasn't real good at it. Definitely not a 'hot stick,' if you catch my drift. The way I hear it, they took him off the gunships after he had a few too many 'mishaps.' But it's not like they can afford to waste a live chopper jock, so they saddle us with him. He gets to play out his tour doin' milk runs. We just fly to all different bases 'round the Delta delivering mail and supplies."

Realizing that this pilot might be happier if we were not on board, I asked if he wanted us to catch another ride down in the morning.

"Hell, yeah! I'd love that. Only problem is, I've got orders to deliver you two down to SEAFLOAT ASAP."

Oh boy! I thought, *we are in a world of shit with the boss.*

As the last package disappeared into the chopper, Ric and I slid behind the door gunners, our backs up against the rear of the pilot's and copilot's seats. We were in full gear with almost everything we would normally carry into the bush except Ric's radio, making a comfortable position impossible. Once settled, we inspected our Stoners, making sure they were locked and loaded as we took off over the Delta.

We were only about thirty minutes out of Binh Thuy when I heard a loud *pop*. Suddenly, grease and oil started dripping out of the hoses in the overhead.

Anthony, who was also the crew chief, looked up to see what was happening.

"Oh, shit!" he yelled.

That was not something I wanted to hear at 2,500 feet without so much as a towel to use for a parachute. Ric and I could do nothing but look at each other and shrug. I thought about how difficult it would be for my family to have me killed around the holidays.

The pilots started yelling at the two crew members as they all started turning valves and throwing switches. In seconds, the helo filled with smoke that quickly poured out through the open doors. We never shut the side doors on a slick to allow for ventilation in case of fire, but I had not planned to test the practice personally.

We descended to under 500 feet while the pilots fought for control. I could hear them frantically broadcasting a "Mayday" in between shouting orders at the crew. We were going down. Ric leaned way out to get a look at the area, trying to get his bearings in case we survived the crash and had to evade the enemy. I tried to do likewise, but from the air, the whole delta looked pretty much the same to me. Endless rice paddies, jungle, and canals. I didn't have a clue where we were. I gave up and started whipping through my list of prayers while desperately hoping the pilot could find a way to get this thing down in one piece.

I felt the engine shudder and stall. The pilot immediately yelled to the copilot that he was putting the helo blades into autorotate to aid descent, which I knew was chopper slang for a softer crash. I looked out again. Considering the fact that we had no engine, and clouds of black smoke was spewing out the doors, we weren't going down all *that* fast. And we still had some forward momentum. It looked like we were might get lucky enough to miss the jungle and crash into the lovely brown water instead.

I grabbed hold as we cleared the trees and angled into an old abandoned rice paddy. The soft mud cushioned our crash as we slammed into the muck and then sank up to the floorboards of the helo with a sickening *slurp*. We landed fifteen feet from a berm that formed a barrier between the crash site and the jungle. Ric and I wasted no time, scrambling out of the damaged bird and climbing up the berm in order to get a better view of our surroundings and provide cover for the crew while we awaited rescue. It was about 1700 hours when we put in, but it was getting dark real quick. A thick cloud cover was rolling in fast from the China Sea.

The pilots and crew stayed in the helo to assess the damage. As they checked it over they found that a couple of the hydraulic lines had been neatly cut halfway through. The cuts were made to ensure it would hold just long enough for the fluids to heat up, then the lines would burst under the pressure. Sabotage, of course. But this was something the crew was supposed to check for preflight. Apparently the preflight check had been overlooked in Tom's haste to get down to SEAFLOAT in time for a quick turnaround.

"Ric, as far as I'm concerned, you're in charge now," I half-whispered to him as we carefully scanned the nearby tree line for unwanted company.

"How do you figure that? We're the same rank."

"Well, you've been in the Navy longer, so that makes you the senior SEAL on this op."

He thought about it for a second.

"Okay. Fine. But only if you're in charge with me."

With that settled Ric pulled back to the helo. He and Tom studied the pilot's map in an attempt to figure out where we had crashed. With the coast currently clear, I slid back down the berm to see if I could help.

"Can we use the radio?"

"The pilots say the radio broke on impact. I haven't checked it out yet."

"So have you figured out where we are?"

"Pretty sure." Ric continued to look at the map.

"So where are we?"

"Right in the middle of Indian Country."

Of course.

On that note I suggested that the door gunners pull their M-60s off the helo and set up on this side of the berm so they could use it for cover.

"Any attack will come from the jungle in front of us, and not the rice fields behind. So set your 60s to cover the tree line."

Behind us, the open, flooded fields provided a natural defense, making it very difficult for anyone to sneak up on us from that direction.

Ric went back to the helo to check out the radio. Even though the pilots seemed certain it had been destroyed, I had faith that Ric could find a way to coax it to life. I climbed back up on the berm to keep our perimeter covered. A second later, I heard yelling behind me from the helo. I turned around to find that the two pilots had taken their pistols from their shoulder holsters and were nervously waving them around. The noise came from the door gunners, who were yelling and cussing at each other as they fought to break their machine guns out of their mounts in the chopper. It was getting darker by the minute. Charlie would be out hunting soon—if he wasn't already on to us with all that noise.

I slid off the berm and stormed over to the ruckus at the downed helo.

"Shut the fuck up! All of you! If you keep making all that racket Ric and I are going to leave you to Charlie's mercy and escape on our own!" That got their attention. "Now bring your weapons and get over here."

While Ric continued to work on the radio, the door gunners managed to finish breaking their weapons loose without the extra noise. I gathered all four of the crew together with me on the side of the berm away from the jungle.

"Okay, listen up, guys. I want you to keep very quiet from now on and listen to the jungle very carefully. We are listening for the sound of metal hitting metal. When Charlie comes, we should be able to hear him well before he gets here. But only if you are quiet." The VC, for the most part, did a lousy job of keeping their gear silent while moving through the jungle. This gave us a slight advantage.

The pilots were still nervously waving their handguns in the air, certain something was going to get them out of thin air. I grabbed both men and placed one on either side of my position with their pistols aimed forward toward the jungle.

"Only shoot in that direction. Nowhere else. Okay?" They nodded. "And don't shoot anything until Ric or I tell you to. Got that? No shooting unless we give the order."

I then placed the two door gunners each next to a pilot on the end so that each of them had a good field of fire on their respective side. I had just gotten everyone settled in when Ric crawled up next to me.

"The receiver is done for. But I think I may have gotten a transmission out before the battery went completely dead. Hopefully someone heard me." The *right* somebody.

Silence reigned as the four crew members looked at Ric and me like lost puppies. They were scared to death and counting on us to save them. After a couple of minutes, Ric looked over at the downed bird, fifteen feet away and about three feet below us, and broke the silence. "I know! Let's see what we got to eat for Christmas. I'm starved."

The crew eased up a bit and smiled as they saw Ric sneak back over to the helo and start unlashing the cargo that was still secured in place. After about ten minutes, Ric tossed some of the packages up to us. They were full of all sorts of goodies. Some cookies, lots of candy, canned soda, and even a few bottles of Yoo-Hoo, my favorite chocolate drink. The crew started to relax a little when they saw that Ric and I were very calmly smiling and enjoying the treats. Of course the calm was all on the outside. We were on hair trigger inside. Our trained eyes and ears were always checking in every direction.

RIC'S brief transmission was picked up by two Seawolves on their way from SEAFLOAT to Binh Thuy. They immediately radioed the base that our chopper was down and that they were returning to SEAFLOAT to assist in the rescue. Mr. Flanagan had Boh call out the troops for a quick warning order—which meant stand by, no drinking, something was coming down quick—and then met the Seawolf pilots on the helo pad. They immediately went to the briefing hooch to go over maps.

"Sir, whoever made that transmission was very professional. He never said he was a SEAL, but he gave us code coordinates. He confirmed that everyone was okay, but that we should feel free to come and get them whenever we had the time."

Mr. Flanagan had worked side by side with Ric as his radioman long enough to recognize Schroeder's style. Ric was smart enough not to mention we were SEALs because every VC in radio range would be looking for us for the bounty.

Boh poked his head in long enough to overhear that we were okay. "So LT, who said those assholes could run their own op tonight?"

The sky had grown dark with lots of low clouds and reduced visibility that made a night rescue mission too dangerous. Flanagan and the pilots determined they would search for us at first light.

IT was a dark, dreary night. Looking up at the clouds moving quickly across the sky, I almost expect to see snow on the ground by morning. It was, after all, only a couple of days before Christmas, and my Midwest body clock said I should be shivering instead of swatting mosquitoes in eighty-degree temperature. As the darkness closed in, the flight crew began to get increasingly nervous. I could hear them swatting at flies. Ric and I brought the four of them in close for a pow wow. I gave them bug juice to put on their exposed skin.

"Don't swat at the bugs," I whispered. "It makes too much noise. You have to lie still."

Ric tapped me on the shoulder. "I think maybe it would be better if just the two of us keep watch without their help."

Looking over at the fidgeting crew as they continued to swat at the bugs, I knew he was right. We had the skills to sit very still and not make a sound. They didn't.

We put the four guys right below us on a dry spot on the berm and told them to catch some sleep if they could. "But don't make a sound."

Ric and I took a position sitting back to back to cover all directions. We could feel each other breathing as our spines touched. When one of us started dozing off and bending forward, the other one would jab him in the spine to wake him up. About 0300, Tom tugged at my boot.

"I have to take a dump."

"You'll have to hold it."

"I can't. Those Christmas goodies were too rich."

"Shit."

"Afraid so. I feel the shits coming on."

Sympathetic to his plight, I signaled to Ric what I was going to do, and then had the guy quietly follow me about twenty-five meters to the corner edge of the berm. I thought there might be a little drainage ditch on the other side. What I discovered was a twelve-foot-wide canal at high tide. It was a narrow ditch with a trickle of water at the bottom when we crashed.

"Hurry up and go," I whispered, gesturing at the canal. "I want you to get in the water, very quietly to do it."

"In the water?"

"Yes, in the water. I don't want every VC in the area to hear you fart—or worse yet, smell an American."

When he finished, I had him crawl back over to Ric and tell him I was going to watch the canal for an hour or so until the tide started to drop. At high tide it was full enough to allow enemy sampans an easy passage.

The clouds gradually receded and the three-quarter moon started rising around 0345. By 0430 it was bright enough for me to make out the helo in the paddy and see where Ric and the guys were posted. As I watched, I suddenly heard the familiar sound of a paddle hitting the side of a sampan. Someone was rowing in my direction from the jungle side of the canal.

I also heard muffled Vietnamese voices. It didn't sound like they had any idea we were there. A voice from farther back up the canal gave the order to pull in to the bank. I heard the sampans crashing in the reeds. I let that noise cover me while I hustled back to the others. I arrived to find that they had also heard the VC. The crew was beginning to panic. They were all ready to run in an attempt to escape what they were sure was certain death.

"Calm down," Ric whispered. "Take your positions with your weapons. But don't you dare fire a shot until we do. There's a good chance the VC don't even know we're here."

The crew responded to the steely assurance in Ric's voice and returned to their positions. But we both knew the situation was getting tricky. If I could see the downed helo easily in the moonlight, then it was likely that the VC would also spot it once they got in the jungle. Even if they didn't know we were there, they would probably come over to investigate.

"We have to get away from the helo," Ric whispered to me.

"I agree. What do you suggest?"

"They're going to have to cross from the canal to the jungle. That will take them away from us. When they do, we can creep along the berm back toward the canal and get some distance from the helo."

We explained the plan to the others and led them along the berm, crawling as silently as possible until we were hidden in the shadows near the canal the VC had just vacated. We settled in to wait.

At 0515, the sun began to peek over the horizon. At almost the same moment I began to hear the sound of aircraft in the distance. I could also hear what sounded like a PBR on a river or canal nearby.

"Okay, guys. If the shit hits the fan, I want you to follow Ric and me up the canal toward the sound of that boat."

All of a sudden, I saw a half dozen VC come out of the jungle toward the downed helo, not forty yards away from our hiding place. They had seen the chopper. I tensed, ready to move if they spotted us. Before they were halfway to the helo, an OV-10 Black Pony screamed out of the sky right over the helo. It was only about one hundred feet off the deck. I wasn't absolutely sure the pilots had spotted the VC, but if they had, they would be calling in the gunships and we would be right in the middle of it.

Ric and I decided it was time to take the fight to Charley. He pulled

Tom, the pilot, aside and told him the plan. I saw Tom's face pale, but he nodded and put his flight helmet on. Ric then told the rest of the crew to stay low no matter what happened.

As soon as the VC started walking toward the helo, Tom rose up on his knees and started waving his arms while yelling out, "Don't shoot! I surrender! Don't shoot!" I was pretty sure most of the panic in his voice was real. He continued to yell and wave, making certain that all the VC could hear and see him.

While the VC focused on the pilot, Ric and I quickly flanked them. As I snuck through the brush, I could hear the unmistakable sound of helicopter gunships. They were very close. The VC tried to watch the pilot while simultaneously watching the sky for the approaching helos. They did not watch out for us. Six VC were no match for our two Stoner machine guns as we popped up behind them and quickly sent them to meet their maker.

Seconds after we stopped firing, two Seawolf gunships appeared overhead circling our position and looking for targets. Two Army slicks came in fast behind them and dropped all of Alpha platoon, plus Frank Flynn and a bunch of his PRUs. They were on the ground in moments, forming a perimeter and checking out the dead VC.

Ric and I collected the aircrew, as well as our composure, and walked toward the downed helo to meet our rescuers. Mr. Flanagan and Boh met us there. Their ugly faces never looked so good to me as they did then. Despite being covered with mud, we must have looked pretty good to them, too. Even Flanagan was half smiling.

"So," Boh said, in that Florida drawl of his, "you boys had a nice vacation? Are you ready to stop goofing around and get back to work?"

Ric and I just looked around, grinned like idiots, and gave Boh a big, muddy, hug.

"Get away from me, you faggots!"

Flynn and his PRUs headed into the jungle, hunting VC, while the rest of the platoon fanned out to enlarge the perimeter. A salvage crew flew in to check the downed helo. They determined it was too badly damaged to fix. They were going to have to blow it. Mr. Flanagan sent Ric and I back to SEAFLOAT with our crew on the repair helicopter to get some rest while they took care of destroying the chopper to make certain Charlie couldn't use it.

After cleaning our weapons and getting some chow back at base, Ric and I finally managed to find some shade for a little shut-eye.

Four hours later we were awakened by the arrival of the choppers bearing the rest of the guys and all the Christmas packages salvaged from the Jolly Green Helo.

"Hey Doc," Jonah Benanti yelled over at me. "I found an open package with my name on it. It was empty. What should I write my mother and thank her for?"

27

It Was the Night Before Christmas and a Truce Was at Hand Which Gave Time for the Viet Cong to Cover a Lot of Land.

IT was good to be back on SEAFLOAT, but while we were gone something had changed. We went out on operations as usual, but our success rate fell dramatically. Somehow the Viet Cong seemed to know where we were going before we got there. It began to appear that our security had been compromised. Every village emptied before we arrived, every hot lead turned cold, and every weapons cache was empty. No one was killed and we managed to avoid being ambushed. But even fresh intel, which was normally very trustworthy, failed to produce any results. At first it seemed that we were just having a run of bad luck. But when it continued to happen we realized the truth: We had a security leak somewhere. Someone on the base was feeding enough information to the VC to allow Charlie to evade us.

Lt. Flanagan decided the only way to solve that problem was to run an op that was so secret that no one but the people on it even knew it was happening. Even we would not know any of the details. He picked a day when no one would expect us to operate at all.

It was Christmas Eve day, and the entire U.S. military declared a Christmas cease-fire and started to wind down to take a couple of days off for celebration. All of SEAFLOAT prepared to party as only the Navy could. Of course the SEALs, having the responsibility as lead party animals, prepared in earnest for a serious multi-day bash. The blistering hot day felt nothing like Christmas to me as Ric and I started to set up the party. I blew up a Santa doll and Ric made a little punch for the platoon. In true SEAL fashion we were already making merry while drinking heavily—but all of Alpha Squad's drinks were alcohol-free. To any watching eyes we gave every appearance that we were starting a party that would turn into a long-lasting bender. And that's just how Mr. Flanagan wanted it. He knew that if any spies were on SEAFLOAT, the word would get back to alert the local Viet Cong that the SEALs weren't going to be going anywhere for quite a while.

The time, our warning order briefing took place in our sleeping hooch, rather than in the regular briefing room. A mix of rock and roll and Christmas songs provided cover music in the background as Flanagan shared his plan.

Shortly after dark, without alerting our scouts or any South Vietnamese, we left the music playing, quietly slipped out the back of our hooch, and boarded one of our STABs to head upriver. My buddy, Jim Gorman, came down from Binh Thuy to drive the boat. The only other people who knew that we were slipping out that night were Mr. Moody and his squad, who continued partying hard to cover for us, and the CO of SEAFLOAT. The CO was a gung-ho Black Shoe commander whom we all respected because he did his job well. We knew we could trust him.

Mr. Flanagan waited until we were under way to give us the details of the patrol order, so that no one outside the mission could hear us or have a hunch where we were going. The thought that we would be able to shoot or capture a bunch of VC with their pants down made us all pretty excited. The mission plan itself turned out to be genius in its simplicity.

We quietly set up a camouflaged position near the mouth of the Ca Mau River as it flowed into Cua Lon, a high-traffic area, and prepared to interdict any VC using the waterway. It was kind of like saying you were going to park where Interstate 5 and Interstate 10 merged to pick out a stolen vehicle. We slid in silent and unseen and hid our boat in the deeper shadows and growth of the left bank. Once settled in, we waited in the darkness like a spider for the right fly. The Christmas cease-fire guaranteed that a lot of boats would be out, but curfew was still in effect, and we were still, after all, in a free-fire zone, so we hoped most of the innocents would stay home.

However, we knew the reality was that a lot of ordinary farmers and fishermen would be out on the river during the night hours. If we didn't want to catch innocents, we had to be careful. Fortunately, a nearly full moon came up only a couple of hours into the ambush. The light gave us a much better view of both rivers from our camouflaged positions at the intersection. But Jim Gorman was our secret weapon. His fluency with Vietnamese gave him the ability to understand the bits of conversation that drifted over to us from the passing boats.

We let a lot of sampans go by and even a few small junks. Gorman could tell by what the people were saying to each that they were peasants and probably not VC—at least not voluntarily. Most of the night passed without the appearance of any likely targets.

Things changed early Christmas morning. While visions of sugar plums should have been dancing through my head, I sat on a Vietnamese river, suddenly at high alert at the approach of what sounded like multiple sampans. Jim observed them through the boat-mounted Starlight scope, which allowed him to see clearly at high magnification even in the dark. He signaled "many VC." Mr. Flanagan whispered something back to him and then signaled us to hit the spotlights.

As the night suddenly turned into day we saw a dozen heavily loaded sampans brightly illuminated by the intense glare from our floodlights. Most of the boats were closer to the other bank than to us. As the light hit them, they turned and started for the shore. Jim yelled at them in clear, commanding Vietnamese to stop and surrender or we would shoot. A few VC stopped and raised their hands, but some of them ignored the order, rolling out of their sampans or scrambling for the shoreline. We opened up on the ones trying to get away, while attempting to avoid hitting those whose raised arms indicated they wanted to surrender.

Someone threw a couple of concussion grenades in the water. The blast knocked out a couple more men who floated on the surface. There were about twenty-five to thirty Viet Cong and a large shipment of supplies and weapons spread among the various sampans. They obviously believed they had a free pass across the river that night, and were caught completely by surprise by our presence.

We stopped firing, but continued to shout at them to keep their hands up. Five of them pleaded with us "No shoot! No shoot! *Chieu Hoi*!" I had Jim tell them to check their buddies to see if any of them were still alive. If they were, I promised to try to help them.

Jim Gorman drove our boat over to the other bank and Mr. Flanagan, Boh, Ric, and I jumped onto the bank. Jim continued to give orders to the VC, who did exactly as he said, all the while carefully watching the weapons Preacher, Benanti, and Ritter held trained on them. Ric carefully checked the prisoners and handcuffed them with plastic snap-ties while Mr. Flanagan radioed for a couple of Swift Boats. He gave them our position in order for them to pick up the prisoners and casualties.

I set about checking for wounded VC. They had never had a chance to fire anything at us, so we had no injuries. Drawn by loud cries of pain, I climbed to the top of the riverbank to find two bodies lying perpendicular to each other in the knee-high grass. One man was still alive and whimpering pitifully. The other lay very still, facedown in the muddy grass. I immediately dismissed the dead man and kneeled down to examine the wounded fellow. His legs had been hit, but he had a good chance to survive with help.

I had just started applying pressure bandages when a sudden movement to my right caught my attention. Turning to look, I saw the "dead" VC wasn't. He had managed to climb to his knees clutching an American-issue bayonet from an M-14 rifle. When he realized I had seen him, he attempted to get to his feet, weapon slightly raised. Before he could stand I spun around and pounced, driving him face-first back to the ground and onto his own knife. The bayonet went through his chest and out his back. But it didn't kill him. He screamed in fury and tried to reach around to grab me.

By this point, adrenaline was racing through me. I couldn't believe this guy had tried to sneak up on me! I couldn't believe he was *still* trying to attack me with a knife in his chest!

"So you want to play rough?" I hissed. "I'll put an end to that!" While still on his back, I pulled my K-Bar out of its sheath on my web gear. Grabbing the thrashing VC by the hair, I stretched his neck tight and slit his throat. He still didn't die. In my panic I forgot the windpipe is about as strong as a garden hose. I had only cut about halfway through it and had missed his carotid artery and jugular vein altogether. Too many John Wayne movies, not enough practical experience. A bright spray of blood and air spurted from his neck as the VC really freaked out, trying desperately to buck me off his back.

Boh, drawn by the initial scream, rushed over to help.

"Shit, Doc! Just kill him! Don't torture the bastard!"

With one hand Boh pulled the VC from under me and sank his K-Bar down to the hilt, into the side of his neck, right between his shoulder blade and spine, silencing him instantly and permanently.

"Did you see that?" I was shaking as I climbed off the body. "That fucker tried to kill me!"

"But Doc," Ric explained patiently, "that's their job."

"Oh yeah. I forgot." But never again. Up until then, I had never had anybody try to sneak up close and kill me. It had never been personal before. Completely focused on my patient, I would probably have been dead meat if I had not glimpsed the movement. It was a serious wake-up call, and I swore that I would never be that careless again.

The Swift Boats arrived around dawn. By that time I had gathered and treated the three wounded VC who did not have life-threatening injuries. We also held eight prisoners. The mortally wounded and dead VC were to be left behind. Once I was certain the prisoners were taken care of, I went among the dying, giving a shot of morphine to any who were conscious and suffering. This time I injected it into their hip to take away the pain but not kill. In each case I left the empty Syrette next to them along with a second dose in case some of their friends showed up to help them. Anyone coming across them would know they had received some morphine and could then make the decision about how to use the second Syrette. Ric and Boh watched me, but said nothing.

Ric and I took the wounded along with our sixty-gunners, Dave and Jonah, on one boat, and Boh took the prisoners on the other. Mr. Flanagan, Preacher, and Ritter rode back with Gorman on our STAB. As we began the run back to base, I decided I had seen more than enough killing and suffering for one morning, especially Christmas morning.

As soon as we got back to SEAFLOAT, I turned over the wounded prisoners to Gary and the new corpsmen and headed off to clean my weapon. I could hear Christmas music blaring throughout the base, but it seemed to be the soundtrack for another world apart from mine. I dragged myself to the showers and numbly washed all the blood and dirt of the night from my body. I was so tired I almost fell asleep in the shower.

"Merry Christmas, Doc!" Mitch yelled as I stumbled past him to my rack.

Others also called out holiday greetings, but I did not respond, too weary to acknowledge the holiday. It certainly didn't feel like Christmas to me. I knew the moment I laid down that I was too tired and stressed to actually sleep, so I got one of my medicinal brandies from my footlocker and downed a few Darovan with it. *That should do the trick,* I hoped.

As I started to drift off, I found myself wondering if I had given the morphine to those dying VC out of guilt for butchering the poor bastard that tried to knife me. Was that why I left extra Syrettes? Was I trying to justify killing by tracking the lives I saved as though there was some kind of score being kept? I didn't have an answer. Mercifully, the Darovan and brandy took effect before I could torture myself further.

I woke to feel someone tickling my feet. I slowly opened one eye and glanced at my watch. It was 1600 hours, late afternoon. I tried to roll over and go back to sleep but the tickling continued until I couldn't stand it.

"Wake up, sleeping beauty!" Ric yelled. "Present time."

I opened my eyes and sat up as Ric ceremoniously presented me with a bottle of tequila. A very *familiar* bottle of tequila.

"Hey, isn't that *my* tequila?"

"Yeah," Ric admitted, grinning, "but it came from our Conex box so . . . Merry Christmas!"

I gave him the finger, and started to lay back down with my bottle.

"Oh, no you don't. You don't think we'd let you drink it alone, do you? I think we need some margaritas here!"

I gave up and climbed out of bed. It took only a few minutes to get out the mix, scrounge some ice, and find the blender, during which time I began to wake up. I spent the next several hours in nonstop margarita making, manning the blender until late that night. Being a conscientious bartender, I stopped occasionally to sample my work, to maintain quality control.

Flanagan even joined us. Loud and cheerful, he was definitely in his Radical Dick persona, though we would never dare call him that to his face. He definitely seemed to be enjoying the party. To my surprise, I was, too. The events of the morning faded a little with each glass.

Sometime that night Flanagan proposed a toast: "To Alpha Platoon! To survivors! We've managed to get through the first half of our tour without sending anyone in our platoon home in a box." Loud cheers sounded from everyone. "I intend to see to it that the second half of this tour is equally successful! There will be no Alpha Platoon casualties! That's an order!"

We all cheered wildly and downed our margaritas. After my close call that morning, I agreed wholeheartedly with that pledge. I poured another margarita and realized I only had a half bottle of tequila left to make more.

"Ric! More tequila over here!"

"We're out."

"So get some from the galley stash."

Ric shook his head.

"Or from the boat support guys? I know they have some."

"No. They don't. Not anymore. I've already snagged them all. There is no more tequila anywhere on SEAFLOAT." He raised his own glass and grinned. "If the CO asks, though, I have no idea what happened to any of it."

The VC would be free to operate that night, because none of us were in any shape to stop them. Now we really *were* on that bender.

Fortunately, it wasn't a problem. After the ambush, the word got out that the SEALs were even more dangerous when drunk than sober. As a result, it was the night after Christmas and all through our AO, not a VC dared stir anywhere near SEAFLOAT.

28

With Friends Like These . . .

OUR Christmas ambush must have convinced the VC their informant was unreliable. Our operational success rate gradually returned over the next several ops. I settled down to business as usual, helping Gary and the other corpsmen when on SEAFLOAT and working in the bush with my squad whenever they went out.

With the advent of the New Year and new decade, however, the flavor of the war began to change. Beginning in January of 1970, President Nixon started pushing hard to speed up the Vietnamization of the war. The Navy was under extreme pressure to train South Vietnamese Navy crews to operate the Swift Boats and other watercraft on their own. Up to this point, the U.S. Brown Water Navy had dominated the boat service, with Vietnamese serving primarily in support roles. But Vietnamization required that the South Vietnamese take over as much of their own defense as possible.

In an attempt to ensure a smooth transition from American control, one or two American sailors always stayed on with each boat for a while, working as advisors to the South Vietnamese crew. This not only allowed the crew a chance to gain experience with professional guidance, it also provided the Vietnamese with an extra safety factor in an emergency. If the shit hit the fan, only an English-speaking American could call in support from other assets.

Most of us didn't care for the ARVN, or South Vietnamese military. Not only were they usually chickenshits, but they were easily infiltrated by the Viet Cong. Most American pilots and military commanders didn't trust them. Rather than risk getting called into an ambush, most American gunships would only respond if they knew an American life was at stake. Boats with an American advisor on board were the only ARVN boats that would be guaranteed air support, or medical evacuation.

The Seawolves and our boat support guys were the exception. They might not come to the aid of any regular South Vietnamese military unit, but they protected our Vietnamese SEALs, the LDNN, or *Lin Dei Nugel Nghai,* with the same determined dedication they gave to us. And we would accept nothing less. We selected and trained the LDNN and though they, too, were Vietnamese, they were our SEAL brothers, as much a cut above the ARVN as we were from garbage. The Seawolves understood and respected that.

Chief Anderson, an experienced sailor, was one of the men assigned to be a Swift Boat advisor for the new Vietnamese crews. He also respected the South Vietnamese sailors he was attempting to train. Anderson believed that if he expected excellence, his crew would live up to the challenge. He was an old salt for this war, probably in his early forties, and had a full squad of little tow headed kids waiting for him back home. When he was on base, Anderson partied with us, though he often joked that he was an old family man and couldn't be expected to keep up with us young SEALs. Shortly after his protestations, however, he usually managed to either beat some of us at poker or drink someone under the table. So much for old age.

Chief Anderson had been on SEAFLOAT before we arrived and was due to rotate back to the states in a few weeks. He loved showing off the latest pictures of his kids, though I couldn't begin to keep any of their names straight. He was proud of his assignment as an advisor, though I admitted I didn't think much of the crew he had been given. He believed he could turn them into sailors worthy of his boat.

Anderson and a number of other Swift Boat advisors often operated their boats in groups in the rivers and canals around our region in order to prevent unauthorized VC shipments from getting through to the major waterways. It was during one of these operations that the VC managed to ambush the little fleet.

Gary had just gone to get some chow, leaving me in sick bay, when the word came down that some of the ARVN Swift Boats had just been ambushed. They had been operating in a river close by and were coming in with casualties. As the first available corpsman, I grabbed some supplies and raced for the dock.

I arrived just as the damaged Swift Boats started to pull alongside. The chaplain arrived behind me. One by one, the American advisors yelled out the status of their casualties to us as they jockeyed for position on the dock. As the reports came in, it was apparent that most of the casualties were inflicted on the Vietnamese sailors, and most of them either were dead, or had received enough first aid en route that they were not in immediate danger of dying.

I was starting to pull the wounded off the closest Swift when I recognized Chief Anderson's boat trying to come alongside. I looked up expecting a status report from the chief, but Anderson was nowhere in sight. I couldn't see him on the bridge or on deck. I could only see his Vietnamese sailors, who all seemed to be in a state of confusion. One sailor stood at the helm screaming something as he attempted to bring the boat in. He was obviously in a total panic.

"*Dai-uy* dead! Rocket killed *Dai-uy*!" he yelled, shifting manically between broken English and garbled Vietnamese.

"What?"

Dai-uy gone. Rocket got!"

It took me a moment to understand what he was trying to say. I finally managed to piece together what happened, something about them getting hit in the bow by a B-40 rocket. He said the rocket strike killed the *Dai-uy*—their name for any American who was in charge. The SEAFLOAT dock was already filled by the other damaged boats, forcing them to pull Anderson's on the outside of one of the other docked Swifts. The current was very fast and they were having a hard time getting it secured to the other boat.

"Where is Chief Anderson?" I yelled again.

The Vietnamese sailors on deck just shrugged their shoulders.

"Where's the chief?" I repeated, louder, repeating it in Vietnamese. When they still had no answer I decided I couldn't wait for them to dock. I climbed aboard the first Swift, pushing a Vietnamese sailor out of my way as I crossed the boat, and quickly jumped for Anderson's boat.

I could immediately see a large hole just below the bridge where the rocket must have hit, and there were chunks of fiberglass scattered all over the bow area. As I scrambled to get on board, the crew on Anderson's boat saw me coming and started jumping off, some leaping into the water, some onto nearby boats. As soon as I hit the deck I grabbed the first guy I could get my hands on and dragged him back onto the deck.

"Chief Anderson!" I yelled. "Where's Chief Anderson? What happened to Chief Anderson?"

I got no answer from the frightened sailor, despite screaming in his face. Then I saw the blood trail leading from the wheelhouse to down below. I quickly released the useless gook and followed the trail.

I found Anderson at the end of it. Colorless. Lifeless. Dead. He had bled out and probably had died within a few minutes of the explosion. I checked for fatal injuries and discovered a surprise. He only had about a three-inch gash on his inner thigh, but it had nicked his femoral artery. It was obvious that nobody had tried to help him when he was hit in the wheelhouse. He had dragged himself below to find something to stop the bleeding. The boat's first-aid kit was still in his right hand. Even without a medic he shouldn't have died. All the ARVN were taught simple first aid, including how to apply a tourniquet to stop the bleeding. Anderson knew what to do, but, weakened by blood loss, he had not been fast enough.

In most cases, his injury would have been serious, but not life-threatening by any means. I had seen and treated many similar wounds. It would only have taken a second for one of the sailors to apply the tourniquet that would have saved Anderson's life. I knew for an absolute fact that every one of those sailors had the skills and knowledge to save him. The fact that he had crawled below to attempt to do it himself was a testament to the worth of his crew.

Staring at his lifeless body, I was outraged. I was also very sad. This man had served his country well, left a widow and a bunch of kids, and all for what? The sailors he had tried to help obviously didn't care about anything but their own hides. I immediately yelled for the chaplain, knowing that Anderson would have wanted last rites.

It took only a moment for the chaplain to find me. I think he had also known Anderson, from the gentle way he performed the ceremony. I left him to his work and went topside, determined to see to it that the careless crew paid for his unnecessary death.

As soon as we finished treating the rest of the wounded, I wasted no time in finding SEAFLOAT's CO. I requested that Anderson's boat crew be brought up on charges of negligence and dereliction of duty. The CO tried to calm me.

"Son, now you know we can't just go filing charges on our allies every time something happens. We can't be sure of what really happened until we get the ruling from Saigon. And that won't happen until the medical examiner there makes his report.

"Given the current situation, I honestly don't think there will be any charges unless the report from the autopsy is conclusive and confirms the crew was negligent."

I told him again what I had found. "How much more conclusive do you want? Sir!"

"Well, if the medical examiner agrees with you, we may be able to do something. I just don't want you to get your hopes up. We have orders to work with the South Vietnamese, and we may not be able to do that if they're afraid of reprisals every time something happens to an American."

I left feeling even angrier than before. I had a bad feeling that the shits who left Anderson to die were probably not going to be punished at all. I spent the rest of the day making sure everyone who would listen knew exactly how I felt about what had happened.

For the next few days, tensions really started mounting between the U.S. and Vietnamese forces stationed on SEAFLOAT. I knew I was the cause, but I didn't care. The ARVN had become as much of an enemy in my mind as the VC. But at least the VC were fighting and dying for what they believed in. The ARVN soldiers and sailors seemed determined to avoid any type of risk or combat whatsoever. They preferred that we do it for them.

As relations eroded, officers from both sides started putting pressure on me to stop placing blame. They insisted it was no one's fault. The tensions I had caused were endangering regular operations.

A few days after the ambush, I was called into another meeting with the SEAFLOAT commanding officer. I was glad to see that the chaplain was already there, sitting in on the meeting. The CO immediately informed me that he had gotten the report back from the medical examiner on Anderson's death. I could tell from his expression that I wasn't going to like it.

"The U.S. Military Mortuary in Saigon has determined that the official cause of death was blunt trauma to the head." The CO watched me as he spoke. "It has been determined that the blast from the B-40 rocket hurled him back off his feet and over the rails to below deck, where he struck his head with such force as to cause instant death."

I was aghast. "But sir, you know that's not possible! That doesn't fit what I found! They didn't even examine the boat!"

He was polite, but firm. "That is the official determination of cause of death. I have no choice but to consider it final." He took a deep breath and went on. "It has also been determined that his crew could have done nothing more to save him. In fact, the senior Vietnamese naval officers on Chief Anderson's boat have been put in for a Navy commendation for getting the crew and boat back safely after the loss of their American advisor."

I felt like I was the one who had been hit by a rocket. Those lazy gooks were going to get a medal?

The CO leaned forward and focused his intense gaze on me. "I know you were Anderson's friend, but I need you to stop causing trouble about this. We need to put this incident behind us and move on. Officially, it was nobody's fault. We still have to work with the South Vietnamese, and we can't do it so long as you continue to insist that they were complicit in his death." He straightened and sighed, "Doc, I really need you to just let this one go so we can get back to fighting the war."

I grudgingly agreed to stop placing blame and just say it was nobody's fault. As I turned to leave, I looked over to the chaplain, still sitting quietly in the corner.

"Hey Padre, remember when you came down on the boat? After I called out for you to give the chief the last rites?" He nodded, but didn't look happy. "Remember seeing the first-aid kit still in Chief Anderson's hand?" He nodded again. "Kind of hard to pick up a first-aid kit if you're already dead." I turned to glare at the CO. "Instant blow to the head, my ass!" With that I turned on my heel and stormed out of the CO's office and officer's country. I didn't stop until I got back to the SEAL hooch, glad for some poker and a badly needed beer.

For the entire remaining duration of my military career, I never said another word about Chief Anderson's death. But I knew he was the one who really deserved the medal.

Anderson's death became a turning point for me. Up until that point, I was willing to work with the South Vietnamese Navy guys, even though I didn't respect them. But the Swift Boat incident was the straw that broke this camel's back. For weeks afterward, I thought about exacting revenge on the men who had left Anderson to die—only to be nominated for a medal for their cowardice. I was very close—too close—to sabotaging their boat and killing them all. Whenever I was alone I found myself thinking about how I would do it.

It would have been so easy to slip under their boat one night and place a charge, then have them sent down the river on a wild-goose chase. I imagined them disappearing downriver in their boat, then a few minutes later: KABOOM!

Who's your enemy now, assholes!

Fortunately for them, my saner side prevailed. They lived to receive their medal. But the war was never the same for me. I realized that our allies were more dangerous in many ways than our enemy.

It didn't help that rumors were running wild about a possible re-creation of the infamous TET Offensive of '68. The late January holiday had been fairly quiet in Southeast Asia in 1969, but we all had enough bloody memories of '68 to pay close attention to the rumors that Hanoi was putting together an even better planned and better armed attack.

As January progressed toward the Tet holiday, the SEALs were charged with beating the bushes to gather intel on any VC activities that might relate to an escalation. By this point in the second half of our deployment, we believed ourselves to be seasoned veterans. We all knew our jobs and the jobs of the squad as a whole. Mr. Flanagan and Mr. Moody started arranging for each of us to take turns as patrol leader for various operations. The determination of who would lead was often decided simply by assigning it to whoever came up with some intel and a plan. That person was then in charge of working the plan and running the operation.

Jonah Benanti, who usually performed as Mr. Moody's sixty-gunner, came across some information on some VC tax collectors who were working the villages in an area near us. Tax collectors were usually linked directly to higher VC operations. The capture of a tax collector would net, at the very least, the tax monies he had gathered, keeping them from Uncle Ho. At best, such a capture might also lead to good intel, other VC, or caches of weapons or supplies. Anything we could capture or destroy left that much less for the VC. If their supply line and tax income were damaged badly enough, they would be unable to mount any kind of effective major offensive. Jonah worked out a plan with Mr. Moody to set up an ambush site near a village that the tax collectors hadn't hit yet. Since no one knew exactly when the tax collectors might arrive at the village, Jonah and Mr. Moody decided the operation had to be run that night. Any delay might give the collectors time to get in and out of the village before we could catch them.

29

Jonah's Whale

WHILE Mr. Moody gave his squad the Warning Order for an imminent operation, Jonah tracked me down in sick bay.

"Hey, Doc, I got some good intel going and we've put together an op for tonight. I'm the PL. Do you want to go out with us?"

"You're the patrol leader?" I made a show of looking him over. Jonah had taken advantage of the relaxed grooming regimen most SEALs followed in country. His beard and hair had grown out in a rather haphazard manner that made him look a little like a cross between a mountain man and a hippie.

"Yeah. Is that a problem?"

"Nope. It just means you really do need me." It actually sounded like good therapy to me. I was ready to seek a little revenge for Chief Anderson's death.

"Then consider this your WO. The PLO will go down at 1800 hours."

"Whooo! Aren't we fancy with all those proper abbreviations?" He was so serious, especially compared to his usual more casual demeanor. "I think this leadership thing is going to your head."

"Just be there. 1800." He turned and left without even a snicker.

After setting up transportation, air support, and other logistics, Mr. Moody and Jonah came back to the SEAL hooch around 1700. Most of us took that opportunity to go for chow, but I noticed that Jonah went to our briefing room to work on his op instead. At about 1745, I gathered up some stuff from the mess and went to the briefing room.

I found Jonah seated at the briefing table, his trademark sunglasses forgotten high on his head, while he concentrated on an array of maps and charts spread out before him. At my entrance, Jonah looked up from his papers, then looked pointedly at his watch.

"You're early Doc. What do you want?"

"Since you ask, a cold beer, a warm blond, and a pizza." I slid into a chair across from him.

Jonah looked disgusted "No really, I'm busy."

"Hey, relax, buddy." I placed the food I had scrounged on the table in front of him. "Here, I thought you might be hungry so I brought you a sandwich and a Coke."

He thanked me and went back to work. He seemed very nervous.

"Don't worry, Jonah. You got me going along. What could possibly go wrong?"

He rolled his eyes, shook his head. "With you along? My mind boggles at all the possibilities!" But he relaxed enough to grab a bite out of his sandwich while I lit a smoke.

Like most of my patrols, Jonah used me as rear security and prisoner handler. Jonah was going to be up front, right behind X.T. Cossee, who would take point. They would be followed by Mr. Moody and the rest of the squad. There would only be SEALs on this op, no Vietnamese.

I finished my smoke and watched Jonah eat the last bite of his sandwich as the rest of the squad arrived for the PLO briefing. We all found a seat and listened as Jonah laid out the plan. He gave a very detailed briefing for what seemed to be a simple op.

We were to go downriver about twenty klicks to a canal, pass the canal, and scope it out while maintaining speed, go another three klicks, pull in, get off and patrol back to the canal we had passed. Then we would patrol up the canal until we reached a fork in the canal. Once there we would set up an ambush. After a couple of hours, the PBR would come back by out on the river, never slowing, so it would sound just like it was on routine patrol and heading home. We would then hunker down and see what came our way.

Every detail was covered. Jonah even went over the process for escaping from the enemy. We hadn't covered escaping the enemy since training. But it was Jonah's first official op as a patrol leader, and he seemed determined to do everything by the book.

In retrospect, this rotating of patrol leaders was a great concept. When it was each man's turn, we all went right by the script we learned in training. This left nothing up to chance. Being thorough and cautious became a trademark of our platoon. Mr. Moody and Mr. Flanagan were both "detail" men. They passed this concept down to each of us. Those of us who became instructors later passed it down to other SEALs.

Unfortunately, not all SEAL officers who became platoon commanders were as concerned about safety for the platoons as they were concerned about medals for their chests. But Mr. Moody and Mr. Flanagan insisted on keeping the big picture as their primary focus. Lots of times when shit started going down and firefights were breaking out all over the place, we were all itching to run and jump in our STABs and race to the action, guns a blazing. Mr. Flanagan and Mr. Moody always made us stop and think things through. They believed it was more important to fight smart than to just fight hard.

They were like the old bulls and we were the young bulls. The young bulls would see a bunch of cows down on the pasture and want to run down and get one. The old bulls would say, "No. Let's walk down and then we can get them all."

We were to leave SEAFLOAT at 2350 that night, so right after the patrol order had adjourned, I hit the rack for a two-hour nap. I thought I was tired, but my mind started racing the minute I put my head down. The briefing had been so thorough that I started playing out the op in my mind. At some point, I dozed off and my thoughts drifted into dreams.

I was on the PBR, ready for insertion. I recall the boat slowing down and pulling into the bank. As usual I was to jump off first, followed by the patrol leader, point man, and radio man.

I jumped off the bow, but this time the boat pushed backward, as a rowboat would. I turned and put my hand out to catch the rope to pull the boat back in. But the other guys just stood there in the bow, smiling and waving bye-bye to me as the boat receded. As they pulled away I heard Mr. Moody whisper, "That will teach you not to come out with my squad flashing that preppy smile of yours."

Suddenly, I was alone. I started to panic. Then I remembered the escape plan from the patrol order. It called for us to patrol up the canal until we made contact with friendly faces. I waited about forty-five minutes, hoping the squad would come back. Then I started quietly walking up alongside the canal into the jungle foliage. I soon smelled a cooking fire and heard American music.

Well, that didn't take long, I thought. *This has to be a joke.* I spotted the campsite ahead and made for it. As I casually strolled into the little camp, I called out to the shadowy figures crouched near the fire, "Is this some kind of a joke, you assholes?"

Just then, the figures all jumped to their feet, AK-47s pointed right at me. They were VC! I immediately opened up on them with my Stoner. But instead of mowing them down, my bullets just rolled slowly out of my barrel, going about five or ten feet before they fell harmlessly to the ground. I turned and began to run, but I wasn't getting anywhere. I found myself running in place as the VC got closer. I heard the music get louder and louder as bullets started slamming into my back, knocking me off my feet.

As I fell, I heard Ric's voice call to me over the loud music.

"Wake up. Wake up, sleepyhead. It's 2300. Curfew time. Do you know where your VC are?"

I opened my eyes to find Ric standing next to my bunk and laughing at me. He was poking me with his finger while holding his tape player up to my ear. I popped up, dazed, but very glad that it had all been a dream.

"Ric, I'm really tired," I yawned. "Why don't you go out tonight and take my place?"

"Yeah, right." He jumped up on his rack and flopped down. "Be sure to turn off the lights when you leave, Doc."

I got up, trying to clear the cobwebs from my head, and gathered my gear.

As I left the hooch, he called out, "Happy hunting!"

We got ready outside in the shadow of the lights coming from inside the SEAL hooch. While we geared up I could hear the guys from my squad opening beers and talking about chicks. We always talked about chicks. We had been in country over three months now, I don't think the government had put enough salt peter in our food because all the guys were getting a little horny. We were stuck in Vietnam as our sexual prime passed us by.

My eyes gradually adjusted to the darkness as I worked in the shadows. I could see Jonah gearing up nearby, looking more like a camo-faced hippie than a mountain man with his bandana tied around his head. I tied my own bandana in place and decided I had no room to pass judgment. We all looked a little scruffy—so much the better to strike fear into the hearts of VC. X.T. was even barefooted, since he was taking point. He said it allowed him to feel for trip wires or other obstructions in the mud.

At 2345, we silently boarded the PBR for the run up to the insertion point. We all knew that from now until insertion, all communication would be limited to whispers. After that, we would observe total silence, communicating only by hand signals.

As we pulled away from SEAFLOAT, I caught a sudden whiff of pungent smoke. Someone was doing some reefer. I sniffed and caught the eyes of a couple of Moody's guys. They smiled at me and quickly flashed me the peace sign. I didn't flash them back, hoping the smell of pot was really coming from the boat support guys on the dock and not the ones who would be at my back.

About forty-five minutes later, I saw Jonah use the Starlite scope to examine the passing shoreline. He checked his map. A couple of minutes later he signaled the driver to turn toward the riverbank. The driver slowed the engine and pulled quickly into the shadows. I crept up to the bow, jumping to the bank as soon as I felt the boat scrape the mud bottom. For a moment I had a terrible feeling that my dream was coming to life. I started to look back, half expecting to see the boat once again leaving me stranded, but before I had time to complete the turn, Jonah and Mr. Moody were at my side. The rest of the squad followed in short order and started taking up their positions. I drew a deep breath of relief as the PBR quickly pulled away to continue its decoy run downriver. Jonah shot me a questioning look, but I just smiled.

We held our position in silence, waiting to see if our insertion had been noticed. I listened to the night sounds of the jungle, attentive for any disturbance, but the only sounds were those of the river as it lapped the bank, mosquitoes buzzing around my ears, and crabs coming out of the mud, their movements making a light popping sound like a man walking through the mud.

After about twenty minutes, Jonah signaled the squad to move out. X.T. took point and led the way while I guarded our rear position and the river. I waited, watching our back until Mitch, who had the position in front of me, melted into the shadows. I followed him into the darkness, carefully trying to stay five paces behind him while casting a glance over my shoulder every couple of minutes to make sure we weren't being followed.

The early morning hours were cool, damp, and quiet as we silently made our way to the side of the canal. We avoided the existing path in an attempt to evade any possible booby traps. Charlie loved to put traps on all his trails, and many a grunt had fallen victim to them over the years. There was no moon and hardly any ambient light. Even with my eyes adjusted to the darkness I could make out very little. Twice I walked into Mitch's back because I couldn't see him. It was slow going. We had to be careful of our footing on the muddy ground while trying to avoid making any noise as we passed through thick growth.

After about two hours of walking, I saw Mitch come to a stop in front of me. Then the signal came back, passed silently from man to man until it got back to me, that we had reached the fork in the canal. It was time to take our positions for the ambush.

The rest of the squad settled themselves into the muck at the edge of the canal, while I climbed up the bank to take up a position above and behind them so that I could more easily cover our rear and both flanks. I liked being up high and dry, but the heavy growth obscured some of my view of the main canal. A fleet of sampans could come down the canal and I wouldn't be able to see them through the tall weeds.

As I settled in, I slid out my canteen and took a long, slow sip. Then I downed a Dexamil to stay alert. Putting my canteen away, I applied a little bug spray around my ears to prevent the mosquitoes from dive-bombing into my head. Attempting to get comfortable, I found an old stump from a mangrove tree that had been fully defoliated. I settled into position, leaning on the stump until I was as ready as I was likely to get. I peeled back my watch cover to check out the time. It was almost 0400. *This shouldn't take too long*. I hoped.

The early morning hour grew very quiet as the night critters turned in. The day critters hadn't gotten up yet. I heard someone in the squad clear his throat and another guy squirming around trying to get more comfortable. Three months earlier I would have considered those severe infractions of the SEALs' discipline to maintain total stealth. Now it was just a little noise. We had never encountered any sort of resistance that could equal our fire superiority, and all of us were getting a little lazy with proper procedures. When a platoon starts getting sloppy and believing the procedures no longer apply, that is exactly when they are most likely to get themselves hurt or killed. Of course, I didn't realize it at the time.

Mr. Moody, like Mr. Flanagan, did not cut corners and was always most concerned about his men. At first light, Mr. Moody crept from man to man to check on us and inform us what the plan was. I was the last in line. As Mr. Moody crept up to my position, he gave me a warm smile.

"Ready to take your breakfast order?" he whispered.

From my position I could see the sun was just about to peek up across the canal. It was still out of sight for the guys down on the lower bank. A slight breeze cooled my backside, and for the most part I was pretty high and dry and quite comfortable.

"Nice place you got here, Doc," Mr. Moody commented. I just smiled and put my finger over my mouth to shush him.

Just as he was about to slide back down to his position, I heard something. I cupped my ear to listen more closely. There it was again. Coughing. *The fish are about to start biting*, I thought. Mr. Moody froze as he too, heard the cough. The VC were beginning to stir—and they were not too far away. We both looked up the canal, trying to figure out which fork the sound was coming from. Noise plays tricks on you near water. We couldn't be sure of the actual location of the VC without more information.

A few seconds later I heard a small diesel engine coming toward our position. Mr. Moody signaled the squad to let them know what was happening. Jonah signaled everyone not to shoot unless he instructed it. As I stared in the direction of the sound, a large junk appeared, visible through the reeds of the canal. Very ornate, red and gold, and unusually well polished for this area, it moved slowly up the canal on the incoming tide. I couldn't make out any people on it.

When it was almost even with our position, the engines stopped. We watched as the junk drifted onto a small mud bar where the canal split. A few minutes later I caught the scent of burning incense. I watched as two men in brightly colored yellow and red monks' robes stepped out on the main deck from belowdecks and walked up to the bow. One carried a drum and played a quick tune while the other belted out some chants. They were only about twenty-five yards away and obviously had no idea we were there. Mr. Moody's eyebrows raised in question.

I leaned over and whispered in his ear, "Charlie's Chaplains."

Mr. Moody glared at me, looking as if he had eaten something very sour. I just shrugged my shoulders and grinned.

We knew the monks were VC sympathizers from the beginning. Up in Saigon they were even prone to lighting themselves on fire to promote the VC cause. What were the odds that these monks in their bright yellow and red robes had come this deep into Indian Country just to hold religious services? Somehow I didn't think so.

A few minutes later I heard shouting from upriver. As I watched, several sampans came down the canal to meet the junk. When they arrived, a VC in black pajamas climbed out onto the junk's deck from down below and started yelling orders. The guys in the sampans started yelling right back. I picked up enough of the conversation to realize that the junk was transporting weapons and supplies bought on the black market. They wanted money from the tax collecting VC in order to go back and get more. It sounded like they were fighting over the cost. As the haggling unfolded in front of us, more VC arrived to unload the junk.

I saw Jonah get on the radio to order air support. He knew these guys were going to attempt to haul ass back up the canal when we tried to take them. He wanted to make certain they had a surprise waiting when they did.

As we waited for the signal to open up, the VC up on the bow suddenly caught a glimpse of X.T., who, as point man, was only a few yards away from the bow. Before he could sound the alarm, X.T. dropped him with a single shot from his 9mm hush puppy. There was no gunshot report, only a splash as the body hit the water. It was followed by loud laughter from the other VC, who obviously thought the man on the bow had just lost his footing and slipped.

Mr. Moody and I used the commotion as a cover to get a better view of the area. We crawled quickly up the dike bank paralleling the river to gain a higher vantage point that allowed us to see more of the canal. Before the VC had time to realize what was really happening, Jonah gave the signal and the boys opened up on the VC, sending bodies everywhere. Jenkins, the radioman, called in an air strike on whatever might be up the canal waiting to come down.

As Jonah and the rest of the squad started pursuing the VC they had missed, Mr. Moody climbed back down to check the damage and make sure Jenkins was also calling for extraction. I held my ground and waited.

Suddenly I saw two brightly dressed forms sneaking off the bow of the junk. It was the two monks. They climbed over the rail, out of the canal, and started sneaking up through the brush right toward me. I found myself faced with a moral dilemma. I did not want to take out a man of the cloth, no matter who his god was. What if their religion was right and mine was wrong? As far as I was concerned, you had to play all the options during a war.

I stepped out of the bush and greeted the startled young monks with a polite, "*Dung Loi, La Day,*" or "Please stop and come here."

The monks stopped in shock, then suddenly started chanting and praying at the top of their voices. To shut them up I quickly handcuffed them and taped their mouths shut. I tried to lay them down, but they resisted and insisted on squatting. I found out later that Buddhist monks are not supposed to sit on their robes.

As I kept one eye on my prisoners and one on the terrain around us, I heard gunships overhead. They came in real low to check me out, then went after the bad guys. About five minutes later our PBR arrived and we started getting ready to extract. I left the monks taped, cuffed, and squatting in the high brush and made my way down to the PBR.

"What about the junk?" Jonah asked. "We can't just leave it."

We all agreed the junk was way too cool to abandon. Mr. Moody seemed skeptical.

"It would make a really cool party boat," Jonah insisted.

Looking at the polished wood and ornate gilded designs, I couldn't help but agree. Mr. Moody relented. It was Jonah's op, after all. We decided to tow our new boat home behind the PBR. We would bring it back to SEAFLOAT as a war trophy.

By the time we finished gathering up all the weapons and loot and had the junk ready for towing, our covering aircraft was low on both ammo and fuel. They had to turn back to base. Without air cover, we knew we had to get the hell out of there or risk getting overrun. X.T. climbed onto the junk and the rest of us headed for the PBR.

"So where are the monks?" Jonah asked as I climbed into the PBR.

"I took care of them."

"So where *are* they?" he insisted.

"What does it matter?"

"Just tell me where they are!"

I pointed over to the bank by the edge of the trail. "Let it go, Jonah. Let's just go home."

"Look, they are the enemy and this is *my* op, so shut the fuck up!" He climbed out of the PBR and stormed toward the spot where I had left the monks.

A few minutes later Jonah reappeared, climbing up onto the junk with an arm full of brightly colored robes. *So much for my attempt to save karma.* I angrily flipped him off from the PBR as we started to move, towing the junk close behind.

Jonah smiled and pointed up to the bank. I looked up. At first I didn't see anything. Then the brush parted to reveal two naked guys in handcuffs, with their mouths taped shut, standing helplessly on the bank. Relieved, I laughed and took up my position at the Honeywell grenade launcher. Feeling much better, I let a few rounds go back up the canal, just to ensure that the VC kept their heads down.

We were still several minutes out from SEAFLOAT by the time Jonah and X.T. managed to get the junk's motor started. Jonah immediately asked us to cut him loose. He said he wanted to come up to SEAFLOAT on his own power. We let them go and proceeded to our dock to SEAFLOAT. It was about 0800 and it looked like everyone had come out to greet us.

"So, where's Jonah and X.T.?" Boh asked once we were on the dock.

As if on cue the ornately finished junk sailed around the rear of SEAFLOAT with two guys in flowing monks' robes on the deck. Jonah, resplendent in his stolen finery, stood solemnly on the bow, beating a drum, as X.T. drove the boat toward the dock. Suddenly all the Vietnamese within sight of the new arrivals starting bowing and folding their hands as if Buddha himself had arrived. They didn't seem to care that the guys in the robes were round eyes.

When the boat got close enough for everyone to recognize the two monks, all the Americans started cracking up. The junk smoothly slid into dock. We all hooted and cheered as Jonah exited onto SEAFLOAT with all the dignity of his stolen station.

30

Take This Junk

I think Jonah's war trophy affected his brain. For the next few days, he refused to remove his robes, acting as if he really was some kind of cleric. He wouldn't allow anyone near the junk, and insisted on sleeping on it rather than in the SEAL hooch. Periodically he would bring out the drum and beat it while chanting something vaguely monklike. I started to worry that he may have hit his head when we weren't looking. X.T. insisted that Jonah had always been a little "off," and that there was no cause for concern.

I got word that some of the Vietnamese brass were disappointed with our operation. I knew it had been a complete success, so I went over to Jonah's hangout near the junk and asked him what he had put in his after-action to rile them up.

"Well, I told them that the VC tax collector must have gotten away, because we never did find any money." He shifted his brightly colored robes and went on in a mock serious tone. "After all, if we had recovered any money, we certainly would have turned it all over to the local Vietnamese authorities, just as the regulations called for. That way, we would be assured that it would end up right back on the black market, providing even more guns and supplies to the enemy."

Listening to Jonah, I realized X.T. was probably right. Jonah was just fine.

"So where is all the money we found?"

"What money?" Jonah looked at me with exaggerated wide-eyed innocence. "Of course, if there were any money, wouldn't it be great if it actually went to the folks who really need the help? After buying some beer for us, of course."

Jonah's op had netted more than a lot of weapons, money, and a neat boat. We also scared the hell out of the VC in their own backyard and disrupted their secret supply line. As a result, the whole area was pretty quiet all through Tet. In fact, most of Vietnam was spared any major fighting during the holiday.

"So can I see your boat?" I had never gotten a chance to see inside the junk since we captured it.

"Our boat," Jonah corrected, graciously motioning me to enter, just as if he were a monk gesturing me into his holy shrine.

Most of the peasant Vietnamese in our region were Buddhist, Christian—by way of the French—or just worshipped their ancestors. As I climbed on board the Buddhist junk for the first time and looked around, I realized that this boat was actually a floating chapel for many of our neighbors. I could smell the pungent aroma left over from incense that had been burning a week before. There was a little altar at one side of the cabin complete with a small hand-carved Buddha. It was built right into the support beam so it could not fall or break or be easily stolen.

It was weird. I could feel the spirituality of the place. It gave me some of the same feelings I got whenever I walked into a church at home. And since Buddha was so important to so many millions of people in this part of the world, I also felt I had better be very careful to avoid desecrating a holy place. Who was I to decide whether Buddhism was as valid as my own religion? After all, as far as I knew, Buddha could have been the same as my God—or at least his brother. I suddenly decided that it might not be good karma for us to keep this boat as a war trophy.

There were several little pieces of incense stuck in the wood near the altar. I lit one, and once it was burning, faced the altar and made the sign of the cross.

"Buddha. God." I paused for a moment. "Now that I have both of your attention, may I please ask that this stupid war come to an end fast? And that our platoon, fellow military men, and especially me, get out of here in one piece?" I chuckled, pleased with myself, and climbed off the junk.

Jonah was no longer on the dock, but several of Flynn's Kit Carsons were there, watching me leave the junk. They immediately came up to me to talk about the boat.

"*Bac Si,* please, give junk to us. Is a holy place. We must return it. Is very bad karma to keep such a holy thing. We will return it to our monk. *Bac Si* help?"

They wanted me to see to it that the junk was given to them, so that they in turn, could turn it over to their local Buddhist holy man. Apparently they, too, were concerned about bad karma.

"But the monks are working for the Viet Cong!"

The leader, an older man, got very agitated. He made it very clear that they didn't give a rat's ass who the monks were working for, holy men were holy men. "Very bad karma to keep such a boat! Must give it back, *Bac Si.*"

Apparently holy was holy no matter what. I realized that it must have been similar for our soldiers fighting in World War Two. Didn't the Germans have Christian chaplains, just like the Americans? *Maybe,* I thought, *God doesn't really take sides in wars. Maybe in God's mind, both sides are equally at fault.*

I told the KCs I would see what I could do, then I left to find Jonah, who had finally removed the robes and returned to the SEAL hooch. After I told him about my conversation with the KCs, he agreed that we should probably let the monks have the boat back.

"But we shouldn't just give it back to them like a present or something. We should let them steal it from us."

"Steal it?"

"Sure. If it really means that much to them, then surely they will have the balls to steal it back—especially if we leave it unguarded."

Of course to steal it they would have to sneak over to the SEAL barge, where we had it tied up, and take it out from under our noses. No big deal. We made a point of leaving the junk unguarded and the area around it virtually unattended. We even dropped a few casual comments about how easy it would be to steal the thing. We did everything but hang a sign on it saying, "Please steal this boat."

Three days later the junk was still there.

By the end of the week it became clear that the boat was not going anywhere without help. I decided the only way to get it back to the monks was to deliver it ourselves. Jim Gorman agreed with me. I grabbed two of our scouts, Tong and Chang, and told them to sail the damn thing down to the village. Jim and I would follow them in one of the STABs to give them a lift back. Taking advantage of the cargo space, I also loaded the junk with extra medical supplies, antibiotics, soap, and some extra rations I found lying around. Jim got on the radio to notify Frank Flynn and his PRUs that we were coming down to his village with a present. The radioman was pleased to hear about the junk, but told Jim that Flynn wasn't there. Frank and a dozen of his men had gone a few more miles down the river chasing some VC that had tried to infiltrate his camp the night before. Flynn's camp was located right in the middle of the village, and most of the civilians there were either related to the troops working for Flynn or to the ones assigned to us.

When we got to the village, the rest of Flynn's guys and their families came pouring out to the water's edge to see the junk. A few minutes later I heard the pounding of a drum. The chiming of little cymbals joined the drum as the crowd fell silent. Then, as if out of the air, a monk dressed in traditional yellow and red robes materialized majestically out of the crowd and stepped forward that he might formally receive his boat. He turned to face the crowd, and barked out a quick sermon. The gathered throng listened attentively. When he was done, they all bowed their heads and kept them bowed while he walked away. As soon as the monk disappeared into the crowd, the villagers quickly unloaded all the supplies we had brought and set about polishing up the junk.

As I helped with the supplies, a couple of Flynn's men approached me to request some medicine and antibiotics.

"What do you need medicine for? Are you sick?"

"Sick, *Bac Si.* Need antibiotics. Number one sick. No feel good."

Both men looked fine to me. "Let me check you out. If you're sick, I will help you."

"No. No. Just need medicine and antibiotics."

There was usually only one reason apparently healthy men would ask for drugs—to sell on the black market. Medicine was a very valuable commodity. "If you need drugs, I will give them to you. But I need to check you out."

"No. No. Is okay," they declined, walking away, all but confirming my suspicions.

"I will give medicine to *Dai-uy* Flynn when he comes back," I yelled after them. "You can get medicine from *Dai-uy.*" Whenever possible I preferred to administer any valuable medicines myself, or have someone like Frank Flynn do it for his people. It was the only way to be sure it really got to those who needed it.

"Hey Doc!" Jim Gorman yelled to me from the STAB. "Hurry up! Your services are needed! There's been trouble downriver. We gotta go!"

"What's up?" I yelled as I ran to join the boat. Tong and Chang were still in the village, so it was just Jim and me on the STAB. By the time I reached the boat, Jim already had his flak jacket and helmet on. He threw me a set as I boarded, then hit the throttle.

"Flynn's boat got hit on extraction," he yelled over the engine noise as the little STAB leaped forward in the water. "One of my guys is hit bad. I just got off the radio."

Your guy is my guy, I thought, *we are all in this together.* I threw the helmet in the back, and donned the flak jacket. SEALs don't wear helmets. I knew it was probably a dumb tradition, but I wasn't used to wearing one and was more comfortable without its awkward weight perched on my head. I don't know how the tradition started, but someone probably figured that if SEALs ever got hit in the head, it was the one place we couldn't get hurt.

I grabbed the large field medical kit, and an M-1 bag, stored in the STAB and made a quick inventory of its contents to make certain nothing had been pilfered since I last checked it. Everything was there. Then I grabbed my Stoner with one hand and the radio with the other. I radioed SEAFLOAT to find that they had been monitoring Flynn's distress call.

"We are launching Seawolves and a Medivac. ETA approximately forty-five minutes," the voice cracked from the radio.

I could see a PBR up ahead. "Roger that. We are almost on station and will render assistance until the Medivac arrives."

As Gorman slid our STAB alongside Frank's larger PBR, I jumped over the rail onto the deck. The first-class boatsman's mate skipper immediately directed me to the bow. His .50 cal gunner had been hit and was being looked after by one of the other crew members. Flynn and his guys had set up a perimeter to protect the vulnerable boat. Apparently the PBR found a booby trap in the canal. The hard way. When the PBR turned into the waterway looking for VC, they tripped the bomb, causing a sizeable explosion. It was a homemade device full of razor-sharp metal fragments. The area around the canal was fairly secure, and I suspected that whoever set up the device was probably long gone.

I hurried in to the bow to check out the wounded man. He lay in the forward gun well, drenched with his own blood.

"So, what's up man?" I smiled with a deliberately casual air in an attempt to reassure the wounded man. There was a lot of blood everywhere, typical of face and head wounds. Fortunately, most head wounds usually looked a lot worse then they actually were.

"I'm hit, you shit!" he yelled. "Are you going to help me or not!"

I knelt down next to him, attempting to get him to calm down so I could check his wounds. "Well, you know we charge extra for making house calls."

For the most part, he had been protected from the shrapnel by the gun well, his helmet, and his flak jacket. His sunglasses saved his eyes from the sharp metal frags, even though both lenses had been broken. As I was dabbing at his facial lacerations, I noticed a deep gash in the side of his neck. I started to touch it.

"Aarghh!" he screamed. I realized this guy was starting to go into shock from the sight of his own blood and the pain. I gave him a shot of morphine for the pain. Once it began to take effect, we slowly lifted him out of the gun well and laid him down on the bow on a dry tarp. I quickly checked the rest of his body and started an IV of serum albumin. He was dehydrated, so I lifted his head to give him some water.

"No. I don't want any. Just leave me alone. Get away from me."

"Sorry, man. You have to have a sip. I need the water in you so I can check for more leaks."

He half smiled as he gulped down a huge swig.

"Doc, don't make me laugh. It hurts too much."

I wasn't upset at his earlier attitude. A lot of wounded get mad at the corpsmen who are trying to help them. Sometimes they just give up on themselves too soon and don't want to be moved because of the pain. It is important to try to keep these patients positively focused. As people get increasingly shocky, phantom pain gets worse, and sometimes people who don't appear to be hurt badly at all just die. Then there are times when guys are all messed up, with loss of limbs, guts hanging out, bones dangling, and worse. You figure, no way is this guy going to make it with this much damage. Then a month later, you get word that they are recovering fine. You never know. It's all in God's hands—and his brother Buddha.

After stabilizing the gunner, I checked the gash in his neck again and realized the reason it wasn't bleeding any worse was because of a big chunk of shrapnel in the hole. I realized I had to keep him from moving his head. Any movement might start a bleeder. Belowdeck on the PBR, they had a portable stretcher hanging on the overhead. Up until now, it had only been used for napping and catching some rays. I had them bring it up to the bow, open it up, and help me roll the wounded fifty-gunner onto it, all the while holding his head in the exact position it was when we moved him onto the deck.

I put a few pressure dressings on some of his wounds, then proceeded to immobilize his head with Ace bandages. I wrapped them securely around his forehead and then stretched them tight and tied them off on the stretcher's handles, repeating the process on the other side.

The bandages would keep his head from rolling from side to side. I also tied one elastic wrap to the crossbar on the back of the stretcher, then looped it under his chin to keep his head from tilting forward and down. I finished the package by securing a rolled flak jacket above his head to keep him from sliding forward on the stretcher, continuing to work until I heard the helos coming in overhead.

There was no place for the helo to land. The skipper directed the Medivac chopper to hover near the bow so we could hand off the stretcher to the crew on board. This was a tricky maneuver for even a very skilled pilot. The pilot brought his bird down low and tried to hold a steady hover just off the bow. Now, Medivac pilots are very brave. It takes a lot of balls to fly into a hot LZ in an unarmed slick to pick up wounded men. But they are neither highly skilled nor seasoned pilots, because if they were, they would be flying gunships instead.

We lifted the stretcher off the PBR's deck and started to put it on the chopper. Suddenly the chopper wavered, lifting a few feet into the air. The sudden movement jarred the stretcher, almost turning it over and dumping my patient. We caught the stretcher and the pilot steadied the bird so we could try again. During the second attempt, I noticed a ton of blood soaking through the bandages. All the shuffling the guy endured must have nicked a bad one. He would bleed to death if it wasn't staunched. I knew I needed to stay with him to stop the bleeding. The second attempt was successful. Once he was on board, I hopped in with him. As we started to lift off, Jim threw me my medical bag and I flashed him the okay sigh.

We had barely started to gain altitude when I heard the ping, ping, ping of bullets ripping through the skin of the aircraft. We were under fire.

"Let's get out of here!" I yelled, trying to hold on to both the frame and my patient. Then I heard a loud "puff" and a couple of "pops." *This is not good!* I thought. *The rounds are going right through the fuselage.* My thoughts flashed back to my ride on the Jolly Green Helo as the chopper started to slew. *"Not again!"*

"Try to stay over the river!" I screamed to the pilot.

"I can't!" he yelled back, frantically hitting switches and fighting the stick. "I can't control it!"

We were sixty or seventy feet over the water and headed for the jungle when the deck suddenly lurched, and I found myself on the outside of the bird, flying without an aircraft. I tumbled headfirst toward the riverbank. I don't remember hitting the ground.

I landed in about three feet of water—which probably cushioned my fall enough to save my life. According to observers, I got up, lurched forward into the mud, rolled over onto my back, and just laid there like a dead fish.

Through my stupor, I heard the explosion as the Medivac crashed into the jungle and blew up. I felt blistering heat from the blast wash over my body. *Oh swell!* I thought. *I'm dead and on my way to hell. I can already feel the fire!*

Boh and Ric were riding in one of the Seawolves, flying escort for the Medivac. After watching my fall, they were in the water and on me in less than a minute. It took several minutes for me to regain consciousness.

When I came to, I started freaking out. All I could think about was the guys on the Medivac and the horrible pain in my head. I just knew I had been shot. Nothing else could hurt that bad.

"I can't hear anything," I screamed. "My head hurts like hell! I've been hit!"

"I'm tellin' ya there ain't no bullet hole, Doc," Boh insisted, firmly.

"Check again. I know I'm hit." I imagined the bullet lodged in my brain.

"We've checked three times, Doc. No holes," Ric verified. "Now come on, let's get you outta here."

They swam me out quickly to the Seawolf helo hovering over the water. Once I was inside, Boh and Ric went back to shore to see if anything could be done for the downed Medivac while the Seawolf pilot headed back to SEAFLOAT.

I had already forgotten everything I had said to Boh and Ric. But some part of my damaged brain realized the other chopper was down and that my place was down there helping the wounded. I had at least one patient down there!

"I need to help them!" I yelled to the pilot, pointing at the column of smoke rising up from the jungle. "Please put me back down there! They need my help!"

The door gunners politely kept me from falling out of a second helo while the pilot ignored my raving.

My brain started to clear by the time we reached SEAFLOAT, but my head felt like it was being crushed by vise grips, and I had no memory of anything that had happened after my fall. I had been taught that a patient with a concussion should not be allowed to go to sleep. That was fine if you weren't the one whose head was trying to explode. I went in to sick bay, took some Darvon with a lukewarm swig of beer, and proceeded to pass out right on the examination table.

31

Where Are the Nurses?

I drifted in a blissful fog of unconsciousness for a long time before I felt myself trying to wake up. I started to regain consciousness, only to run into a wall of pain that drove me back down into darkness as I passed out again.

That cycle continued for hours as I seesawed between dark oblivion and half-conscious pain before finally managing to fight my way back to full awareness. At first, I was afraid to open my eyes, knowing the light would make the pain start again. As I lay there, eyes still shut, I realized I was clean and cool. I could feel an oxygen mask on my face. *Man, I must have really been hurt bad. They sent me home! I must be in Great Lakes at the naval hospital.*

I smiled, thinking of the nurses there, and opened my eyes.

Instead of nurses, I found myself surrounded by the much uglier faces of Gary, Ric, Boh, and the two corpsmen. *Oh shit! I'm not hurt and I'm definitely not at Great Lakes!*

"It's about time!" Ric was obviously relieved. "It's been fourteen hours! Where have you been? I can't find the key to our Conex box and we need some more tequila."

Oh God! Back with my loved ones, again!

"S'nice to see you too!" It hurt to talk, but at least the ringing was gone from my ears. "Did any one else make it? I don't remember anything."

"'Fraid not," Boh replied. "You were the lucky one. After you fell out, the helo crashed in the jungle and exploded on impact. No survivors."

He must have seen the look on my face. "You couldn't have done anything. They died in the explosion."

For the next few days I kept mostly to myself, sleeping as much as I could. My rotation to go on R&R was coming up soon. I would be meeting Vicki in Hawaii, so I spent a lot of time writing to Vicki and the rest of my family, and re-reading letters from home. Nobody back home really had a clue about what I was actually doing and I made a point of keeping it that way. I found it was best to keep family in the dark. After all, I was a corpsman and, as far as they knew, I had a cushy little job in a field hospital taking care of the wounded or sick. I could see my mother going into hysterics if I ever told her the truth: "Oh by the way, Mom, I spend my days killing VC. Just the other day I was the only survivor of a helicopter crash. I only have a small bump on my head, though I can't remember what any of you look like. But I'm sure I'll be good as new after I get a few more kills."

Things were pretty quiet in our area for the time being. I had almost two weeks before my scheduled R&R with very little to do. When a Medivac chopper stopped over at SEAFLOAT, bound for the hospital ship *Repose*, I decided it was a good time to visit the hospital ship. The *Repose* was anchored out in the South China Sea, only about thirty minutes away by helo. She had been assigned to that location in anticipation of heavy fighting over the Tet Holiday. I arranged to hitch a ride with the Medivac, then set about gathering some trade goods for the trip. I had never been aboard a hospital ship, but I knew corpsmen well, so I packed a bunch of VC flags, K-Bar knives, and other assorted war souvenirs for trade. We had to fly over the heart of Indian Country to get to the South China Sea, so I dressed accordingly in full web gear with all my weapons at hand. I knew too well what could happen if a helo went down in hostile territory.

Surprisingly, even though this was my first time back in a helo since the day of the crash, the flight did not bother me. I had become so used to flying in a helo that it seemed as natural as any other means of transport. It helped that I had almost succeeded in blocking out the entire crash from my mind.

As we landed on the flight deck, a couple of corpsmen ran up to the helo pushing a gurney. I realized they expected casualties. Before we were completely down, one of them started helping me out of the helo while the other grabbed my gear.

"Where are you wounded? Are you bleeding?" The corpsman was pulling at my web gear looking for signs of injury.

I smiled, pulling away and patting them on the back. "I'm fine," I yelled over the rotor noise. "I'm a corpsman in SEAL Team One, and this is a social call."

I was met by disbelief in both their faces.

"Corpsman my ass!" the tallest one shouted back gesturing at all my weaponry. I admit I definitely didn't look like any corpsman they had ever seen. Besides my web gear, I was carrying my Stoner machine gun and had two LAAW rockets, my pistol, K-Bar, and assorted hand grenades all strapped to my web gear. Oh yeah, I did have a little tiny medical kit at the top of my web gear between my shoulders.

The medical pilots vouched for me as they exited the helo. One of them grinned and said "Yeah, haven't you ever seen a SEAL before?" I think he was enjoying the whole thing.

I followed the pilots into air ops and reported aboard. I asked permission, as a visiting corpsman, to meet with supply and talk with a few doctors. Surprisingly, everyone was very cordial, if somewhat awestruck. The guys on the *Repose* were not used to seeing a fully geared field corpsman—unless he was arriving feet first on a stretcher. Most field corpsmen only visited the hospital ship if they were shot up, usually because they'd been working with the marines.

I had only been on board for a few minutes when I heard a voice call my name.

"Greg? Greg McPartlin? It *is* you."

I looked up to see a vaguely familiar face.

"It's Tom Smith. Remember me? We trained in Key West together."

Now I remembered. Tom Smith had been one of the corpsmen who trained with me in Key West. He was also one of the thirteen who washed out. It had worked out well for him. He had landed a cushy gig on the *Repose* and didn't have to worry about crawling around in the mud or getting shot at. He had been on the hospital ship for almost a year and his tour was almost over. His time on board also made him one of the senior guys in his division. He insisted on giving me the royal tour of the ship, introducing me around as his friend the SEAL. The ship itself was impressive. It was literally a floating hospital, complete with real operating rooms, wards for various types of patients, and nurses. I especially liked the nurses.

Tom apparently liked them, too. "Yeah, and if I hadn't had that damn swimmer's ear, I would have been a SEAL too," he bragged to the nurses, the other corpsmen, and anyone else who would listen. "My buddy Greg and I would have been shooting VC together."

I smiled and played along. He was a bit of a blowhard, but he was valuable as my point of contact on this little excursion. If the tale helped him to impress his friends, it certainly didn't hurt me. I no longer had any doubts about my status as a SEAL.

After noon chow, I walked through the wards, talking to some of the wounded Marines and sailors from our area. I had been the corpsman who initially treated some of them, and had known others as comrades in arms. They shared a different sort of camaraderie with me than with the other corpsmen on the ship, because we had been in "combat." Unlike the other corpsmen and doctors they saw, they knew I understood everything they had endured.

As I walked through the wards, I couldn't help but notice that the patients were getting some great gourmet-quality chow. There were steaks and lobsters and all kinds of delicacies. I hadn't seen food of that quality served outside an admiral's reception. Perhaps it was the Navy's way of saying "thank you" for their sacrifices. All I knew was that I had to get a couple of cases of those steaks to bring back home.

I started talking to the cooks, and discovered that one of them really needed a VC flag and a captured commie weapon. Fortunately I happened to have both. I also found a supply guy in search of war trophies, and even the master of arms, who really needed a K-Bar, a VC flag—oh yeah—and his picture taken while holding my Stoner.

The awesome look and scarcity of Stoner machine guns made mine an instant hit wherever I went with it. I was out on the fantail of the great ship showing the weapon to Tom when the CO of the *Repose* came out to meet me—and see the Stoner. I could tell he was more impressed with the weapon than with me.

"Yes sir, this is my Stoner 5.56mm belt-fed, gas-operated machine gun. Would you like to test fire it off the fantail, sir?"

I could tell that he couldn't believe the offer. "No. I couldn't," he declined. But I recognized the hungry gleam in his eyes. "Does it really shoot as fast as people say? A thousand rounds a minute?"

I held the weapon out to him. "Why don't you see for yourself, sir?"

He took it from me, almost lovingly caressing the stock and barrel. It was very quiet and the waters were calm as we stood at the back of the big hospital ship, looking out on the South China Sea. I flashed back to that day at MACV headquarters as the captain stepped over toward the edge of the fantail deck.

"Uh, sir, perhaps I should warn you that the last time I did this, the whole base went on alert. Shouldn't we tell somebody we're going to be shooting back here?"

The captain stopped and looked at me for a moment. "You have a point, son. And I know just the thing. I think a general-quarters drill is just what we need to break up a boring afternoon, don't you? Hold her for me?" He handed the Stoner back to me. "I'll be back in a moment."

I watched him walk over to where his aide was waiting, near a rear hatch. The next thing I knew the GQ alarm started to wail. Suddenly, guys were scrambling everywhere, putting on their helmets and life jackets and racing to man their battle stations.

The captain's voice broke through the wail as he used a remote speaker system to address the crew. "Now hear this. This is a drill. This is your captain speaking. I will be test-firing an actual U.S. Navy SEAL Stoner machine gun off the fantail in sixty seconds. This is only a drill."

I looked over at Tom and rolled my eyes as the captain hung up the microphone and jauntily strolled back over to us, a big grin on his face.

"Now we can see what she can do."

I handed the weapon to the captain and showed him how to take the safety off. He pointed the barrel toward the water and prepared to fire.

"Fire when ready. Use only quick, short bursts on the trigger." I stepped back to give him room.

He pulled quick, expending about five rounds. He stopped for a moment, grinning like a kid with a new toy, then held the trigger down and fired into the sea until the ammo box was empty—a ten-second burst that expelled almost one hundred rounds.

"Captain!" I yelled. "I told you quick short bursts! Shit! You almost cooked my barrel!" I ran to him to reclaim my weapon. Stoners fired at such a high rate of speed that firing too many rounds at once could cause the barrel to heat up to the point that it became red hot. When this happened the metal often warped to the point that it would no longer fire correctly.

"Wow!" He carefully handed the weapon back to me, a look of admiration on his face. I quickly checked it over to make sure it wasn't damaged. The barrel was too hot to touch, but looked as though it was okay.

By this time a crowd had gathered, drawn by the sound of machine gun fire. They all wanted to see my Stoner. I let them look at it, but I was now down an entire box of ammo. I only had two extra boxes on my web gear. I didn't feel comfortable traveling around with less than three hundred rounds, especially with a weapon that could shoot a thousand rounds a minute. Of course the *Repose* didn't carry ammo for a Stoner, but the ships armory did have 5.56 shells. I ended up picking up the discarded links off the deck and borrowing some 5.56 ammo from the armory. I clipped them together to make another belt of ammo and loaded that in the box of my Stoner. Once again I was grateful that the ammo, if not the links that held it, was interchangeable with other weapons.

The captain was very nice and even invited me up to the ward room for supper. I declined, saying I had to clean my weapon, and I really wanted to spend some time with my friend, Tom. That last was bullshit. I just didn't want to sit around with a bunch of officers grilling me about life in the jungle.

Unfortunately, I did not manage to avoid getting grilled about my life. During dinner with Tom and the other corpsmen, I mentioned the helicopter crash in passing. Some of them had heard about it. After dinner a funny little man with thick curly hair that stuck out at odd angles cornered me. He reminded me a little of a mad scientist. He turned out to be a shrink. The man wanted to know my feelings about the crash, and how I was dealing with them, and how my life had changed.

"I really don't want to talk about it." I didn't remember most of what happened, and I certainly didn't want to dwell on it.

"But they say you almost died. I believe people are changed by proximity to death. Such things fascinate me. If you could just tell me what you saw and felt."

"But I . . ."

"It usually helps to talk about it. And it would definitely help me in my research on the near-death experience."

Since he was so persistent, and seemed unable to take no for an answer, I decided to lay it on him thick. *Analyze this!*

I described the helo being hit, adding a nice embellishment about how my whole life started playing out in slow motion. He hung on my every word as I described the helo screaming toward the jungle as I flew out the open doorway into the river, crashing with such force that I sustained a concussion and was knocked out. At this point, I started really laying it on, telling him how I saw myself rising above my limp body as it lay in the mud. All was quiet and peaceful as my religious beliefs played themselves out in my mind.

"I heard music, and saw the hand of God reaching down through the clouds to take me home to his heavenly kingdom. I was so thrilled and excited," I told Mr. Shrink, "until I started to regain consciousness, and the hand of God pulled away from me before I could grab it. Then my head felt like it was splitting into pieces. As I was coming to, my ears started ringing so loud I couldn't hear anything else. My vision was blurry, and I was very disoriented. Everyone says I just sat there, dazed, with a blank stare on my fact, looking out toward the center of the river. I didn't even notice my rescue helicopter coming in."

"My goodness. Thank you for sharing that with me. That's really quite an amazing story."

"Yeah. I thought it was pretty amazing myself—especially since I just made most of it up. Fact is, I don't remember anything about the crash itself. My memories start sometime after I was rescued. The only reason I know what happened is because other people told me." I had him now.

"Fascinating."

Instead of being put in his place, he looked like one of those science guys who has just discovered a new species of bug.

"Of course your subconscious knows what really happened."

Huh?

"How do you know it wasn't your subconscious mind telling the story just now—the real truth that you haven't faced?"

Now I was really confused. I thought I was really going to bullshit this guy, and instead he did a complete 180 on me with his psychoanalytic crap. All without batting an eye. I always thought I was good at bullshitting. But I'll bet Mr. Shrink ended up with a very lucrative practice when he got out.

After that, I needed a drink. I ended up staying aboard the *Repose*, playing poker and drinking Navy brandy all night. The next morning I went into the radio room at air ops to see if I could hitch a ride back to good old Solid Anchor.

Unfortunately Solid Anchor, or SEAFLOAT as I knew it, was not exactly a hot destination. Our little home away from home was not a place anyone wanted to go unless he had to—and at the moment, it looked like no one had to. I spent the morning striking out. Finally, around noon, I managed to get in contact with a pair of Seawolves out of Binh Thuy who were en route to Solid Anchor. I convinced them to detour by the *Repose* to pick me up.

"It will be worth your while. I promise!"

Since these guys usually fly in pairs, I convinced both of them to land on board the ship. I was on the pad, waiting for them, with a large pallet stacked full of medical supply boxes and a few friends. As soon as they touched down, I ran up to the lead pilot's door and pointed to all the boxes. I signaled not to shut down, this would only take a minute and not to answer his radio. He looked at all the boxes, shrugged and signaled okay. On my signal, my new friends formed a line, along with the door gunners and me, and we quickly loaded the boxes onto both helos. I boarded the lead helo and we lifted off.

I put on a flight helmet so I could speak to the pilot over the intercom.

"Thanks for coming to get me. I really appreciate the lift."

"No problem." He glanced back at the boxes filling his helo. "So are you planning to open your own hospital? That's a *lot* of medical supplies."

"Yeah, something like that." I smiled and reached for a case of large battle dressings. I opened the case. "Look inside." I pulled up the top bandage so he could see the four-dozen lobster tails filling up the rest of the case.

He grinned, smacked his lips and rubbed his hands together. "That will definitely cure something!"

I had them radio SEAFLOAT to let my platoon know I was inbound. "Be advised, will need assistance offloading some sensitive SEAL operating equipment."

"Roger that."

I knew my guys would understand I had some goodies coming in with me.

We landed on SEAFLOAT, and offloaded all the boxes of frozen delicacies. Ric and Mitch walked over to the empty choppers and looked inside. They seemed disappointed.

"So where are they?" Ric asked.

"They who?"

"The nurses," Mitch filled in. "You were on a hospital ship, weren't you? A hospital ship filled with lovely young nurses? When we got your message, we thought surely you were bringing back some nurses!"

I really felt stupid. After reviewing my message, they had all gotten their hopes up. I didn't even think about bringing anyone out to SEAFLOAT, let alone some nurses. I was saved by the fact that the lobster tails and steaks were starting to thaw. It was time to light the charcoal on the old fifty-five gallon drums and get out the beer. It was barbecue time!

Frank Flynn and some of his KCs were on SEAFLOAT. They had come up from Nam Can for a little intel briefing and op planning. Once they heard about the barbecue they were more than happy to join in, even bringing along some local dishes to add to the feast. I knew better than to ask what any of it was. Vietnamese food didn't always look appetizing, but some of the shit was pretty good—especially if you put enough Nuc Bam, or Vietnamese hot sauce, on it. Of course, like most SEALs of my era, we put hot sauce on everything. We always had a big jar of jalapeños on the bar to challenge your manhood—and ignorance. Of course most of my pals who are still around today require an Alka-Seltzer after a bread-and-butter sandwich.

When Flynn caught sight of me at the barbecue, he looked as if he had seen a ghost. "The last time I saw you, Doc, you were falling out of the sky from a Med-ever chopper."

I grinned. "Lucky for me I hit headfirst. Otherwise I probably would have hurt myself."

32

Salty SEALs

A couple of days later, after having a morning Coke and a smoke in sick bay, I heard the mail chopper coming in. It was only about a week before Valentines Day, and all the guys aboard SEAFLOAT were getting goodies from their loved ones. My mom had promised to send me a box of her homemade Toll House chocolate chip cookies, so I hurried to the helo pad to see if my package had made it. It is amazing how great something as simple as homemade cookies can taste when you are so very far away from home.

I started helping unload all the mail sacks when I spotted a stack of *Stars and Stripes* magazines. I picked one up to get a better look. The cover featured Jane Fonda, but not as I had last seen her in the movies. A few weeks earlier, while in Binh Thuy, I happened to catch her in the new movie, *Barbarella,* which featured Miss Fonda wearing some very revealing spacey costumes—when she was wearing any clothes at all. At that time, I thought that she was a real hot babe, though the only thing I remembered about the movie was how little clothing she wore through most of it—and that she was fooling around with some big guy in wings up in his giant nest.

On the *Stars and Stripes* cover, not only was she wearing a lot more clothes, but she was also wearing an NVA helmet and sitting on a North Vietnamese antiaircraft gun. I flipped to the article. Apparently the photo had been taken just outside of Hanoi during her visit to North Vietnam. *Her visit to North Vietnam?* A number of nonflattering expletives came immediately to mind.

The article went on to say that it was thought, at that time, that she might get arrested upon her return to the United States. The charges were most likely to be treason and aiding and abetting the enemy. I put the magazine back on the stack in disgust. The next box off the helo was full of movies. Curious, I checked the movies in the box. Sure enough, *Barbarbella* was among them.

I closed the box back up, grabbed my package of cookies and a copy of *Stars and Stripes,* and ran off to show the article to Ric. Of course, he immediately had an idea. He went out to the helo pad and grabbed the whole stack of *Stars and Stripes* and took them to our hooch so that no one else would see them yet. We then went to visit the chief in charge of SEAFLOAT's fun and recreation to suggest that he show *Barbarella* that night.

"Yeah, Doc, here has already seen it, and he says it's good."

"Yeah. Jane Fonda naked. Lots of boobs and ass," I supplied.

The chief was probably as desperate for female flesh as the rest of us, so he readily agreed.

During evening chow, I kept telling the rest of the platoon about the movie, and how hot Jane Fonda looked. After getting the guys aroused with my descriptive adjectives of Jane's attributes, Ric passed out copies of *Stars and Stripes*. Mitch was so pissed, he immediately wanted to lead the platoon on a body snatch op up North—her body, that is.

"Whoa, that's way out of our AO," Boh cautioned. "I figure somebody up north will get her."

"We need to make a statement right here." I agreed. "We need to blow up the projector and screen."

"Hey," Boh interrupted, "not before I get to see her naked ass up on the screen. If she's as hot as you say, I want a look before we destroy anything."

Most of the guys agreed. We decided to go to the movie with Boh. Once he had seen enough, then we would take action.

We thought we were the only ones who knew what Ms. Fonda had done. We hadn't counted on the fact that one of the helo door gunners had already read the article while in the air. About fifteen minutes into the movie, the door gunner stood up and threw his soda can at the screen. "I've seen enough of this traitor!"

They should have stopped the movie right then, but they didn't. Most people didn't know what the door gunner was yelling about. The projectionist kept the reel turning and Jane Fonda continued her on-screen antics while the door gunner and others got more riled. Finally Boh had had enough. He stood up and put about three shots from his 9mm pistol through her face. *Then* they shut off the movie.

We were all pissed off as we stormed back to the hooch. We couldn't believe our government was stupid enough to allow this broad to do this, or that they showed even greater stupidity by allowing that movie to be distributed to the troops at the same time she was appearing on the cover of *Stars and Stripes*.

We had been in country about five months now and had become pretty salty SEALs. We had done a lot, seen a lot, and begun to understand a lot more. The war was definitely changing—and so were our attitudes. No one talked about winning the war anymore. We just concentrated on our little piece of it. We won our battles ninety percent of the time. Everything else seemed far, far away.

I began to understand why the SEALs only served in country for six months at a time. It had been almost five months and I was beginning to lose my focus. I could feel it. I found I didn't always pay much attention during the patrol orders. On ambush, I caught myself dozing off. Part of the problem was that I wasn't nearly as scared as when I first came into country. In fact, I was beginning to fear going home. What was my future?

This war was winding down, especially for the SEALs. I had changed. I no longer dreamed of becoming a doctor. I didn't want to stay in the service. I didn't want to go back home to Lake Forest. I didn't want to do anything in particular. I was losing my ambition. My drive was gone and my focus was wavering badly. The black "brothers" had a saying: "Ain't nothing but a thing." They used it whenever anything happened. Someone could get killed, or get promoted, and all they would say was "Ain't nothing but a thing."

It wasn't until I heard one of our guys say it that it struck home. One of the Seawolves had come under enemy fire and lost a door gunner. As I was putting the door gunner into a body bag, one of our guys walked by, glanced at the body, and said "Ain't nothin' but a thing." I looked down at the body of the dead boy and felt chilled. *Nothin' but a thing*. It was gut-check time. I needed something to remind me who we were, and what being a SEAL meant.

Just as I finished with the body, Boh came running up. "Get your gear! We have a helo down!"

Mr. Flanagan and Mr. Moody were both up in Binh Thuy, so Boh was in command. I zipped up the body bag and scrambled to get my gear. The platoon was ready to go in minutes.

"Doc, you, Ric, Mitch and me on the first bird, and the M-60 gunners behind us on the next bird, and the rest of you stand by to back us up."

We did a quick radio check while Boh unfolded a map on the deck. The whole platoon huddled around as Boh indicated the crash site on the map. "The helo went in here, near the river."

It was a familiar area. It was also crawling with VC. The thought of going in there midday made my blood run cold. I jumped on board the first Seawolf. We lifted off immediately without waiting for the second bird. The pilots and Boh were monitoring radio communication with the downed helicopter.

"There were six people on board," Boh reported, "including two passengers from Binh Thuy, two door gunners, and the two pilots."

Oh shit, I thought, *Mr. Flanagan and Mr. Moody might be on that bird.* I could tell from everyone else's expressions that they were thinking the same thing.

We were over the crash site in about ten minutes. From the air, I could see the downed helo lying on its side in the middle of a rice paddy. I could also see that the VC were moving in fast from at least two directions. We flared in fast and hard, right next to the crash, our door gunners blazing away from both sides of the chopper as the number of VC began to grow. I bailed out without waiting for the helo to touch down, followed by Boh, Ric, and Mitch. The Seawolf immediately lifted off, opening up with rockets and mini-guns to drive the VC back to the trees.

I couldn't see any VC between us and the river, but they were everywhere else. Boh radioed the other helo to insert Dave, Jonah, X.T., and John and their sixty-guns in that open area. He ordered them to set up a firing lane that would allow us to evade in their direction.

I was the first to reach the downed helo. Four guys were already out. The pilot and one door gunner had been partially trapped on the side of the helo that was embedded in the rice paddy. They were still struggling to get out. It turned out the two passengers were boat-support guys coming down from Can Tho with some spare parts for one of our boats. Other then being white as ghosts they both appeared to be okay, though neither of them carried any weapons. As I checked them out in the shelter of the fallen bird, Mitch gave one a pistol and a few grenades and the other a LAAW rocket.

"But don't use any of these unless all of us are dead. Got that?"

They nodded, unable to speak.

Mitch poked his head around the other side of the helo to check the progress of the two men still trying to work free from the wreckage. Ping, ping, ping! Bullets bounced off the helo close to Mitch's head.

"Cover me, Doc!"

I crawled behind the broken tail section of the helo, which lay like a fallen tree across the paddy. Bullets were flying everywhere. I slowly peered over the tail behind the barrel of my Stoner to find a sea of black pajamas converging on our position. The closest VC were less than thirty yards away, crawling toward us through the waist-high grass and shooting away. I glanced back to see Dave and Jonah setting up their heavy sixty-guns behind us. They were too far back to see the VC clearly in the grass. I looked back at the approaching enemy and opened up on them. My red tracers were like laser beams, pinpointing the enemy as my bullets smacked dully into mud and flesh alike. I expelled all 150 rounds in about a minute. As I ducked back down to reload, Jonah and Dave's M-60s opened up on the enemy my tracers had marked, making hamburger of those they hit.

"Hey Doc! You want to do some bandaging while we do the shooting?" Ric yelled sarcastically as the two remaining crewmembers scrambled out from under the helo. "I think one of these guys is hurt."

I scooted over to where they huddled behind the helo and started checking them out. By the grace of God, nobody had taken a bullet. I didn't even find a cut big enough to stitch. The door gunner couldn't use his leg. It looked like he might have broken it in the crash. I grabbed an air splint out of my medical bag and wrapped it around his leg to just above the knee. After I zippered it shut, I had one of the boat support guys inflate it while I finished reloading my Stoner. I felt much better once I had slammed down the feed tray. There are few things worse than that feeling of complete nakedness you get when you're caught in a firefight with a weapon that isn't ready to fire.

One of the Seawolves made a quick pass overhead. They had already expended all their rockets and their mini-guns were empty, so they were reduced to just using their door gunners. But the gunners could still do some damage with their M-60s. Incoming fire slowed for a moment after the pass. But both the Seawolves were out of ammo and low on fuel.

As the gunships returned to base to refuel and reload, I felt as if we were being left behind. I could hear wounded VC calling out for help from where they lay in the rice paddies. I also heard a lot of yelling coming from the tree line as the VC tried to regroup and coordinate themselves to mount a final attack on us before our guardian wolves came back.

I noticed that the second half of the squad had formed a skirmish line at the edge of the rice paddies with Jonah and Dave covering both flanks with their M-60s.

"We need to fall back with the others!" I yelled to Ric.

Ric was on the radio with some pilots. He shook his head at me then spoke into the mike. "Black Pony, this is down chopper. Do you have us yet? Over!" He pulled the mike away from his mouth to yell to me. "Hold your position. Keep firing."

I looked up to see a wave of VC leave the trees to begin an assault across the paddy. They were moving fast and low. Ric tossed out a smoke grenade which landed right in front of them. The wind blew the green smoke in their direction as we continued to fire on them.

"Black Pony, this is downed chopper. Can you identify yet?"

"I got green smoke, over," the pilot replied.

"Fire on smoke and downwind for two hundred meters," Ric instructed.

"Roger that."

A moment later, I heard the roar of engines as the OV-10 Black Pony fixed-wing aircraft dropped from the sky overhead and started blowing the shit out of everything in front of us.

"Fall back," Boh yelled, indicating the skirmish line at the edge of the rice paddy. "Let's get out of here!"

I led the injured gunner, crew, and the two boat support guys out first while Boh, Mitch, and Ric covered us from behind the downed helo. Once we were clear, Ric and Boh then lit up the helo with some incendiary grenades and hot-footed it back to our position.

By then, our gunships had returned with extraction helos. They were ready to pick us up on a dike to the rear of our position. We leapfrogged back to them in precisely the manner we had been trained, all the while maintaining fire superiority on a force that was much larger than ours. As we loaded the helos for our extraction, a lone Marine A-4 jet contacted Ric on the radio. The pilot had been monitoring our firefight, and now offered his services.

We lifted off and had just cleared the area when the A-4 came screaming in underneath our chopper to drop a five-hundred pound napalm bomb right on top of the downed helo. *Bull's-eye!* As it exploded, its expanding fireball rolled toward the enemy. Seconds later, the entire tree line burst into flames and a thick black cloud rose into the air. I watched the flames expand into a conflagration that covered the entire area. Anyone caught within half a mile in front of that downed helo was incinerated within moments. I thought about the fact that the government was always looking for numbers of kills and emphasizing the enemy body count. Well, if the government was ever looking for a high enemy body count, they got one that day. And there were no American KIAs.

Later, as we all silently cleaned our weapons, I realized that something had changed—for all of us. We had regained our focus and our drive.

"Guys," Ric broke the silence, "did any of you notice that Doc here was having so much fun shooting VC that he put the splint on the door gunner's *good* leg?"

They all laughed.

"Nah!" I retorted, "I was just checking to make sure he wasn't faking. Then, I put it on the right way."

Apparently we had regained our sense of humor as well.

"Man, did you see that Marine A-4 cook the crap out of those gooks?" Mitch had been talking of nothing else since we landed. "That was so cool!" Mitch loved to fly, so it was not surprising that he had fixated on the jet and the napalm run. I understood perfectly, since my brother Fred had been an A-4 pilot himself a few years earlier. He was my hero. He was also the reason I joined the Marines. Of course I had left the Marines after that short—and almost fatal—tour of duty to join the SEALs, because it was safer.

Fred never bragged about his heroics like some fighter pilots, but I knew there were a lot of Marines who owed their lives to his accurate, close-in air support and bombing precision. I knew he had done for others just what that Marine pilot had done for us today.

After chow, while most of the guys were playing cards or listening to music, I went over to my homemade desk and wrote my brother a letter. I told him all about what a good job his brother Marine pilot had done in protecting his little brother SEAL's ass. Then, of course, I had to pimp him about how comfortable his job was. He got to sit in the cozy, cushioned fighter jet seat instead of having to hump his butt through the jungle with seventy pounds of gear and ammo. I also told him all about what a hairy firefight we had been involved in that afternoon—knowing he was the only one in the family who could understand—and that I must be maturing, because it scared the shit out of me. A scared SEAL is a safe SEAL. A SEAL who is not scared is just a plain idiot.

Thinking of my brother reminded me that I would be seeing Vicki in a few days. I was looking forward to the rest and relaxation break in Hawaii, but I had no idea how things would be between Vicki and me. We were both just twenty years old, had only been married for about ten months, and hadn't seen or spoken to each other in over four of those months. I knew that those months had changed me. And where my brother, as a fellow soldier, understood those changes, I did not know if Vicki ever would. I wasn't sure we even knew each other anymore. She was my wife, but it was the guys in the platoon who were my family.

33

Who Do You Think You Are?

THE day before R&R began, the local weather deities decided to rain on my head—literally. It rained all day and into the night, the heavy drops pounding on the corrugated metal roof of our hooch like a frenzied drummer. Between the pounding rain and excited anticipation of my trip, I got very little sleep, tossing and turning all night.

By first light, the rain had slowed to a light drizzle. I gave up on sleep and glanced at my watch. It was 0430 our time. Vicki was probably already on the airplane on her way to Hawaii from Chicago. I looked out at the dreary warm rain, took in the ever-present smell of jungle rot, and thought about how different our two worlds had become. Hawaii would be our meeting point between those worlds, a welcome dose of civilization for me, and a touch of exotic wildness for her.

My reverie was broken by the commotion of Mr. Moody's squad returning from an overnight snatch-and-grab op targeting a high-level VC. They were laughing and cheering and patting each other on the back. I climbed out of my rack, pulled on pants and a T-shirt, and padded over to get an update.

"So how did it go? Did you make contact?"

"Oh, we made contact alright!" Mitch laughed, green camo paint running down his face from the rain and sweat. "It was raining so hard that the gooks never heard us comin'. They were all holed up trying to stay dry. We sneaked right in and grabbed the target right out of his hooch before they knew what hit 'em."

"Yeah, his bodyguards figured something was up right about the time we were leaving," Jonah added, stripping his heavy sixty-gun for cleaning. "They tried to stop us. Bad mistake."

"No shit! You missed a great firefight, Doc!" X.T. grinned like a drunken schoolboy. "We took out about half a dozen of those mothers without getting a scratch!"

"You shoulda seen Jonah rockin' and rollin' with that pig of a sixty-gun!" Mitch continued, throwing an affectionate arm around Jonah's neck in a mock headlock while pulling off his headband. "Chalk up another saga for the legend of the 'men with green faces!'"

I knew the high they were feeling. I had experienced it myself on many occasions. Cheating death makes you giddy. All combat veterans share this same experience. Many won't or can't talk about it, fearing no one will understand where they are coming from. It's impossible to understand unless you have been there. Watching them, it seemed surreal that I would be sipping Mai Tais on the beach in a few hours while my own squad was out in the bush.

I left the guys to their celebrations and went to our storage area. Outside of the hooch, the base was very quiet. Most of the SEAFLOAT crew were still in their racks at this hour. I walked slowly over to the Conex box I shared with Ric and unlocked its heavy door. It squeaked in protest as I swung it open, the sound echoing loudly through the early morning stillness. I climbed inside. There, in a dim corner of the large container, almost hidden behind our radio and medical equipment, sat my R&R suitcase. The small, black, civilian-looking bag contained my dreams and memories of the real world. I hadn't checked it since we left Coronado, and I wanted to see what Ric had borrowed from it since then. I pulled it out of the box and opened it up. Surprisingly, everything was there, even my Hai Karate aftershave and my Right Guard spray deodorant. It also contained a few polo shirts, some shorts, and a pair of slacks with a sportcoat, a white shirt, and a tie. I put in my shaving kit as well as some war trophies I wanted Vicki to take back to the states with her.

I wasn't scheduled to leave until the mail chopper showed up around 0900. It was still about forty-five minutes before breakfast, so I closed up the Conex box, picked up my suitcase, and walked slowly over to the chow hall to grab a cup of coffee and a donut. As I sat down alone at one of the tables I could smell breakfast cooking. From the aroma, the cooks were doing their usual magic with powdered eggs and spam.

A cook I hadn't seen before poked his head out of the kitchen and yelled at me. "We're not open yet! Come back in an hour."

Yeah, right! I glared at him. Before the new guy could get into trouble, another cook leaned over and whispered something to him. The only word I heard was SEAL, but his face went a little pale as he withdrew quickly back into the kitchen. I put my suitcase on the table next to me and took out my traveling orders. A few minutes later, the new cook came out bearing hot muffins fresh from the oven.

"Sorry. I didn't realize you were a SEAL," he apologized, placing the muffins in front of me.

I laughed. "Hey, man, no big deal. You're new and you don't know me from Adam. It's not like I was just coming off an op where I hadn't eaten for a day!"

The cook smiled and returned to the kitchen. As I took a big bite of a sweet, warm muffin I realized that I never gave a thought to the mess-hall decorum that the other sailors had to follow. For the little over four months we had been at SEAFLOAT, we had the run of the kitchen and chow hall. The staff and Vietnamese were only allowed in during prescribed meal hours, but SEALs were allowed in anytime.

About twenty minutes later, Boh and Ric walked in.

"I've been looking all over for you," Boh said, pulling up a seat beside me. "We just got an urgent radio message from SEAL Team One headquarters in Coronado."

"A message?" I was curious now.

"Yeah." Ric sat down across from me. "Apparently your wife can't make it."

I was shocked. My stomach balled up in a knot as I turned back to Boh.

"Why not? What happened?" Visions of Vicki being in a wreck or something worse flashed through my head.

"Well, I'm not quite sure, but I heard that Gary Shaddock met her flight when she landed in San Diego. Apparently he took her to the Trade Winds to party. Last anybody heard, they ran off together."

Gary Shaddock? I didn't think she even liked Gary.

"Vicki never liked you that much, anyway." Ric grinned and grabbed a muffin. But Boh's face was perfectly serious.

"This isn't funny, guys. What's going on?"

Then they both broke into laugher. Boh shrugged his shoulders and patted me on the back. "Give her a kiss for us, will you Doe?"

They both stared at me, waiting for the color to return to my face. I started to laugh. They got me good. I wish I had thought of it first. I would have pulled it on Jim Loeding when he went to see his wife a month earlier.

"Yeah, will you two try not to have too much fun while I'm gone, okay?"

Moody's squad came into the mess for breakfast, famished after their night in the field.

"Hey Mitch!" I gave Mitch my keys to Ric's Conex box, so that he could help himself to medical supplies while I was gone. "Try not to use everything up before I get back." Even though John Mitchell was a machinist's mate by rate, I had helped him become the duty doc for Mr. Moody's squad. If he ran into any problems putting Band-Aids on holes in people in the field, I would either talk him through it on the radio or go in, if possible, on a Seawolf, acting as a Medivac. John had gotten pretty comfortable with his medical stuff, even helped stitch a few wounded Vietnamese scouts that came in. He grinned at me, still streaked with camo paint, and pocketed the keys.

At about 0900, after half a dozen cups of coffee and a pack of cigarettes, I heard my freedom bird, otherwise known as the mail chopper, come in right on schedule. I quickly threw on a relatively clean pair of tennis shoes and pulled a Hawaiian shirt over my T-shirt. Grabbing my suitcase, I jumped abroad for the quick run back up to Binh Thuy. SEALs were one of only a few military men allowed to wear civilian clothes while traveling in country. Most others were required to wear uniforms of some type at all times.

Shortly after arriving on Binh Thuy, I hitched a ride on a CIA Air America plane. The pilot was one of Don Scully's friends, whom I had met during our adventures with the CIA a few months earlier.

"Doc, we're going to give you the royal treatment all the way to Saigon."

I smiled and settled back to enjoy the whole hour-long flight. Once we landed at Than Sun Nhut, he bypassed the terminal and taxied directly over to a big old Pan Am 707, sitting alone on the tarmac.

"I radioed the Pan Am pilot to tell him you were coming. They are expecting you."

I thanked him and climbed out of the helo to find the Pan Am pilot waiting for me at the foot of the boarding stairs. He greeted me with a cold beer, then had a stewardess run a copy of my orders in to the office to get them stamped. As she left, the pilot proceeded to pick up and carry my bag onto the plane. Puzzled, but pleased, I followed him onto the plane. Once on board he introduced me to the rest of his crew.

"It's great to meet you guys, and the beer is terrific, but why the special treatment?"

"Son, when the CIA says they are bringing me a genuine Navy SEAL war hero to go on R&R and they pull their plane right up to ours and request I give you the royal treatment, you don't say no. And you don't ask the CIA any questions. If the CIA thinks that highly of you, then so do we."

All right! I thought as I took my seat in first class, put my suitcase in the overhead, and popped another beer. I lit up a cigarette, closed my eyes, and leaned back, enjoying the luxury of first-class seats. A disturbance at the hatch caught my attention, and I opened my eyes to see two Army MPs climb aboard and stop at my seat.

"Are you McFarlin?" the shorter one asked, holding a copy of my orders in his fist.

"The name's McPartlin. How can I help you?"

"You want to get off the fucking plane now?"

"Excuse me?" I said through gritted teeth.

The other man reached for my arm. Before he could grab me to pull me out of my seat I intercepted his hand, twisted it backward and up behind his back while bending it at the wrist.

"If you insist on talking to me in such a rude fashion or try to grab me again I will break your fucking arm!" I whispered loudly in his ear while increasing pressure on his arm. The other MP, a Barney Fife type, started to go for his pistol.

"I wouldn't do that if I were you," I warned. "I will kill you with one blow before the barrel ever clears your holster."

He froze for a moment. He could tell I wasn't bluffing.

"Now I suggest we all stay calm and get off the plane together and see what the heck is going on here."

They both nodded, and I released the guy I was holding. He held his arm awkwardly. I don't think he was used to harassing someone who knew how to defend himself.

I let them lead the way off the plane while they explained what they knew.

It seemed the Army 2nd lieutenant in charge of the terminal took offense when the stewardess brought him my R&R orders instead of having me deliver them myself. He was the one who told the MPs to go drag my ass off the plane.

In the terminal there were at least a hundred guys milling around waiting to board the plane. Now they would probably have to wait even longer because some Army official felt I had stepped on his toes. The officer in charge, a chunky guy who definitely didn't look as though he had ever missed a meal, was waiting for us and he was steaming mad. I could tell immediately that he was a typical Army rear-echelon puke, unfit-for-duty-asshole junior officer with delusions of grandeur.

"Do you want to tell me why you didn't go through proper check-in procedure?" he yelled, apparently not caring if the waiting men overheard him or not. "How the hell did you even get out on the tarmac without checking with me? Just who the hell do you think you are?

Admiral Zumwalt? No! You are a mere Navy E-5 Corpsman. And what do you think you are doing running around out of uniform?"

He continued to scream, his volume increasing by the minute as he listed my sins. I tried to be very diplomatic, gritting my teeth as I listened quietly to his tirade. After all, his job as an Army travel agent was obviously highly stressful and dangerous. Who even knew what the casualty rate was among travel agents? They were probably on some secret VC hit list. He was definitely on mine.

I waited until he finally wound down, his face red and puffy from the effort, then spoke, in as calm a voice as I could manage. "Sir, I'm sorry about getting footprints on your head by not going through you. My plane taxied me right up to the Pan Am jet where the captain greeted me and offered me a beer and a seat in first class. Everything was fine until your thugs tried to physically remove me from the plane. Which by the way, sir, was a truly dumb move. And now, when I come in to calmly straighten things out, you start yelling at me like an idiot. And to answer all your other polite questions, I have this." I handed him my MACV-SOG ID card along with my standing orders granting me first-available flight on all planes, including jet fighters. SEALs all were ejection-seat qualified just for that reason. These orders granted me a seat on any available plane I wanted or needed to get to my destination. According to these I could bump almost anyone but the pilot. Or the stewardess. Stewardesses were almost as good as nurses.

This guy had never seen credentials like mine before. He demanded I step into his office so he could verify that I wasn't a Russian spy or something. Behind closed doors and away from the men waiting to depart, I gave him about five more seconds to examine my IDs before I snatched them from his hand.

"Look, *sir,* I am Navy SEAL Corpsman Greg McPartlin, SEAL Team Two. I have just come from our base at Solid Anchor and I am on my way to see my wife in Hawaii—who, by the way, I have not seen in many months. I *strongly* suggest that you avoid doing anything further to impede my travel plans."

The 2nd lewey just looked at me, his face getting redder by the minute. I was starting to get a little upset myself when the base Navy

Commander walked into the office. Apparently, word of my predicament had reached him. He focused on the 2nd lieutenant with a look that could shred stone, never even glancing in my direction, but his words were aimed at me.

"Doc, go get back on the plane and go see your wife in Hawaii. And please, try not to damage any more MPs." His unwavering stare never left the Army junior officer, who seemed to shrivel under its impact.

"But sir, he . . ." I started to defend myself.

"Go now," he snapped, "Please! No more trouble."

Moments later, as I sat there in my first-class seat, watching all the other guys board the aircraft, I couldn't help but smile when a lot of them shook my hand or patted me on the shoulder. "Way to go, man!"

"You showed him!"

Apparently, the Army bureaucrat had made *lots* of friends before I got there.

One uniformed private stopped at my seat and stared at my brightly colored shirt. "That was really somethin'. Is it true you are only an enlisted man?"

His question caught me completely by surprise. "*Only* enlisted?" I forced back. "Who do you think is fighting this war? Sure as hell isn't assholes like that 2nd lewey back at the gate!"

Those within earshot of me all let out a cheer. The stewardess had to tell everyone to calm down. Once the noise quieted, the chaplain got on the intercom to speak to us. At first, I wasn't listening closely, but then he caught my attention.

"And for those of you who do not have wives joining you in Hawaii, please be careful. Always use a condom."

I thought that was pretty funny. I had never heard a preacher talk about sex before. After a quick "Our Father," he gave us all his blessing. That really meant a lot to me. When he had finished, I said a few more private prayers and began trying to remove myself from the war.

The plane turned onto the runway and began to race over the tarmac. A loud cheer erupted throughout the cabin as the wheels lifted off. I toasted the guys sitting around me, then drained my beer, reclined my seat and lit up a smoke. I was tired but too excited to sleep. I closed my eyes, trying to think of my wife and me lying on a beach, but the only images in my mind were of the war. The only thing I could smell was jungle rot.

I listened as the guys around me started telling war stories. They were a combination of Marines, soldiers, and a few sailors. The stories did nothing to help me in my quest to escape from the war. I opened my eyes for a moment and a Marine leaned over to talk to me.

"You're a corpsman, right?"

"Yeah."

"You don't know how lucky you are! At least you don't have to get into firefights in the jungle."

Yeah, right. "Yeah, I'm a real lucky guy, okay." I closed my eyes and turned away from him, hoping he would get the message.

A few hours later, a stewardess tapped me on the shoulder.

"Please bring your seat upright, sir. We're preparing to land."

The plane was quiet as I rubbed the sleep from my eyes and looked around. A lot of guys were looking out the windows, pointing to this little spit of land off in the distance. I heard the engines throttle back and felt the vibrations change as we began our approach into Honolulu. A few minutes later, when the Pam Am jet's wheels touched the runway, everyone cheered again and there were tears all around.

I was surprised to discover I had the same butterflies infesting my stomach I usually got before inserting on every op. It was fear of the unknown. I reached for my bag from the overhead only to discover that my hands were sweating. As soon as the cabin door opened, I smelled clear tropical air. My stomach calmed and I felt cleansed as the aroma of orchids wafted into the plane, inundating my senses. I stepped from the aircraft to be greeted by a lovely young Hawaiian girl who hung a fresh lei over my head and gave me a quick peck on the cheek. The MPs were there to greet us, as before, but these guys were different. They *smiled.*

Hell, I thought, *why not? They get to work in paradise.*

"We will get you guys through customs as fast as we can," a tall, well-groomed MP announced. "Those of you that don't have to clear customs, come with me."

I gave it a shot, alone with some senior-looking personnel, and sure enough, after a quick look at my IDs, the sergeant waved me through. Unlike the 2nd lewy back in 'Nam, this officer had seen IDs like mine before, and knew who they belonged to. I retrieved my IDs and started to walk away.

"McPartlin?" The sergeant stopped me. I turned back to find his hand extended. "You guys are doing a hell of a job over there and don't think people don't know who you are." I took his hand.

"Thanks!" The handshake was warm and sincere. "I really appreciate your kind words. They mean a lot."

It was really great to know that someone back in the world noticed and appreciated our work. That kind of thing made up for a lot of 2nd lewey assholes. With a big smile on my face, I headed toward baggage claim and the bus to Fort DeRussey, location of the R&R processing center.

Since I didn't have to clear customs, I was one of the first to board the bus. As a result, it seemed to take forever for the vehicle to fill up, and there were four other buses behind ours. I considered taking a cab to Fort DeRussey, but figured I had bent the rules enough for one day.

34

Wives and Brothers

AFTER an interminable wait, the bus finally pulled out of the parking lot onto the city streets. I had a weird moment of culture shock when we drove onto a modern highway instead of the muddy streets of a third-world country. Up to that point, I had not believed I had left Vietnam—at least not deep down. The sight of broad avenues, well-tended tropical gardens, and palm trees proved that I was no longer in Southeast Asia. But it was the fresh, balmy breeze, thick with the sweet smell of tropical flowers and clean ocean spray, which finally convinced me I was in paradise. I had not really realized how much the pungent stench of jungle rot had permeated my senses until it was gone.

The bus rolled into the process center and squeaked to a stop near a mass of good-looking young women—wives and girlfriends awaiting our arrival. I was the first one off, stepping into their midst as soon as the doors opened and scanning the crowd. Vicki spotted me first and came running up, half laughing.

"Somehow I would have bet you would be the first to arrive!" She threw her arms around me in a soft, perfumed embrace. I had almost forgotten how it felt to hold her.

"Well, you would have won the bet—if there had been any takers."

She looked a little different than the last time I had seen her. She wore her hair longer, more "mod" than I remembered. Her dress was short, and brightly colored. It definitely looked good to me after months of green and brown. After a quick stamp of my orders, we were off to the Ala Mauna Hotel for a week together in paradise.

We spent the next week doing the complete tourist thing: the luaus, the Don Ho show, the island tours, mopeds, waterfalls—everything to keep busy and anything to avoid being alone together. It took only a few hours to discover that we didn't have a lot in common at this point. Hell, truth was we hardly knew each other before I left, and now both of us had changed quite a bit. We were almost strangers. She had gone back to college in Illinois, and, like most of the college set, agreed with the antiwar crowd. I knew from her letters that she was sympathetic to the movement. She felt justified in the strength of her antiwar beliefs. But because she respected me and my work as a SEAL, she never demonstrated or showed any outward support for the antiwar movement. Respect did not ensure understanding, however.

"I don't get it, Greg. Why don't you just quit and come home?" We were having after-dinner drinks on the beach. "You could just tell them you've had enough. It's time to get back to your family."

"Vick, it doesn't work like that. I'll be home when my tour is over. It won't be that long now."

"I can't understand how you can let them send you back there!" she pouted. I don't think she really grasped the fact that being in the military during a war was a little different from a regular nine-to-five job in the city. I couldn't just put in eight hours at the office, wave bye to the VC, and then hop back to the suburbs for cocktails at the country club.

Throughout the rest of the week, we found ourselves fighting over nothing. By the fourth day, I think we were both anxious for our seven days to be over. I tried to keep things positive by talking about the future. Since I only had about seven weeks left on my tour of duty in country, Vicki decided to go ahead and move back to our apartment in Coronado instead of staying with her folks in Lake Forest. She had met and befriended a lot of team wives and girlfriends and said she was anxious to set up house on her own. I think the truth was that she wanted to get away from her parents.

The tension dissipated on the last day as we packed and loaded our bags in the taxi. The cab dropped me at Fort DeRussey, then left to take Vicki on to the airport to catch a flight to San Diego. I watched the cab pull out, wondering if she would look back. Sure enough, Vicki turned around and mouthed "I love you," while waving goodbye. I smiled and waved back. I think we were both relieved it was over, and very confused about our feelings. I missed her already, but I was glad our time together was over. Hell, face it; nineteen is too young to be married unless you are from the Ozarks.

I jumped onto the bus to find myself looking at about a dozen teary-eyed men. I greeted them with a big, cheerful smile.

"Well, men," I announced, good-naturedly, "now that we have spent time with our wives and families, it's time to get back to Vietnam and our true loved ones!"

Howls and fingers were raised as a bunch of the guys flipped me off. I just smiled back brightly and took my seat.

I STARED out the window as the Pan Am jet lifted off the Honolulu runway, watching as the island gradually receded into the larger blue of the vast Pacific Ocean. The island was still in view when the memory of sweet Hawaiian orchids faded, to be replaced by the memory of thick foliage, mangrove swamps, and muddy water. Fifteen minutes into the flight, Vietnam returned to my senses as if I had never left, and all my thoughts were of my platoon. I smiled as I dozed off, thinking fondly of how much razzing I was going to get from Ric when I got back. I had brought one bag, but had filled my empty seabag during the trip, and was going back with two. Both were safely stowed in the overhead compartment—my suitcase filled with my stuff, and the seabag filled with goodies for the guys in Alpha Platoon.

Unlike the boisterous cheer of the flight out, the mood on board was very somber by the time we touched down in Saigon. It reminded me of the difference between the Friday night flight to Las Vegas and the Sunday flight back home, broke. It was raining when we landed at Than Sun Nhut airbase that evening. Water and wind blew into the cabin the moment the stewart opened the door. He stood back, waiting for the stairs to be wheeled up to the plane, then announced our arrival.

"We have now landed in Saigon," he announced. "Please be sure to check the overhead storage bins and the area around your seats for any personal possessions at this time."

Everyone gathered his luggage and packages in preparation for deplaning. I collected my two bags from the overhead and waited my turn to exit. It was strangely quiet as men shuffled off the plane heading back to the war. Only the captain stood in the doorway. He wished every man good luck, shaking the hands of any who were unburdened by packages.

I noticed, as I walked by, that he was wearing a Vietnam service medal.

"How about coming back with me for a couple more weeks in the jungle—just for old time's sake?"

He smiled. "Sorry, I'd love to, but I'm afraid I can't. I have to fly back to Hawaii tomorrow afternoon. Can I have a rain check on that?"

As if it heard him, the rain came down harder the moment I stepped out of the plane onto the stairway. I looked back at him, standing in his nice, dry plane. "Smart call, captain." He smiled and waved a good evening as I descended the steps.

It's funny, I noticed the smell immediately—that overpowering mixture of overripe produce and wet, rotting plants that permeates the entire Mekong delta region and most of South Vietnam—but this time it didn't bother me. It actually seemed familiar and somewhat comforting, almost as if I had come home.

I walked over to the terminal and checked in along with the rest of the passengers. Some corporal clerk looked at my papers, stamped them, and said "Next."

"Can you direct me to the MACV-SOG office?" I asked. Only then did he look up at me.

"Why do you want to know?" He seemed suddenly very nervous.

"Why do you ask?" I showed him my ID card. He told me it was two terminals down and inquired if I needed a ride. I thanked him. He immediately yelled over to some private, who ran right up to him. He whispered something in the private's ear. A few seconds later the private, a tall, blond youngster with an M-16 on his back stepped smartly over to me.

"Right this way, sir. Do you need help with your bags?" Without waiting for my reply, he picked up my seabag, which was loaded full of stuff for the guys. "Man, what's in here? Bricks?"

"Not quite. Girlie magazines, fuck books, booze and other contrabad. So be careful. And don't call me sir. My parents were married. Doc will do." We headed for his jeep, with him carefully hefting the heavy bag.

He set my bag into the jeep then tossed his M-16 beside it. At my surprised expression he grinned. "It's not loaded."

I climbed into the jeep wondering at the point of carrying an unloaded weapon, but I decided it must be base protocol or something.

"What's your name?"

"Jason, sir." He glanced at my civilian clothes. "Are you some kind of a medic?"

"At this point, I'm not sure," I responded, hesitantly.

The MACV offices were all dark by the time we pulled up in front. Everyone had secured for the day. The private looked a little perplexed as he stared at the locked building.

"It's okay. You can just drive me over to the MACV compound. I'll have them call back to let your corporal know where you are."

"I don't know if I can do that." Jason seemed really nervous. "Their compound is off base and I'm not supposed to leave the base. Besides, it's getting dark."

"Don't worry." I opened my suitcase and pulled my 9mm parabellum pistol from under a pair of socks. "Everything will be fine." I chambered a round, then tucked the gun in my waistband. "Move over, honey, I'll drive." He was looking at me a little like a deer caught in someone's headlights. "Just load your M-16. If we need it, it won't do much good without bullets."

Jason vacated the driver's seat and quickly scrambled to grab his rifle and load it. I scooted behind the wheel, smiled reassuringly, and drove us out the front gate and down to "to do" steet. The young private's gaze darted everywhere as we worked our way through the press of the early evening crowd. Apparently, he didn't get out much. For me it was the same old story. The streets were littered with the usual bunches of young men—men who should have been serving their country—instead, racing around on mopeds trying to hassle GIs. One kid on a scooter came up on my side of the jeep trying to sell something. I waved a five-dollar military pay certificate in front of him. The MPC immediately got his attention.

"This is yours if you can lead me on the quickest and shortest route to the Presidential Hotel."

The boy's eyes lit up. "You number one GI. I go quick! Follow close!" He pulled his little scooter right in front of the jeep and started honking his horn and ordering people to get out of the way. "*Didi Mau.* Very important GI in jeep!"

Since I wasn't wearing a uniform, and the private was, people started pointing at young Jason, assuming he must be somebody special. They never gave me a second look. After all, I was only the driver, in a wild Hawaiian shirt. It put a whole different spin on urban camouflage.

"They're all looking at me, sir."

"Just smile and wave at the crowd, Jason. You're their hero—at least for the moment." I didn't bother to add that most in the crowd would have gladly slit his throat for his watch.

We soon pulled up to the Presidential Hotel. A bunch of GIs, mostly Marines, loitered out front, smoking and drinking beer. "I thought we were going to the MACV compound? It's secure there." Jason was growing increasingly twitchy as he watched the locals on the street watching him. "What are we doing here?"

"This is where I get off." I handed our guide the promised five bucks, and the kid sped off on his moped. "Why don't you come in and join me for a beer?"

"No sir! I have to get back on base. I should never have left." The private was starting to freak out. "I can't believe I let you talk me into this." His voice began to quaver and rise in pitch as he climbed out of the jeep. "I'm going to get in serious trouble for this. They'll probably send me to a godforsaken infantry company—probably somewhere in the fucking highlands. People die there. Lots of people. I'm probably going to be *killed* because of you. I'm practically a dead man and it's all your fault!"

The GIs gathered in front of the hotel watched the growing spectacle with obvious interest. That gave me an idea.

"Anyone need a ride to Than Sun Nhut?" I yelled. A few guys had early morning flights, and came over to the jeep. "You can have my ride. Just deliver the jeep and this private back to the corporal at the R&R center."

"Great! Thanks man!" They grabbed their luggage and tossed it into the jeep.

Jason still looked upset and sullen as his new passengers climbed in, but a young Marine sergeant stepped up to the private and said something in his ear. Jason immediately straightened out, jumped in the driver's seat, and drove off to the airport.

"I guess you'll have to buy *me* that beer, Doc." The Marine sergeant, obviously well lubricated, had a big smile on his face as he watched the jeep drive off. "So how's it going Doc? And why the civilian clothes?"

"Do I know you?" There was nothing on my person to show that I was military, much less a corpsman.

The young sergeant laughed and, oblivious to any onlookers, proceeded to pull down his pants. He pointed to a large eight-inch scar on his inner thigh. "I can't believe you don't remember me, pecker-checker, especially after all that time you spent with your head between my legs."

A curious crowd started to gather, drawn by the sight of the drunken sergeant with his pants down around his knees.

Now I remembered him. "Gunny Peterson! I can't believe you're still alive." I had patched him up during my first tour as a Marine corpsman after he caught a nasty bit of shrapnel.

"Thanks to you, Doc." He pulled up his pants, and threw his arms around me in a big bear hug. He turned back to his men, one arm still around me. "You can thank this squid that you have me around to take care of you. Without Doc here, I would have died up in Hue during Tet of '68."

His men came forward to meet me, a few of them shook my hand and one, whom I sort of remembered from those days, grabbed my bags as Peterson and I headed into the Presidential's lobby. At the desk I asked the silver-haired papa-san for the key to 601. That was the prepaid room always exclusively reserved for Navy SEALs.

"No more key. Other SEALs take."

"What other SEALs?"

"Come this afternoon. SEALs up in bar now."

"Holy shit!" Peterson whooped on overhearing our exchange. "Doc's a SEAL! Now *that* explains the civies."

"Don't worry, Sarge," I grinned at him, "you still scare me."

He laughed, as we proceeded to walk arm in arm to the stairwell and up to the rooftop bar. We barely fit up the stairs with Peterson on one side and one of his guys on the other.

The overwhelming aroma of dirty mop buckets assaulted my nose as I stepped into the smoke-filled room. I think Peterson was too drunk to notice. The jukebox blared out some antiwar shitkicker song as I scanned the gloom. I immediately spotted my buddy Ric sitting over in a corner, with a couple of guys from the advisor's group and some Air America spooks. He was shithoused, with two hookers in his lap, one on each leg. Spotting me at the door, he jumped to his feet, almost spilling his girls on the floor.

"Holy shit!" he exclaimed, staring at the Marines hanging off of my arms, "Doc's gone fag on us!"

"Yeah, Ric," I yelled back. "These are some of the guys I used to sleep with before I started sleeping with you!" Everyone laughed, started shaking hands, then out came the beer, the broads, and the booze.

The next morning, Ric shook me awake to offer me a drink. I had no memory of the previous night's festivities, but judging from the pounding in my head, I must have done some serious partying. Once my eyes finally focused, I saw that Ric was offering me a tray with coffee, a beer, and a Coke on it. I opted for the Coke. He took the beer and fed the coffee to the trash can. Ric had been sent to Saigon to drop off some classified intel the platoon had gathered while I was gone. There had been too many leaks in the regular chain of command, and apparently this was pretty serious stuff about some double agents who were working in our area.

After a breakfast of hot rice and about six more Cokes, Ric got us an Air America helo ride to Binh Thuy. Later that afternoon, we hopped a Seawolf from Binh Thuy back down to SEAFLOAT. Strangely enough, it felt good to be back on SEAFLOAT with my platoon. After spending R&R back in the world, I no longer had any doubt about who had become my real family. All the guys were happy to get the treats I had brought them. A few of them had gotten banged up while I was gone. As soon as I hit the hooch, they came forward for treatment. While none of the wounds were serious, some of them were sustained as much as a week earlier.

"So why didn't you guys just go to sick bay and let Gary or one of the other corpsmen patch you up? Why wait for me?"

"I'm sure those guys are okay," Jim answered. "But you're our Doc."

"Yeah," Dave confirmed, "nobody was hurt bad, so we figured we could wait for you. You were only gone ten days."

Nice to be wanted, I thought to myself as I treated a week's worth of minor cuts and bruises.

35

Once More Into the Breach

IN the wee hours the next morning, I was awakened from a very deep sound sleep by an urgent tug on my shoulders. I forced one eye open a little. It was still dark, so I started to drift off again. The tugging resumed, more insistent this time, and someone jerked my poncho liner off of me.

"Doc, wake up! Get up quick, Doc!" Flanagan's whispered words slowly penetrated into my sleep-fogged brain. "They need you over in sick bay. Lots of casualties coming in. Two Swift Boats were attacked. One was blown up, the other is bringing in all the casualties."

Casualties. The words finally registered. I forced myself up, quickly poured a half a canteen of water over my head and grabbed a towel to wipe the sleep from my eyes. It was still pitch black outside. Flanagan saw that I was awake, and quickly brought me up to speed.

"The Swifts picked up a group of AVRN regulars. They were ferrying them up to Can Tho when they were ambushed with B-52 rockets by the Viet Cong." I nodded and pulled back my watch cover. It was 0440 hours. My jet-lagged body, still on Hawaiian time, said it was even earlier. Everyone else was still sleeping, but I made no attempt to be quiet as I quickly threw on a T-shirt and flip-flops and headed for the side door of our hooch. A couple of the guys awakened by the disturbance, mumbled to me to stop making noise. In answer, I stopped at the door and flipped on the overhead light. The sudden brilliance was greeted with a chorus of groans and profanity.

"Sorry to disturb your beauty rest!" I yelled. "But we got a bunch of wounded guys coming in. Their Swifts were attacked. If you guys could spare a few minutes, I could use some help."

The groans immediately stopped as all the guys rolled out of their racks and started throwing on clothes. Most of the members of our platoon had learned enough advanced first aid that they easily could have qualified as medics anywhere else.

I arrived at sick bay just as the first couple casualties were carried in to the room. They looked bad. Gary, as senior corpsman, was acting doctor at this point, and had his hands full.

"Doc, I'm glad you're here." He flashed me a grateful smile as he looked up from his first patient. "I need you to go down to meet the incoming boats and start a triage. Don't send anyone else up here until we see what we've got."

I understood immediately. SEAFLOAT's sick bay was only about ten feet wide and fifteen feet long with one examining and surgical table in the middle of the room. It was never designed to handle large numbers of sick or wounded. We were only equipped to treat simple ailments and limited emergencies on a small number of patients. Even then, we could only stabilize serious cases while waiting for a Medivac out of Binh Thuy. Without triage we would soon be overrun and no one would get good care. Ric and Dave arrived as I grabbed a stethoscope and a field medical bag. I had them grab some serum albumin and some IV kits and asked Dave to tell the rest of the guys to meet us on the dock.

We arrived at the slip to find the place in chaos. The crew was attempting to pull men and bodies off of the boat. People ran around yelling in both Vietnamese and English, while wounded men screamed for help. The carnage was unbelievable. Blood and mangled bodies filled the boat and littered the dockside, adding to the panic and confusion. All of the casualties were Vietnamese sailors and soldiers.

"I need a dozen body bags." Preacher and Ritter left to get them. I turned to the rest of the guys. "Clear the area of anyone who's not hurt. If they're not wounded and not a medic, I want them off this dock!"

I was daunted by the sheer volume of dead and wounded. There must have been fifty or sixty men on the boat at the time the rocket exploded. There was nothing but debris left of the Swift Boat, and not much more of some of her crew. None of the men aboard had escaped injury. As we pulled guys off the surviving boat, the dock became so heavily coated with blood that I couldn't keep my flip-flops on. The sticky gore pulled them right off my feet. I finally had to have someone get me my coral booties. The dive booties were designed for slick wet surfaces. Fortunately, they worked on blood as well as in the water, giving me secure footing as we worked through the long process of sorting the dead and wounded. First, we tried to locate and stabilize the worst cases so they could be Medivaced to the hospital. The rest of the wounded were treated on the dock or sent up to Gary in sick bay. The dead were left on the dock.

First light was fast approaching by the time we had finished moving a dozen of the worst cases out to the helo pad to await Medivac. We received word that the choppers would launch from Binh Thuy at sunrise, so I left Dave and Mitch with the wounded on the helo pad while I went back to the dock. There were still injured men on the boat, many of whom were in no shape to get off on their own. It had been almost two and a half hours since the ambush. I climbed back on board the Swift Boat and began helping the rest of the injured off of the boat. A lot of the wounded had died during the trip to SEAFLOAT for lack of basic first aid. Both of their medics were killed in the initial explosion. But no one else even tried to give any assistance to the rest of the casualties. Either they didn't know how or they didn't care. I had a sinking feeling in my gut, realizing that the same inability to render aid that the ARVN had demonstrated in Chief Anderson's death was surfacing here—with even more disastrous results. Many of the dead had noncritical injuries. Even some of the men with minor wounds were in such shock by the time they arrived that they were in danger of dying without immediate attention. Glancing up to see Ric and Boh working on patients on the dock, I was very glad that our entire platoon took medical training seriously.

As the sun started to peek over the jungle, I heard the rotor beats of several helos approaching from the north. *They must have launched early*, I thought. *Maybe it will make the difference for someone*. The instant the helos touched down, my guys loaded four men at a time onto each Medivac and sent them on their way. By 1000 hours, we managed to get all the critically wounded off on their way to the field hospital in Binh Thuy. But the sun had risen well above the tree line to beat down mercilessly upon the dockside. Flies, drawn out of the jungle by all the blood and the stench of death, started swarming over the area. The dock, still littered with the dead, had the look and smell of a charnel house. We quickly filled the body bags as best we could and loaded them on two of the undamanged Vietnamese Swift Boats so they could be taken to the Vietnamese Army post, a few miles upriver.

Once all bodies and patients were clear, the SEAFLOAT crew quickly turned on the fire hoses to wash down the blood-soaked decks. The powerful spray from the saltwater pumps scoured the gore from the area and washed it into the river until the waters of the Cua Lon ran red. The bloody water pooled around SEAFLOAT until the out flowing tide carried it down stream. Numb and exhausted in both mind and body, I rinsed my hands off with one of the hoses, then lit a cigarette and watched the red pool move away from us and out to the sea. In a little while, the river would erase all sign of the carnage she had witnessed. In many ways, I mused, the earth was a healer, too.

I put out my cigarette butt and went to sick bay to help Gary clean the place up. He already had a good start on it, so it didn't take long to put everything back in order. Once we were done, I took a long, cool shower—not that there was a choice, we didn't have hot water. The shower was refreshing, but I was already sweating again before I finished drying myself. The heat in our hooch was unbearable, so I quickly put on my swimsuit, T-shirt, and sunglasses. My flip-flops were ruined, so I found some new ones. I was too hot and too wired to rest. I needed something to do that would keep me busy so I wouldn't have to think. I grabbed my Stoner, went back to our cleaning tables, and began to take it apart. It had been almost two weeks since I had last fired it. The salt air could corrode metal pretty fast and Stoners were especially susceptible to jamming or misfiring if there was any dirt or corrosion in the mechanism.

The cleaning tables were in a shaded, quiet area behind our sleeping quarters. A breeze, just enough to keep comfortable, blew in off the river. I worked alone for about fifteen minutes, trying not to think about anything in particular, just focusing on the motion of cleaning my weapon.

"Hey, Doc," Ric called from inside our hooch, "do you want a soda? I'm buying! I'd offer you a blond, but they don't have any of those in stock."

"Yeah, thanks. A soda sounds good. Wanna join me while I finish up?"

He brought the soda out and placed it on the table near me, then pulled up a seat and sat down to watch. I jammed the bolt in, sighted down the barrel to be sure it was clean, and laid the gun on the table. Sitting down next to Ric, I opened my soda, took a big gulp, and fumbled for a cigarette. He looked at me funny as he gave me a light.

"Hey, man, is everything okay?"

I didn't answer him, just sat there for a few minutes, quietly sipping my soda and puffing on my cigarette. Then, my eyes suddenly began to well up. Tears streamed down my cheeks and out from under my sunglasses. I tried to wipe them away without being too obvious. Ric, not wishing to bust me, got up and walked over to the edge of the barge and spit some chew into the river.

"You know Doc, a lot of the SEAFLOAT guys were really impressed at how you took charge of things this morning. They said that was a heckuva job you did at the boat slips, handling all those casualties like that."

"Thanks." The tears just came faster. I couldn't stop them. Then I just broke down like a baby. "Shit, Ric. My R&R sucked, and so does this war. I am sick of killing people one day, only to spend the next day patching up others that look just like them. For all I know, I could be sewing people up just so they can shoot at me! Two days ago I was on the quiet beaches of Hawaii with Vicki. This morning I'm trying to patch pieces of people back together on the bloody rivers of 'Nam. Damn it, I can't handle the transition. It's all too fast! I don't think I can do this anymore!

"And look at me. I'm drinking all the time. Whenever we're not operating we're drinking, and that just makes it worse. I get even more depressed."

"Doc," Ric pointed to my soda, "that's a Coke."

I refused to acknowledge his attempted humor. "Yeah, this time. It won't be tonight!"

"Hey, man, hang in there. You'll be fine. The tour's almost over. We've only got a few weeks to go."

Of course, that was part of the problem, too. I was getting a short-timers attitude because we only had four or five more weeks of regular operations. Then we would start to stand down and begin the task of breaking in a new platoon. I could tell I was losing my nerve. I was becoming scared of my own mortality. I didn't want to go out anymore. I just wanted to hide somewhere until it was time to go home.

I was feeling real sorry for myself when my thoughts were interrupted.

"Doc? Doc? Doc McPartlin, where are you?" a voice called out from beyond our hooch.

"Back here." I quickly scrubbed my hands over my face to remove any trace of watery eyes. "What's up?"

The voice belonged to one of the Swift Boat crew guys.

"There's a problem down at the Annex. They need you, Doc. One of the Kit Carsons, I think. Frank Flynn sent a boat to get you."

That's the thing about war. It doesn't give you time for self-pity. I grabbed my Stoner off the cleaning table and checked out with Mr. Flanagan. Then I put on my gear, grabbed some medical supplies, and raced to the waiting boat. I arrived on the dock to find Boh and Ric already on board.

"What are you guys doing here?"

"Well," Boh said as he helped me load my gear onto the boat, "it seemed like a nice afternoon for racing a boat up the river. Gives me a chance to see what this baby will do, and it's a great way to cool off! Besides, Mr. Flanagan is still worried about all the double-agent crap that's been surfacing. He doesn't want his Doc falling into some trap, so he sent me and Ric to cover you."

"Yeah, right, Boh. I know your lyin' because your lips are moving." I looked over at Ric. "And as for you, you just want to check and see if there are any new chicks down at the Annex."

Boh looked offended. Ric just grinned as he pulled the throttle back and we took off. The village was five miles upriver. At 60 mph, it only took a few short minutes to get there. As we approached the beach and tied up to the floating piers, I noticed that the village was about twice as large as it had been just a few weeks earlier. Walking in, I discovered that they even had some shops set up. I looked into one shop to see what they were selling, and was shocked to recognize the merchandise. Some of it was the stuff that we had given them. Frank Flynn came up to greet me and noticed the direction of my gaze.

"Frank, they're selling the supplies we gave them!"

"Just think of it as democracy and free enterprise at its best. We *are* supposed to be teaching them our ways." He smiled.

Looking at all the American food and supplies in the shops, I thought that they might be learning a little *too* well. "So what's the problem?"

"Well a high-level VC Chief *Chieu Hoyed* to his brother, who happens to be one of my Kit Carson scouts."

"Great! So what does that have to do with me?"

"I think he surrendered to us because he heard we had a doctor. His wife is pregnant, and is apparently having problems with the delivery." Frank led the way to his compound in the center of the village. "So we sent for you. They just brought the woman in from the jungle. She's on a stretcher behind the compound."

Frank's compound was fairly small and simple. A few hooches and some tin buildings set a little apart from the main village that surrounded it. He had no actual infirmary, but he did have a small, screen-enclosed area he had built as a mess hall. The room had a roof with a couple of lights hanging from it, and two picnic tables in the middle. It would do better than trying to work in the dirt.

"Bring her stretcher in here and put her on the table."

I opened my medical kit and began laying out instruments on one of the tables while Ric, Bob, and Frank quickly brought the moaning woman into the mess hall and placed her stretcher on the other table. As I started to wash my hands, the midwife from the village came in with her assistant. Ignoring me, she started to check out my patient.

After a second, she looked over at me and grinned her mostly toothless grin. "No problem *Bac Si*, baby come now."

I quickly shook my hands dry and stepped over to her side, to find the midwife already holding the baby's head. She was lightly pulling the shoulder out, just as she had probably done a hundred other times. Before I could turn around and grab my stethoscope, she had the baby completely out and had snipped the umbilical cord with her garden shears. I took the baby from her, cleaned it up, checked the vitals, and wrapped it in one of the big, clean battle dressings I used as a receiving blanket. The mother, in the meantime, slid herself to the edge of the table and was sitting over a pail, bearing down hard. She delivered all the afterbirth into a bucket the midwife placed there for that purpose. When she was done, the midwife checked the pail, handed it to her assistant, then came and took the baby out of my arms. She looked at it coldly, showing no more emotion than if it had been a piece of firewood, and handed it to its mother.

"Leave now!" she commanded the woman sternly in Vietnamese. As the mother slid off the table, the midwife turned to me and continued in broken English. "Baby VC. Just like mother. Both VC. Should have killed both."

Ric and Bob just stared as the mother and baby walked away. The midwife stayed long enough to clean the room, then left, without a glance at any of us.

"Well, I see my work here is done." I started packing my stuff back into my medical kit, feeling more than a little useless.

"Hey, Doc." Frank put a hand on my shoulder. "I'm really sorry about the wild-goose chase. But for what it's worth, I'm certain your presence made an impression on the father. The fact that you were here at all will probably be worth some good intel from him."

"Yeah, sure, anytime."

On the ride back to SEAFLOAT, I watched the sun slowly drop below the western horizon and thought about how strange the day had been. I had spent the morning in a desperate battle to save lives, only to be upstaged that afternoon by a third-world mama-san.

As we reached the SEAFLOAT dock, I turned to Boh and Ric. "This has sure been a weird day."

"No shit, Doc," Boh agreed.

"I think we all need steaks and margaritas."

"Lots of margaritas," Ric agreed as we tied up the boat. We all went back to our hooch, secured our weapons, and fired up the blender.

A few hours later, sitting there with my closest friends beside me, sipping cold margaritas, I discovered I no longer felt like hiding from the war. I was still stressed and exhausted, but the worst of the depression was gone. I wanted to do my job again, and do it well. At least as well as that mama-san, anyway.

36

Leader of the Pack

FOR the next week or so, everything was back to normal—or as normal as anything can be when you're living on a barge in a river and fighting a war in the jungle. I had managed to put my fears and wariness aside to focus on doing my job. In between ops, I did more than my fair share of pulling pranks and partying with the guys to keep the tension from building up.

I thought those pranks might have gone a little too far when Mr. Flanagan caught me at morning chow.

"Doc, come see me as soon as you're done."

Oh shit! What did I do now? My mind raced back over the last several days trying to figure out what I might have done wrong—or at least what indiscretions he might have discovered. Whatever it was, I didn't think it could be good news. Looking at the remains of my breakfast, I decided I wasn't hungry anymore. Setting aside my plate, I stood up to follow Flanagan.

"I'm done now, sir." I wanted to get this over. My concern must have shown.

"Relax, Doc. You're not in any immediate trouble—that I know of." He looked more closely at me. "You look like the cat that swallowed the canary. Did you do something I haven't heard about yet?"

"Of course not, sir. I'm a model sailor," I assured him, fingers crossed behind my back.

Flanagan looked unconvinced as we walked toward the briefing room.

"Well, Doc. It looks like it's your turn to lead an operation. And I've got one all picked out for you."

Lead an op? "But I'm only a corpsman. I can't lead an op!"

"Try that on someone who'll buy it, Doc," Flanagan snorted. "Besides, this is a very special op that is uniquely suited to your talents."

"How is that?" As we stepped into the briefing room, I was wondering which talents he had in mind. The scouts were waiting for us.

"We have received intel on the location of a VC rest-and-recovery area, and we want to go in."

A VC rest-and-recovery area was basically a makeshift hospital by any other name. But of course, Americans didn't target hospitals. So it was a rest-and-recovery area.

"The reason you're leading this one," Flanagan continued, as he led me to a table covered with maps and photos, "is that, if you screw up, hospitals usually don't shoot back."

"Thanks for the vote of confidence, LT!"

"And two, you will be able to identify crucial medical supplies to determine which ones should be destroyed, and which we should confiscate for ourselves."

I had never run an op myself before, but I certainly knew the drill. After spending an hour or two looking over the aerial photos, talking to our scouts, Tong and Zuom, and going over the intel, I managed to formulate a plan. I ran it by Mr. Flanagan to get his advice and recommendations.

From the photos, it looked like easy going. The VC rest area was just off a main river at the south end of the U-Minh forest. It was located about a hundred meters up a wide canal, which at high tide could handle any of our boats. It would have been easy to just race up the river, jump off and hit the ground shooting. That way we could just blow everything up and then let God sort it out. But that wasn't my style. I decided we would insert about a mile upriver from the VC rest area, patrol about a hundred yards inland, and then sneak in their back door at first light.

When I finished explaining my plan to Mr. Flanagan, he smiled and shook his head. "Doc, I can't figure you out. You're always the first one to bitch when our ops require too much walking. But now, when it's your turn, you have us patrolling a mile or so into the shittiest terrain you could possibly find!"

"Yeah, but by going in undetected we can set up a perimeter behind the VC rest area. Then we can take them by surprise and we probably won't have to do a bunch of shooting. And besides, as you pointed out, hospitals don't usually fight back—at least not real hard."

"So how do you plan to avoid too much shooting? There will still be armed guards."

"Yeah, but not a lot of them. Once we're in place, we wait for first light. At dawn, we call in one of our boats from the river and have them patrol—very loudly—to the mouth of the canal, which is about 100 meters away. That should draw out any armed sentries or guards. Once they come out of their hooches, they will be looking toward the river—not toward us. We should be able to take them out without shooting any medical people or wounding their patients."

"I see." He raised an eyebrow. "You do realize that they are *all* VC."

"Yes sir. It's kind of a professional courtesy on my part."

I went on to detail how we would then secure the area and take prisoners of the entire staff. I would check out their patients and then decide what to do with them. If they had anything of value, we would collect it to bring out while destroying anything else. We would then extract out to the main river, call in air support, if necessary, and get the hell out of there before all the VC in the area descended upon us.

"Good plan. It could work." Was that actually approval in his eyes? "Who's your point man?"

"Since I'm the patrol leader, I thought you would be my point man."

He appeared to consider for a moment before answering. "Actually,

I shouldn't take point on this one. I think it will go better if I patrol right behind you. Choose another point man."

I thought about it, and realized he was right. He would be more effective behind me.

"How about Jim Ritter?" Jim seemed to be the one who always took the heat when something went wrong in the platoon. And it usually had nothing to do with him. I thought he deserved a chance to be out front and lead the squad in.

"Good choice," Flanagan agreed. "Warning order at 2345 hours?"

I realize he was *asking* me. "Yeah. Forty-five minutes."

"I'll announce it."

With some time left, I went back to our hooch to get some gear and go over the plan in my head. I wanted to be certain I hadn't forgotten anything. Most of the guys were there, playing cards or listening to music. I went to my rack to gather my stuff and my thoughts.

Fifteen minutes later, Flanagan came in, drawing everyone's attention. "Warning order, half an hour. First squad." He hesitated, waiting for the usual buzz of excitement to die down.

"Doc will be patrol leader on this one."

"What?" the entire squad moaned in chorus.

"Doc? Patrol leader?" Dave looked at me over his sunglasses as if I had suddenly grown horns. "You're shittin' me!"

Ric got up and put his arm around my shoulders—just a little too tightly for comfort. "Buddy, if you get me killed, I am gonna haunt your ass forever!"

Despite the razzing, by 2345, the whole squad sat quietly in the briefing room as I gave the warning order. I assigned positions, gave a brief description of the target, and specified the weapons and equipment to be carried—almost as if I actually knew what I was doing. Mr. Flanagan stood next to me the whole time like a proud big brother.

When I finished, Flanagan took the floor. "Find some shade and get some rest. Patrol order will take place at 2000 with departure immediately following." As everyone filed out, he turned to me. "Good job—so far. That was very professional. Almost like a SEAL would do it."

For a moment, I thought I saw a hint of a smile on his face. "Why don't you go get a soda, I will meet you back here at 1900 to go over your patrol order."

I got my soda and returned to the briefing room. I was nervous. In that moment, I felt the pressure Mr. Moody and Mr. Flanagan must have known all the time—pressure born of the knowledge that you are responsible for the lives of others that work with you. Sure, I always jumped in and took charge when it came to casualties, but I had never before been the officer in charge on an op. And this was my op. Mr. Flanagan pretty much let me plan the whole thing on my own. Methods of insertion and extraction, backup support, weather, radio signs, even briefings to essential personnel—including the commanding officer of SEAFLOAT—were up to me. As OIC, I would even have to write the official after action report and submit it to Captain Schiable back at SEAL Team One.

I sat down at the briefing table and studied the aerial photographs again. I wanted to make certain my plan was solid before lives were on the line. We were getting pretty short on our remaining time in country. I knew that, at least for this tour, this would be my one and only chance to lead an op; my only chance to prove once and for all that I was a real SEAL—at least to myself. So far we had enjoyed a perfect record with no injuries worth mentioning. We never discussed how lucky we had been out loud in order to avoid jinxing ourselves, and I certainly didn't want to do anything to ruin that record.

I started the patrol order at 2000 hours right on the button. This would be our fiftieth combat op as a squad. Over the last several months, we had become a well-oiled machine. We all knew what our jobs were and we also knew what everyone else's job was. I tried to be very thorough throughout my briefing and was rewarded as the squad gave me their full support. Once the details were released, the guys, being consummate professionals, immediately focused on the critical areas of the plan.

"You're making us walk in?"

"I can't believe your making us hump through that muck all night."

"Yeah Doc, I thought you hated long walks. What gives?"

"It figures. Give the man a little power and it goes straight to his head!"

"Hey, guys, it won't be that bad. After all," I reminded them, "our objective is a rest and recovery area."

"So?"

"So we can rest and recover when we get there." I grinned brightly at my own humor. Ric looked like he wanted to throw something. Everyone else just looked nauseated.

Mr. Flanagan stepped in to go over the chain of command for the op. It was always important to know the command order to keep the squad functional in case of casualties. "Doc's in charge, then me, Boh, and Schroeder. And if all of us get it, the rest of you can flip a coin."

Flanagan then turned to me to dismiss the briefing. The squad sat quietly, awaited my orders. *Oh boy! I'm really in charge!* "Dismissed. See you at the boat." *I could get used to this patrol leader stuff.* "Hey Dick," I called to Lt. Flanagan as everyone started to leave, "grab me a soda on your way out, okay?"

"Sure, Doc. Sure. I'll get you a soda. But don't press your luck!"

After enjoying my cold drink, I geared up and met the rest of the squad at the boat dock. Everyone was in gear and well painted with camo cream to blend in with the shadows and foliage. We had been doing this so long now that each man had developed his own distinctive style of camo design, ranging from "just slapped it on" to "dangerously artistic." Jim Ritter had even put a little camo cream on his bare feet, since he did not want to wear boots while on point.

"Smoke 'em if you've got 'em," I directed, tightening my bandana around my head to keep the sweat out of my eyes, "'cause once we pull away there will be no more smoking until extraction." The night was warm—dry for a change—and very still. I knew that the odor of American tobacco would drift a good distance under these conditions. I didn't want the VC to smell us coming. There had been many ops where we had been able to smell the VC before we saw them, and I'm sure they could often detect us the same way—but not on my op.

As we pulled away from the dock, everyone flipped their cigarettes into the water, no questions asked, and began applying bug juice. The insect population would be out in force on such a calm night, especially along our planned route through the jungle, so we all slathered a generous helping of repellant on our exposed skin. Bug juice also had a distinct smell, but it was only strong immediately after application. The hour-long boat ride would allow plenty of time for the odor to dissipate before insertion.

With nothing left to do but wait, the squad hunkered down for the ride downriver. As patrol leader, I moved close to the boat pilot and kept checking my map and the radar to verify our position. Mr. Flanagan pretended not to watch me, but I swear he was staring at me through closed eyes.

About a mile before our insertion point, I signaled our pilot to cut back on the twin Jacuzzi motors. He pulled the throttle back, and the engines grew so quiet that I almost couldn't tell they were still running. We glided through the water in near silence for the last mile, then, at the chosen spot, slid the boat slowly and quietly up to the riverbank, coming to a stop in the mud only a few feet from shore.

Once the boat grounded, I jumped off the bow, trying not to make a splash, and quickly took a position behind some bushes. I studied the area carefully for a few minutes to be certain we had not been spotted. All seemed quiet, so I signaled the rest of the squad to come ashore, watching as they quickly flowed off the boat and melted silently into their positions, shadows barely visible in the moonless night. As the last man debarked, the boat slowly backed away from the shore and ghosted into the darkness, leaving us in total silence.

We waited, keeping perfectly still, for another five minutes just to be certain. Then I gave the signal to move out. Ritter cautiously took point, checking for booby traps as he felt his way along with his bare feet. If there were any trip wires along the way, he was more likely to find them safely with his bare toes than with boots. One by one, we followed his lead, careful to make as little noise as possible. We were in an area no American or South Vietnamese soldier had ever traversed. This was Charlie's backyard, and he felt safe there. We hoped to change that.

After about an hour of slowly working our way through the bush, Ritter came across a well-traveled trail. From its placement, it appeared to lead right into the VC rest area. It made sense that they would need a clear path to bring in their wounded. It was also not likely to be heavily booby-trapped. The trail allowed us to pick up the pace a little, so that we found ourselves at our target about two hours earlier than expected. The hooches of the little recovery village loomed out of the shadows, only slightly darker than the surrounding night. As we approached I could hear moaning and coughing coming from several of the hooches.

The lack of moonlight made everything very dark, aiding us as we took up our positions along the edge of the camp. The only light came from a small fire in the center of a little courtyard between the hooches. There were several men gathered around the fire, talking and laughing. It looked as if they were passing a bottle around. *So much the better for us if they're shitfaced*, I thought, finding a spot among the bushes only about twenty-five feet away from the group. I couldn't see if they had weapons or not because they were too close to the fire. I knew that looking toward the fire would quickly dull my night vision and leave me vulnerable.

A few moments after I settled into place, one of the VC got up and walked directly toward us. I tensed as he stopped a few feet in front of me, looking right at my position, then relaxed as he proceeded to open his pants and take a piss. I was staring directly into his eyes, but he never reacted. He was obviously well lubricated, and had probably been staring into the fire for a couple of hours. He probably couldn't see two feet in front of himself, much less a man hiding in the bushes. I was fortunate that he didn't decide to water my particular hiding spot—one of the hazards of being invisible. After he was done relieving himself he walked back toward the fire, grabbed a bottle of something and disappeared inside the nearest hooch. His buddies soon followed.

Within a few minutes, all was quiet except for the occasional cough or moan. I checked my watch. It was 0440, about an hour before first light. The last embers of the fire went out a few moments later, leaving the area in deep darkness. Sitting there, I felt chilled to the bone despite the fact that I was still sweating. This was the true joy of being a SEAL, waiting for hours in cramped, silent stillness for the moment of action.

I finally took a big gulp of water from my canteen just as the eastern sky started to lighten. The coughing from inside the hooches gradually intensified as the injured VC began to wake up. It wasn't long before there was enough light to make out shadows of people moving about. It was time to call in the boats to create our distraction at the mouth of the canal. I signaled Ric to make the call. He immediately returned the all-clear sign. He had already sent the call without waiting for my signal. I flipped him off, but he just smiled back. We all knew everyone else's job as well as our own. We even knew what each other was thinking. The signals were superfluous. We were a killing machine in sync and it felt good.

A few minutes later, I heard the sounds of Jacuzzi engines as our boat arrived at the mouth of the canal. The boat pilot even dropped his boat into neutral and raced his engine a few times, just to be certain the VC heard them. Several VC grabbed their weapons and gathered near the fire pit, looking off toward the canal. As I watched, a sentry ran up to them and announced that there was an American boat on the canal. He said it looked as if the enemy boat was drifting by itself. The motor was running, but the crew seemed unable to get it in gear. One of the VC laughed and gave a quick order. It was a perfect target. Moments later two more VC arrived, lugging B-40 rockets to destroy our boat. Now there were eight men gathered in the courtyard. They all squatted down as the first one began drawing attack plans in the dirt.

When they turned to stand up again, they discovered Ric, Flanagan, Ritter, and me standing ten feet behind them, our weapons' barrels trained on their heads.

37

Saints and Demons

TONG stepped out of the bushes, loudly announcing our presence while ordering the VC to drop their weapons and surrender. One man was a little reluctant to release his weapon. Without hesitation, Tong stepped forward and shot him in the face. The other seven quickly jumped to their feet and threw their arms straight up into the air, their eyes wide in terror as they watched the faceless man slump to the ground.

With the guards and sentries neutralized, the rest of the squad set about securing the hooches. They dragged everyone who could walk out to the courtyard, patients and medical personnel alike. The prisoners screamed and begged us not to shoot them. *"Chieu Hoi! Chieu Hoi!"* Tired, sick, hungry, and very, very frightened, I could tell they were desperate to surrender. They kept looking into our painted faces, folding their hands, and bowing toward us as if we were some kind of gods—or demons. I knew stories of the "men with green faces" had been spreading among the Viet Cong. I could only imagine the nightmares these poor souls must have had about actually running into SEALs like us. Ric called in the boats while Frank handcuffed the prisoners with plastic cuffs. Mr. Flanagan and Boh started searching the hooches for weapons and other booty while I went to check on the VC patients who were too badly wounded to walk.

"I think maybe they got some dead ones in there." Boh indicated a run-down hut that apparently served as the critical ward.

I stepped inside, and gagged. The horrible stench of rotting flesh almost overwhelmed me. Worse than rotting meat, the stench of gangrene and infected wounds permeated the hooch. Five or six people lay inside. While they weren't dead, most of them were pretty close to it, staring into space with the glassy stare of the terminally ill. Choking, I got out of the hooch before I puked.

"Holy shit!" I gasped, trying to pull fresh air into my lungs. If that was the VC idea of medical care, it was a joke. It was certainly a far cry from even our worst field medicine. I understood why our prisoners were so eager to surrender. Most of them faced a more torturous death from VC "rest and recovery" than from our enemy guns.

"This is disgusting," Boh agreed, choking as he emerged from another hooch. "We should just torch the whole place. Let the fire clean it out."

I couldn't let that happen. "No. These poor bastards have suffered enough." Boh didn't like it, but I think he understood. I took a deep breath and went back inside to see if any of the critical patients had a chance for survival. It only took a few minutes to confirm that most of the men in that hooch were terminal. With better medicine and hygiene from the beginning, it might have been different for some of them. But by the time I got there, there was not much that could be done. Most of them were rotting to death. They wouldn't survive being moved, but I certainly didn't want to just kill them outright, either, though it was starting to look as though I would have no choice.

One of the prisoners seemed to be reading my mind. "*Bac Si?* I speak American. Are you *Bac Si*?" I turned to see a silver-haired, older Vietnamese man calling to me from the group in the courtyard. He was apparently one of the medical personnel.

I nodded. "I am *Bac Si*."

"Let me help. Please, do not kill them." He gestured to the hooch with the terminal cases inside. "I will care for the sick. I will stay. Please do not kill them."

I waved him over. In a mix of English and Vietnamese he told me that he was one of the medical assistants. He pleaded with me to let him stay behind to take care of the dying men and begged me to take the others prisoner so that they could get some real medical care. "No one want be VC anymore. Most never want to be VC. No choice. Become VC or die. I never want to be VC. I given no choice. You *Bac Si*? Please help *Bac Si*. In the name of Jesus Christ, please help."

I called Mr. Flanagan over to discuss the problem. I could see that he was moved by the entire situation. None of us had expected to encounter so much suffering in a so-called rest-and-recovery area.

"It's your op, Doc. I hardly think this man or those dying bastards are any danger to us. If you want to leave him behind with the terminal cases, go ahead."

I pulled the old man aside as the squad secured the rest of the prisoners for transport. "We are going to leave you and your patients behind. Collect the medical supplies you need for them. We're taking the rest with us."

"I understand." He bobbed his gray head several times.

I handed him two boxes of morphine with twelve Syrettes. "This is morphine. Only for those suffering the most. Understand? Only those in very great pain."

Again he bobbed his head.

"Do not inject it into a vein unless you want that person to die immediately. Understand? If you put it in the vein, they will die."

He grasped the boxes of morphine and the Syrettes tightly to his chest as if they were the most precious gift he had ever received. "I understand."

I left him to join my squad on the boats.

"Bac Si?"

I turned back.

"I will pray to our Lord Jesus Christ for your safety. Thank you for such kindness."

Surprised, I could only smile back. I had no words that could match his.

At the waterfront, two boats waited. The prisoners had all been cuffed and locked onto a second boat for transport while my squad waited aboard our original insertion craft.

"Mr. Flanagan, you can take it from here," I called to him. "I'll ride with the prisoners and look after the wounded."

Flanagan smiled and waved me on. It was normal for me to ride with the prisoners and wounded, but as I climbed aboard the boat and looked at all those old, pathetic faces, I suddenly felt twice my age. Unlike most of the VC chiefs we usually targeted, these men were all just peasants forced into joining the Viet Cong. None of them had any rank or really gave a shit about the "revolution" they were fighting. They had done what they were forced to do, all pawns in a nasty game of war.

As we started back downriver, I radioed our results back to base. Since none of the prisoners had any valuable intel, I was told to dump them at a nearby Vietnamese Navy base, and not to bring them back to SEAFLOAT.

"Roger that."

I signed off the radio and turned around to find one of the boat crew members, a new kid who had only been in country a couple of weeks, roughing up one of my prisoners.

"Water please. Water," the prisoner pleaded in Vietnamese. He was a well-worn, older man who looked as though he had been through a lot during the war.

"What did you call me? I'll show you!" The kid, obviously a trigger-happy gook hater, grabbed the man and shoved him hard enough to jar his teeth, despite the fact that the man was helpless with his hands bound behind him.

"*Chieu Hoi! Chieu Hoi!*" the old man insisted, desperately trying to surrender again, but the kid wasn't listening.

"Back off!" I pulled the kid off the prisoner.

"Why? He's just a gook."

"Back off or I will cut the handcuffs off little Charlie here and let him kick the snot out of you!"

"That old man?"

"That old man is probably a better fighter on his worst day than you'll ever be. And right now I need a good reason why I shouldn't let him kick your ass! He only asked you for water." The kid must have realized I was serious, because he took one look at my face and pulled away quickly, moving as far from me as the boat allowed.

Once he was gone, I gave the man a drink from my own canteen, checking to be certain he had not been hurt. As soon as the other crew members saw what I was doing, they started bringing more water to the back of the boat so all the prisoners could have a drink. I think once they saw that I respected these old Viet Cong, they realized I must have a reason.

Fact was, many of these VC had been fighting and suffering for a long time. Some of them carried four or five nasty scars from old wounds. Very few chose to be involved in this war. Now they only wanted to be out of it. I gave the wounded men a few clean bandages and some disinfectant soap for their wounds, and passed out some cigarettes to a few of them. They were very grateful for the consideration. Some of them thanked me as though they had been rescued instead of captured.

When we reached the small Vietnamese Navy base, both boats pulled up to the floating dock. Several ARVN sailors and officers were waiting for us. We off-loaded the prisoners onto the dock and handed them over to the custody of the South Vietnamese. The ARVN officer brusquely thanked me as if I was delivering a load of groceries, then turned away as I joined the rest of my squad in the SEAL craft for the remainder of the ride back to SEAFLOAT. As soon as we pulled away from the dock, the South Vietnamese sailors began confronting the prisoners. I watched helplessly as the sailors roughly confiscated my cigarettes and soap from the wounded men. A moment later the sailors started bashing the handcuffed prisoners with their gun stocks, knocking several of them to the deck. I glanced at our pilot to see my disgust mirrored in his face.

"It's amazing how brave these young jerks are when they're fighting helpless old men." I didn't try to hide my bitterness.

"Yeah. You'll also notice they're never the ones out risking their asses patrolling the river." He nodded toward the unused patrol boats tied up at one of the base docks. "We are. Even though it's *their* river."

"Gee, could it be the chickenshits are afraid of facing those old men when they're not in handcuffs?"

He laughed, but there was no humor in it. I glanced around the boat to see the entire squad watching the welcome our prisoners received. They said nothing, but their stares were cold.

Once we were out of sight of the Vietnamese base, I tried to focus my mind back on business. There was nothing more I could do for those prisoners, but as patrol leader, I still had a responsibility to my squad. The op wasn't officially over until after everyone was debriefed, the confiscated materials were cataloged, and the paperwork was done. I pulled Mr. Flanagan aside to discuss the op and get suggestions about how I should handle my debriefing of the squad. According to him, the op was successful. We had achieved our objective with no casualties on our side and only one shot fired and one enemy death. But it didn't feel like a success. In my mind, I could still see those old men watching me from the dock as I left them to the tender mercies of the ARVN.

As soon as we arrived at base, I made my way to the CO's office and debriefed him quickly, then went to meet my squad. I found them behind our hooch, in the weapons-cleaning area, laying out all the material they had collected from the camp. There were a couple of AK-47s, some carbines, and a lot of outdated medicine. It was not much of a haul, and none of it had any serious value.

"Hey, Doc." Boh knelt above a large canvas sack. "Lookee here. I snagged their heroin stash! Charlie tried to hide it, but he did a piss-poor job!" He gleefully opened his sack and dumped a dozen plastic wrapped white powder pouches at my feet. "They hid their dope way up high, on some shelves in a dry area near the medicines."

I immediately recognized the pouches. But everyone was watching us. In an attempt to avoid embarrassing Boh in front of the squad—or worse, pissing him off—I played along. "Yeah, great." I scooped up the packets. "I'll have to check these for purity." Boh grinned like a Cheshire cat. I waited a moment for everyone else to lose interest and return to their tasks, then leaned over to whisper in Boh's ear. "This isn't heroin."

"What? Sure it is!"

"It's sanitizer. We use it in sick bay to sterilize water and instruments against bacteria."

"Doc," he laughed, then whispered back in his slow southern drawl, "ya better not be kiddin' me just so you can sell this shit on the black market!"

"Come with me over to sick bay and I'll show you." I handed him the packets and led the way into sick bay. We walked over to the clean area where I drew his attention to the shelves above the sink, neatly stacked with identical plastic-wrapped packets of white powder. As he stared, I took his packets out of his arms and added them to the rest. "It's okay. At least you found something useful. You can never have too much sanitizer!"

"I'll be damned! Coulda sworn it was dope."

He was quiet as we walked back to the SEAL area and began to clean our weapons. While I stripped my Stoner, I congratulated myself for managing to avoid embarrassing Boh in front of the guys.

"So I heard you found heroin, huh Boh?" Mitch came over to welcome us back.

"Well, as it turns out, Doc here was so nervous out there, it being his first op as patrol leader and all, that he had me bring back a bunch of soap packets 'cause he thought they were dope!"

Everyone laughed. I just grimaced, stifling a strong urge to throttle Boh right then and there. "Why you . . ."

"'Course he done pretty good. He was real thorough and everything went off real smooth, just like clockwork." He looked at me and smiled. "I would be proud to go out on any op Doc was leadin'."

My hot retort froze in my throat. Boh never gave compliments, but that was the closest thing to praise I had ever heard come out of that cowboy's mouth. The fact that it was aimed at me left me speechless. Maybe I had done something right after all if Boh said he would follow me again. I looked around and saw the rest of my squad nodding in agreement. I forgot all about being mad at Boh.

I wasn't in any hurry to volunteer for patrol leader again. This op had given me a serious respect for all patrol leaders, especially men like Lt. Flanagan, who led patrols on a regular basis. But at least if I had to lead again, I knew I would have good men at my back.

Exhausted from my close call with command responsibility, I napped most of the next day. I was planning to sleep until evening chow, but Ric had other ideas.

"Wake up, sleepyhead!"

I lifted the cover on my watch. It was 1600 hours. "Why?" I yawned. "We got an op?"

"Better than that. We got neighbors."

"What? On the river?"

"Yeah, they're bringing in a couple of barges and ships full of Seabees. They're gonna be anchored downriver from us. Apparently they're here to rebuild the town and construct a new base on shore."

"The Annex?" My fuzzy brain could only think of one town, the little village the natives called New Nam Cam and we called the Annex.

"Not the Annex. The original city. Old Nam Cam. The one the Viet Cong destroyed. Apparently we've done such a good job of driving Charlie out of here that the government has decided to rebuild the city. They want to make it the new gateway to the South China Sea."

I thought about the ruins I had seen upon our arrival in the area, and had trouble imagining it as a thriving city, much less the "gateway to the South China Sea."

"Boh says there's even talk of moving SEAFLOAT ashore once construction gets under way."

"They'll have to call it something else then. Sure won't be SEAFLOAT or Solid Anchor if they run it aground. Maybe Landfloat? Solid Mud?"

Ric snorted and threw a flip-flop at me.

I ducked, then got up and donned a shirt and some flip-flops to go see our new neighbors. In a war where success usually meant nothing more than staying alive, it felt good to know that the SEALs had actually accomplished something tangible. Over the last two years, the SEALs were responsible for breaking Charlie's stranglehold on the region. Even though there was still VC activity, the area was now considered "pacified."

I found the rest of the platoon standing at the water's edge, looking downriver. I followed their gaze to see several huge barges working their way up from the sea. We spent the rest of the afternoon taking turns watching their slow, steady progress. By nightfall, the barges reached their anchor point, about a half mile from SEAFLOAT, and ships started to arrive, bringing engineers, civilian construction crews, and the Seabees. Frank Flynn stopped over to visit us on his way to greet the new construction crews. He was excited about the reconstruction because it meant that his people would finally be able to return home.

"Most of the villagers have gotten used to thinking of the Annex as home, but the fact that we are rebuilding their town means a lot to them. It's the first real proof they've had that we can win this thing and give them their lives back, possibly even better than before."

38

Assault on Nam Cam

WE decided to join Frank and welcome our neighbors in person. Ric, Boh, Mitch, and I followed him to one of the civilian barges that housed the construction workers. The level of luxury they enjoyed amazed me. Unlike the tiny little bar on our barge which had soda, bottled beer, and sometimes tequila, theirs had a real bar set up with tap beer and a full assortment of hard liquor that put our limited menu to shame. They even had a piano and a jukebox. I felt completely spoiled among all that luxury. We all had a great time—right up to the point where we ran out of money. Then we had to go back to SEAFLOAT.

Several days later, Ric and I went to the ruins to check on the friends we had made and see how the construction was progressing. In those few days, the Seabees and construction crews had transformed the ruins to the point that I barely recognized our original landing zone. They had cut the dense jungle overgrowth, which had been threatening to engulf the area, and created a large clearing along the riverfront. A new perimeter fence slathered with barbed wire protected the cleared area. Inside, the workers were constructing the structures that would eventually be the new Navy base within the fence.

I remembered my arrival on this spot, over five months before, when we came in on the helo from Binh Thuy. It seemed a lifetime ago we were jumping out to form an armed perimeter defense against the unknown perils of the jungle. The place had been deserted then, except for occasional use as a landing zone. It had changed a lot. Construction workers, both American and Vietnamese, as well as Navy personnel from both countries, scurried busily throughout the area, with additional Vietnamese Navy personnel moving in daily.

"So the word is that they plan to move the men and materials off SEAFLOAT and into the new base in a month or so. Think they'll have it ready?"

Ric looked thoughtful. "I dunno. Fact is, I've gotten so used to bedding down on the river that I don't think I could get used to living on dry land. I'm glad our tour will be over before the move actually happens."

I nodded. That was as close as any of us had come to actually saying it. We were getting short. We all knew we were only a couple of ops away from standing down the platoon. The new platoon was scheduled to come in country within the next ten days, and we were scheduled to return to the world two weeks after that. We all tried not to act short and jinx ourselves, but the inexorable creep of the calendar constantly teased us. The last few ops were always the most dangerous because it was so easy to lose focus when you were thinking about how little remained of the tour rather than the job.

"I hear the new platoon is mostly veterans."

"Yeah," Ric confirmed. "All vets. The only thing we'll have to show them is the way to the bar."

The fact that our replacements were all experienced SEALs would make life much easier for us. There would not be any of the same types of problems we had experienced while learning our way around the bush.

"Speaking of the bar, let's get back to ours."

Ric grinned and we left the workers to their labors. It was St. Patrick's Day and I was looking forward to drinking green margaritas and Irish whiskey. When we got back to base, we discovered the cooks had even cooked up some corned beef and cabbage that wasn't half bad.

Frank Flynn came over to join us for the party.

"Watch it, Ric. Drink too many of those margaritas and you'll give a whole new meaning to the phrase 'men with green faces.'"

"Shit, Frank," Boh laughed, "there ain't enough tequila in all of 'Nam to turn that boy green!"

"So when are your villagers planning to move into the new digs?" I was curious, since the construction seemed to be going well.

"No time real soon. And you guys should stay away from it, too. Especially at night."

That got my attention. I looked at Ric, who shrugged. We hadn't seen any problems while we were there earlier in the afternoon.

"Why?"

Frank took another gulp of his margarita and frowned. "There's no damned security. Everyone over there believes someone else is in charge of security. The construction crews say they have nothing to do with security, the Seabees say the Navy is supposed to provide security, the Navy says it's the Vietnamese Navy's job, and the Vietnamese Navy says okay, and then they all spend the nights sleeping on their Swift Boats. The whole place is wide open except for the few Seabees standing guard around their own area."

Most of the platoon was within hearing and started drawing closer as Frank spoke. Lt. Flanagan had put his own drink aside and was listening intently.

"So you think there might be trouble."

"I'm sure of it. My scouts say the Viet Cong are planning to hit the new base hard. Probably soon. Though they're not in a hurry to cross swords with you. I think you've bloodied a few too many noses around here. My intel people believe they might be waiting until the current SEALs—meaning you—rotate out."

"They know our rotation?" Preacher looked genuinely surprised.

"It ain't like it's a big secret or nothin'." Boh laughed. "They can count to six, same as us."

"Apparently, they are waiting for the next platoon because they assume it will take a few weeks for the new platoon to get up to speed."

"Wrong assumption on Charlie's part!" Ric blurted. We started laughing. Frank looked puzzled until Flanagan explained.

"We're being replaced by a veteran platoon. Most of them will be on their third or fourth tour. I think this might even be number five for one or two of 'em. They've got more experience than *we* do. They'll be up to speed before they land."

Of course, there were only about four or five hundred active SEALs in existence, so it was not unusual to have seasoned pros returning for additional tours of duty. With a long war like this one was turning out to be, it was a very good thing that SEALs liked their job enough to keep coming back for more. If SEALs had followed the attrition rate of most of the rest of the military, doing only the one tour required, we probably would have been unable to continue operations for more than a year or so. Fortunately, Charlie didn't know that. I found myself almost jealous of the fun the new platoon was going to have in the first few weeks after we were gone.

"So it sounds like the new base is in need of some experienced security." Lt. Flanagan grinned broadly. "Let me check with the CO. We might be able to help." He retrieved his drink, then he and Frank went off to plan, leaving us to finish the margaritas.

"Guard duty?" Mitch seemed offended. "Just 'cause the ARVN are too damn lazy to do it themselves?"

"Hey. It's easy duty," Ric countered. "There'll be little or no risk. We can ease on down in preparation for going back to the world without worrying about making a short-timer's mistake. And we can visit that cushy bar a lot!"

"I think it's a fitting way to stand down," Boh agreed. "No humpin' through the bush, but we'll still be useful. Besides," an almost evil grin lit up his face, "Charlie sure as hell won't be expecting *us* to be pullin' guard detail! If we do it right, the VC will still think the place is wide open!"

Matching grins slowly spread among our faces as we all started to realize the possibilities.

The next day, we began providing surreptitious security for the workers on the shore. The Viet Cong had no idea that we were there, watching the perimeter of the new base while it was being built. By day, we occasionally wandered casually around the construction area. At night, we staggered a series of well-hidden two-man listening posts throughout the area so that we would know when the VC tried to come in close. When movement was detected, one man radioed in the coordinates so that someone at the firebase could fire mortars at the enemy position. If we were lucky, someone would actually launch a mortar in that direction. If we were incredibly lucky, they might actually hit the coordinates we requested.

Throughout the next week or so, a number of our LP teams spotted movement and radioed for mortar support. Sometimes the mortars flew, creating a great light show on impact, but no one ever found any bodies. Gradually, we noticed that one particular LP seemed to be reporting more movement than the rest. After the third night of increasing activity around that particular LP, Ric and I decided that that post was the one for us.

"I think Charlie's up to something, and I think LP 4 might just be the place to stop him," Ric told me after the morning briefing.

"I'm with you. But it won't do any good if we wait for one of those mortar rounds to accidentally bop him on the head. I'm sick of waiting for someone else to shoot my target for me."

"So let's take matters into our own hands. Forget callin' in anyone but our own guys. We'll just lay low and quiet—let them get in real close. And then blow their butts away."

"Yeah," I agreed. "After all the damage they haven't taken from the mortars, they should be feeling pretty safe by now."

We both knew the VC would never anticipate that type of ambush. They knew SEALs were too important to ever do anything as menial as base security, and that the Vietnamese Navy were too chickenshit to go toe-to-toe. They were right about Marvin the ARVN, but dead wrong about SEALs.

We clearned the plan with Lt. Flanagan and then presented it to Frank Flynn and the rest of our platoon. Frank said he thought the increase in activity might be leading up to something.

"We're patrolling the river tonight, just in case."

Before going out that night, Ric and I armed ourselves to the teeth.

We had pop flares, grenades, rocket launchers, and M-60 machine guns. And, just in case they managed to get in close and personal, we had our good old trusty Stoners. Boh also loaded up, then took Jonah and Dave and their sixty-guns to man the LP closest to our location.

Once we reached our LP, we even set up claymore mines around our position, just as if we were rigging an ambush deep in the bush rather than guarding a construction site. Our LP, situated between the tree line and the new base, afforded us an almost unobstructed view of the ground between the deep jungle and the site.

Once darkness fell, we waited silently in our lair for our prey to arrive. By now, we had perfected the art of absolute stillness. Blending into the darkness, we became one with the shadows, in perfect sync with each other. We knew exactly what the other was thinking and feeling. A bright three-quarter moon rose until it hung low in the sky overhead, illuminating the barren defoliated area that stretched for a hundred yards or so in front of our position.

We didn't have long to wait. As I watched, shadows started moving into the open area, clearly silhouetted against the moonlight. The VC were coming in. I was almost giddy with anticipation as we watched them brazenly make their way across the clearing, not even attempting to make use of the cover provided by the few remaining trees as they headed straight for the construction site. I spotted about ten of them wearing satchel charges on their backs and another half dozen or so carrying AK-47s. They were obviously sappers, coming to sabotage the base.

Ric quietly radioed Boh and the sixty-gunners at their LP, some distance to our south.

"Copy that. We've got movement confirmed at LP 3. I make it at about a dozen." They were coming in at Boh's position as well. The radio crackled again. This time it was Frank Flynn. He and his men had set up a little farther down the river.

"Confirm Victor Charlie, .05 klick South." They had spotted the remaining force setting up to attack. Apparently, Charlie had decided this was a good night for an all-out assault on the base. I tensed in anticipation as I watched the shadows approach.

Ric turned back to the radio as Flanagan passed the word. "Let them get within twenty-five yards of your position before engaging. First LP within twenty-five yards is to initiate contact."

A few minutes later, the sky lit up over Boh's position as he and the sixty-gunners opened up, shattering the silence with the rapid-fire staccato of the pigs as they started rocking and rolling. At the first sound of gunfire, the VC in front of us began to run toward the perimeter fence in a desperate attempt to get their satchel charges over the wire. They were running right at our position, completely oblivious to the fact that we were there. Their mistake. As they reached the invisible twenty-five yardline, I started to crank off the claymore mines. Explosions rocked the night as the charges went off, taking out anyone caught in their kill zone. Ric opened up his M-60 on those who made it past the claymores. Suddenly, a firestorm erupted in front of us, forcing me to duck low to protect my face. The satchel charges the Viet Cong were wearing were cooking off, exploding right on their backs, each one setting off the next nearest in a grisly chain reaction. They must have screamed, but I could hear nothing over the gunfire and explosions. Some of the VC continued to run toward us, forcing me to open up with my Stoner to bring them down.

Within ninety seconds, our part was done. I heard more gunfire and a lot of yelling as Flynn's men engaged the main force a couple hundred meters away, but except for moaning from the wounded, everything in our area was quiet. Ric and I held our position until dawn without having to fire another shot. We said nothing for the rest of the night, each glad for the other's presence.

As the dawn broke, I got a good look at the night's work. The carnage that lay in front of our LP was unbelievable. There were bodies and parts of bodies strewn all over the place. An arm here or a leg there was about all I could recognize as being human. The satchel charges, designed to do serious damage to concrete and steel, had made a complete mess of softer flesh and bone. We estimated our body count at seventeen to twenty. I couldn't tell for sure based on the remains. The only thing that was certain—there were no enemy survivors at our LP.

As I looked out over the mass of broken bodies, the dead and the dying, I realized that the VC were not the only casualties. Something inside me had broken. I felt nothing. No remorse, no shock, no concern for the suffering. Up until that moment, I had always believed the part of me that was the healer would always be stronger than the part that had been trained to kill. But at that moment, both were gone, and I felt empty. Yet I knew I would do it all again tomorrow. It was my job.

A couple of hours later, after cleaning our weapons and downing a few beers, I told Ric, "It's time for this SEAL corpsman to go home."

WE rotated back to the world two weeks later, leaving the new base in the capable hands of a crack SEAL platoon that continued to spread the legend of the men with green faces throughout the Ca Mau area. We had done the impossible, ending our tour with no casualties despite participating in over forty operations each, deep in enemy territory. Nam Can was successfully rebuilt and became a safe haven for Frank's Kit Carsons and the local villagers until the fall of South Vietnam in 1975.

After my return home, I was awarded the Bronze Star for meritorious service and the Navy Commendation Medal for heroic achievement. Ironically the Commendation Medal was awarded for saving the life of a VC chieftain while under fire. I had deliberately turned down a Purple Heart for that same operation, but had apparently not managed to avoid medals altogether.

All of the men in my platoon earned medals, and none of them were Purple Hearts. At the time, I thought they were just jewelry to go with the job. Now I realize they were something more. They were a symbol of our team's survival in the rite of passage known as Vietnam.